Building iPhone OS Accessories

Use the iPhone Accessories API to Control and Monitor Devices

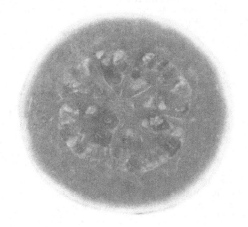

Ken Maskrey

Apress®

Building iPhone OS Accessories. Use the iPhone Accessories API to Control and Monitor Devices

Copyright © 2010 by Ken Maskrey

ISBN-13 (pbk): 978-1-4302-2931-5

ISBN-13 (electronic): 978-1-4302-2932-2

President and Publisher: Paul Manning
Lead Editors: Clay Andres, Tom Welsh
Technical Reviewer: Dean Kaplan
Editorial Board: Clay Andres, Steve Anglin, Mark Beckner, Ewan Buckingham, Gary Cornell, Jonathan Gennick, Jonathan Hassell, Michelle Lowman, Matthew Moodie, Duncan Parkes, Jeffrey Pepper, Frank Pohlmann, Douglas Pundick, Ben Renow-Clarke, Dominic Shakeshaft, Matt Wade, Tom Welsh
Coordinating Editor: Mary Tobin
Copy Editor: Katie Stence
Compositor: MacPS, LLC
Indexer: Julie Grady
Artist: April Milne
Cover Designer: Anna Ishchenko

Distributed to the book trade worldwide by Springer-Verlag New York, Inc., 233 Spring Street, 6th Floor, New York, NY 10013. Phone 1-800-SPRINGER, fax 201-348-4505, e-mail orders-ny@springer-sbm.com, or visit www.springeronline.com.

For information on translations, please e-mail rights@apress.com, or visit www.apress.com.

Apress and friends of ED books may be purchased in bulk for academic, corporate, or promotional use. eBook versions and licenses are also available for most titles. For more information, reference our Special Bulk Sales–eBook Licensing web page at www.apress.com/info/bulksales.

The source code for this book is available to readers at www.apress.com.

To JB, for helping me make it through this endeavor.

Contents at a Glance

Contents

About the Author

KenMaskrey began working on engineering projects when he was ten years old and his uncle Charlie would bring him miscellaneous electronics parts from the TV repair shop where he worked. Mr. Maskrey built his first "homebrew" computer at 16 years old and the next year was programming COBOL at a major Florida bank to organize archived paper records covering nearly a century.

After graduating college and serving in the USAF, Mr. Maskrey worked for a number of aerospace firms including IBM, TRW (now Northrup-Grumman), Loral Aerospace, Lockheed-Martin, and TRW. Spending most of his time in Advanced Research departments, Mr. Maskrey specialized in developing rapid prototypes to demonstrate proof-of-concept ideas leading to large multimillion- and sometimes billion-dollar projects.

Mr. Maskrey was fortunate enough to see the dot-com boom and bust firsthand while working in Silicon Valley during the last half of the 90s and most of 2000. From there, Mr. Maskrey retired at age 43 to live on Maui and teach windsurfing at Kanaha Beach Park. After only two years of rest, Mr. Maskrey went back to work at the Air Force Maui Optical and Supercomputing Station (AMOS) specializing in advancing the software performance of the 3-meter optical telescope at the ten-thousand-foot top of the island.

Eventually unable to continue working for "the man" and having had five years of the isolationist lifestyle on a small island, he left again to study filmmaking at the Colorado Film School in Denver. Mr. Maskrey wrote and produced several shorts and feature films, including the movie *Text* about a series of killer text messages at a Colorado high school that was widely distributed on DVD.

After experiencing the closed nature of the film industry, Mr. Maskrey turned back to engineering and opened an Apple repair shop in Parker, Colorado focusing primarily on iPhone repair. This gave Mr. Maskrey a unique insight into the device and, after the announcement at Apple's WWDC 2009 of the accessory framework, he turned to developing accessories for iPhone OS devices.

Now, with the formation of Global Tek Labs, Mr. Maskrey has assumed the role of Principal Engineer where he designs and develops not only single iPhone accessories but complete solutions for customers from areas such as retail, restaurants, customer service, law enforcement, and social media.

About the Technical Reviewer

Dean Kaplan is founder and owner of Kapsoft (founded 1996), a technology consulting firm that specializes in software applications for deeply complex engineering applications. Kapsoft is a member of the Made For iPod/Works With iPhone program and is currently involved in advanced Accessory development for the iPhone platform. Dean is also an expert in RF (Radio Frequency)/Cellular Radio Test and Measurement systems. Dean is creator of the iPhone Sketch book (Apress) and has a line of UI Stencils for iPhone-iPad development (available at MobileStencil.com). Dean writes a contemporary blog at DeanOnSoftware.com. Follow Dean on Twitter at @Kapsoft. Dean currently resides in Haverford, PA. He received a Bachelor of Science in Electrical Engineering from Temple University in 1982.

Preface

With the announcement at WWDC 2009 of the EAAccessory Framework, I had two instant thoughts: (1) this is really cool and could make someone a lot of money, and (2) I'm probably already too late. This second thought was because, at the time, there were probably about 100,000 apps in the App Store and it had been around a year, I think. I thought there was no way I could develop all the cool accessories I had in my head before other people and companies had done it and it'd be just like the App Store.

But I decided to try anyway, always keeping an ear out for what was going on in the accessory world. The obvious first project was a credit card reader for the iPhone. From my shop, Mac Medics, I repair anywhere from two to ten iPhone screens a day, six days a week. It makes me a nice little bit of green. What I learned was that at least three-quarters of my customers were business people who used their iPhones for business. Most of them really would have liked to have a way to accept credit cards on their iPhones.

At the time, there were several apps that did just that, but no accessories. A software-only solution has two problems: it is manual entry so prone to mistakes, and processing a card this way results in higher merchant fees. A physical reader solves both problems. So off I went, still keeping an eye on what was happening in the market.

Eventually, I turned out a nice product that, I feel, blew away any competition. What competition might you ask? Well, I won't get specific, but if you do a little research you'll see that, as I write this in April 2010, there's really only a single product out there that's been delivered. One other is expected to deliver shortly. Regardless of whose product is better, the moral of the story is: hey, there's not a whole lot of stuff out there!

This is why I wrote this book. I'm saying to all you inventors out there that missed out on the App Store craze, here's your chance. It's nearly a year since Apple opened the iPhone to developing accessories and I'm still struggling to find co-patriots in this new frontier. My technical reviewer Dean Kaplan is probably the only other individual I know of…well, maybe a couple others. For me, I'd like to see more competition. Why? Because if this area of accessory development doesn't start getting some membership, I could see it going away…think Apple TV.

Two things to note about this book (do I always talk in twos?): first, much of the stuff you'll really want to know about is covered by a non-disclosure agreement with Apple and I can't and won't talk about them. Second, although a lot of focus is on software and getting started with the EAAccessory Framework, I'll also cover the costs associated with developing accessories. I talk about costs in terms of hardware and software/firmware skills you'll need as well as time and money.

Understand at the start, developing accessories for the iPhone will cost you some green. You'll of course need to join Apple's Made For iPod/Works With iPhone (MFi/WWi) program to learn the secret handshake, but that'll only get you in the door. You're going to need time and money to do it right. With this book, I am hoping to give you a little insight at the start to see what is involved—at least as much as I can given Apple's NDA.

Now for the good news, since the initial launch of the MFi/WWi program several companies have begun offering iPhone accessory development kits. Because I use Microchip PIC controllers in most of my work, I'll point you to the Microchip web page to see an example. No, I didn't get anything free from Microchip to say that—not that I wouldn't take a free development kit if they sent me one…hint…hint.

But seriously, several companies now offer kits like Microchip that get you started much more quickly. If I'd had one when I started, it would have cut two to three months of time in my development process, so check them out.

I could go into a chapter-by-chapter discussion of what's in this book, but you've seen the table of contents and I know that you get it. If you've picked up or (hopefully) bought this book, then, yeah, you get it.

I'm sort of obligated to describe whom this book is for, but, in essence, it's for anyone who has a really cool idea for an iPhone accessory and wants to make it real. You will need some knowledge and I assume some level of expertise in iPhone software development. Mainly, you should have developed a couple projects using the iPhone Software Development Kit and deployed it to an actual iPhone device, i.e., not just the simulator. At least one of these projects should be your own design, not just copying a project from another book and compiling. As with just about everything, a good understanding of TableViews helps as you use them a lot. I think it's the iPhone software drug of choice.

Other than that, I say go for it. If you read my bio, you saw I started engineering at a young age. My first gizmo was developing a laser gun where I basically plugged a metal bar to the electrical outlet with the cord from a lamp. Can you guess what happened when I (some would say stupidly while I would use the word inquisitively) plugged it in? Warning! I take no responsibility if you decide to wire your iPhone to an AC outlet and plug it in.

Last words—have fun with it. The frontier I talked about is still there, at least for now. Be an explorer if you dare and see what you can come up with.

What is an Accessory?

Chapter 1

Accessory Overview

You've read the iPhone programming books, downloaded the free iPhone software development kit (SDK) from Apple, compiled and executed the sample programs, and maybe even developed a few programs of your own. You may have upgraded to an iPhone developer so you can run your apps on a real iPhone in order to show your friends. Many of you might have developed an app for the iTunes/App store and are waiting to rake in the big bucks.

Then you read the bad news, fifty thousand apps in the app store. A couple months later seventy-five thousand…then, eighty-five thousand, one hundred thousand, and it keeps going up. Your unique little app that nobody could have possibly thought of has a couple dozen competitors. Great news for Apple, but what about you? Your app is now down on the fourth or fifth page in the list—the ones that nobody ever looks at. You're in the noise!

How do you get out of the noise and make your app something unique, something that everyone wants to have?

Being Different

The key to establishing dominance with your iPhone application, even though it might be short-lived, centers on being unique. Your app needs to be different from the rest of the pack. You want to stand out. Imagine being the first person to come out with a meet-up application or developing the first flight simulator app for the iPhone. You could charge whatever you want (within reason). We've all heard the rags-to-riches stories. Steve Demeter, developer of *Trism*, made $250,000 profit in two months. Bart Decrem, CEO of Tapulous and developer of *Tap Tap Revenge*, has seen millions of downloads.

Unfortunately, and no one is saying this out loud, but, for the vast majority of us, those days are long gone. Or are they?

At the Apple Developer's Conference in 2009, Apple made an announcement almost as significant as the iPhone itself. Apple was opening up the hardware interface to the iPhone for developers to create new accessories of their own. And with that announcement, we have all been given the chance again to be there at the start of something, possibly the start of something big.

Accessories

What is meant by *accessory*? For the purposes of this book, an accessory is defined as *any external hardware device that connects to the iPhone via the dock connector at the bottom of the phone* or *via a Bluetooth wireless signal*. In this book, to avoid confusing the reader, I will focus only on accessories that are physically connected to the iPhone by attaching at the 30-pin dock connector.

I know what you're thinking. The iPhone is a portable, self-contained device which got us away from all the cables associated with keyboards, mice, game controllers, tablets, and the like. Why would you want to bring all that junk back onto your desk?

The answer is simple. Functionality. Adding an accessory to the iPhone adds functionality. The addition of functionality increases the usefulness of the iPhone and makes it more valuable. Many people who thought the iPhone was just a fancy phone, music player, and/or gaming device now see a real value to the device.

Uses of Accessories

Take, for example, a jewelry designer who sells her products at weekend craft fairs. She probably takes cash or checks, but the cost of accepting credit cards seems out of her reach. Sitting in a tent, far away from an Internet connection or maybe even power, she simply can't afford the typical $1000 cost of a wireless Point of Sale (PoS) terminal. But pop a small credit card reader onto her iPhone and she has instant connectivity via the phone network to her merchant services account and the online database of her products. The instant connectivity to her merchant services account lets her know that she won't be dealing with bounced checks and that she will be getting paid.

Point of Sale and small business applications provide an easy target for iPhone accessories, and the benefits are not only confined to small off-site businesses. Imagine a restaurant where your server can swipe and process your card right at your table. Your card never leaves your sight freeing you to no longer worry about someone making a copy of your card and leading to possible identity theft. See Table 1–1 for other potential applications.

Table 1–1. *iPhone Accessory Potential Usage*

Area	Accessory Examples	Market Potential
eCommerce	PoS Terminals	
	Electronic Wallet	
	In-store Purchases	
Medical	Glucose Monitor	
	Blood Pressure Monitor	
Diagnostic	HVAC Measurement	Specialty area
	• temp	
	• voltage	
	• airflow	
Entertainment	Game Controller	

Other areas of eCommerce potential include the concept of an electronic wallet. Imagine a set of banking accounts kept on your phone—checking and credit—instantly accessible for any type of purchase. Scary, isn't it? Now imagine that it was only usable by the owner of those accounts identified biometrically through a device connected to your iPhone. Without your fingerprint on the sensor, the information is completely useless.

Think about going to the local big-box retailer, or even your local chain grocery store. They provide an in-store WiFi that allows your iPhone app to see all the products on the shelves. You get a map of where it is and can tally up the total in your cart. With a small bar-code scanner connected to your iPhone this becomes simple.

Medical accessories provide a huge potential area of development. Think about a blood glucose monitor that attaches to your iPhone and keeps a database of all your measurements and graphical tracking of history. It's only a small leap to imagine that it could warn you ahead of time of possible events that you could prevent. Or, imagine an accessory for taking your blood pressure that records the time and date of each reading. When you go to your doctor, you no longer have to remember to bring the several handwritten pieces of paper; you just pass him off your file and he can instantly see your progress.

Game controllers, measurement devices, e-commerce applications…think of anything there is a reasonably sophisticated electronic device for now, and imagine how it can be replaced with an accessory and an iPhone.

Table 1–1 shows only a few of the potential areas that have now become your *new frontier* as an iPhone accessory developer. You now have the potential to be one of those rags-to-riches stories from the early days of the App Store. That's what this book is about.

Accessories: A View From Above

A while back, accessory was defined. To reiterate: an accessory, for the discussions in this book, is *any external hardware device that connects to the iPhone via the dock connector at the bottom of the phone.*

Before digging into the details of accessories, let's first talk a little bit about the iPhone. Figure 1–1 provides one view of the major components of an iPhone.

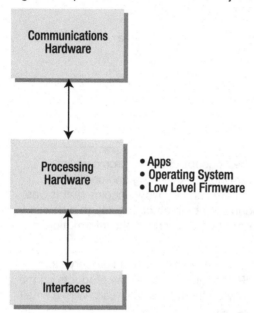

Figure 1–1. *Basic iPhone Organization*

From our point of view as accessory designers, the iPhone has three basic parts:

Communications Hardware: After all, the biggest part of iPhone is **phone**.

Processing Hardware: The tiny computer inside the phone.

Interfaces: How you get into and out of the phone.

> **NOTE:** The development of hardware accessories is not limited to just the iPhone but the iPod Touch as well. Wherever iPhone is used, be aware that iPod Touch may be used as well.

For this discussion, the phone section will not be of concern. It's not that the phone couldn't play a significant part in the overall application. For example, a credit card terminal relies heavily on connectivity to the user's merchant services account and inventory database. But that connectivity is dealt with in the iPhone app that communicates with those services. Normally, following the good practices of software compartmentalization, those services would reside within their own controller with its own set of properties and methods.

> **NOTE:** Although this book focuses primarily on the software aspect of interfacing with hardware accessories, the system architecture and hardware aspects will be covered in order to provide background for the reader wishing to construct his or her own accessories.

As developers of accessory components for the iPhone, we understand that we need to deal with the interface component. The device connects via the 30-pin dock at the bottom or possibly via wireless using Bluetooth. To make the accessory physically work with the iPhone, it must have either a mating 30-pin connector or be capable of using Bluetooth.

> **NOTE:** As stated earlier, Bluetooth accessory interfacing will not be covered in this book.

Finally, in the middle of Figure 1–1 sits the processor. I believe that the processor is what makes the iPhone unique among its peers. In my day-to-day life, I own and operate a Macintosh repair shop, although 90% of my customers are iPhone users who have either cracked their screen or dropped their phone in water. There are a few other problems that come up, but these two are far and away the vast majority.

What I have discerned from over one thousand iPhone customers is that iPhone users look at the device in one of two ways: they see it as a phone or they see it as a small computer.

Which group is correct? Well, that doesn't matter, but what does matter is the group that sees this little piece of technology as *something more* than a phone, seem to get a lot more use from it.

This group understands that at the heart of this phone is a small but powerful computer. A computer that is general purpose in nature and that you can instruct to do your bidding.

The little computer at the heart of the iPhone performs three basic functions:

Low-level hardware control of the internal circuitry

Runs a slimmed-down version of Mac OS (iPhone OS)

Executes user created programs (apps)

Figure 1–2 shows the inside of a 3G logic board with all its constituent parts.

Figure 1–2. *iPhone 3G Logic Board*

You can easily see all the complexity that is packed into approximately six square inches. Compare that to the logic board in a Macbook Pro shown in Figure 1–3. Taking the larger surface area of the Macbook Pro into consideration, you could conclude that the two are virtually identical in terms of complexity.

Figure 1–3. *Macbook Pro Logic Board*

At the system level, our accessory must deal with all three of these areas of processor function: the App, the OS, and the low-level control code in the iPhone.

To make the accessory useful, we develop an App that interacts with its user. This will, of course, appear as one of the multi-colored icons on the iPhone's springboard or home page.

Let's say a merchant uses an iPhone with a small credit card processing terminal. Along with that accessory hardware, there exists an app that the merchant uses to access the functionality of the reader.

A customer approaches the merchant with the items he wishes to purchase. The merchant starts the app on his iPhone and quickly taps the items from an inventory list the iPhone downloaded from WiFi or maybe the 3G network. Once entered, the merchant selects the shopping cart from the app and gives the customer his total.

The customer hands the merchant his credit card. The merchant connects the reader to the iPhone at the dock connector and then the magic happens. To begin working with the iPhone and its operating system, the reader must do several things. First it must conform to pinout, voltage, and other electronic signaling specifications from Apple.

> **NOTE:** To gain access to iPhone specifications, you must join the Made For iPod/Works With iPhone program at Apple. For more information, go to `http://devworld.apple.com/ipod`.

In addition, the reader must meet all the protocol specifications designated by Apple. The reader must assure the iPhone that it is a legitimate piece of hardware and properly functions with the device. It must prove that it will work with this *type* of device, say an iPhone but not an iPod Touch. And it must prove that it is designed to work with an app that exists on this particular iPhone.

Once the synchronization of iPhone and accessory has been accomplished, which generally takes less than three seconds, you're ready to rock. The merchant swipes the customer's card, and the app sends the data securely to the processing house to either approve or deny the purchase. In either case, the merchant has increased her assurance against fraudulent transactions by using the accessory.

> **NOTE:** Credit card processing transactions are subject to additional requirements beyond those of Apple. For example, transactions to/from merchant service sites are encrypted and secure over SSL. Also, no personal data can be kept or stored on either the reader accessory or iPhone. For more information, go to `https://www.pcisecuritystandards.org/`.

NOW, YOU TRY IT

<u>Plugging in the iPhone Game Controller</u>

Assuming you've purchased the Game Controller console that accompanies this book and have downloaded the aPONG game from the app store, let's get started.

1. Start the aPONG app from your iPhone springboard and go to the setup page.

2. Notice the state of the controller link icon in the upper-right corner of the screen. It should appear red and broken.

3. Connect the controller to the bottom of the iPhone at the dock connector and watch for the link icon to change from a broken red icon to solid green.

4. Note the time that it takes to change from Broken/Red to Unbroken/Green. During this period, the accessory and iPhone OS and the app have made their connection and have agreed to work together.

5. Remove the game controller and notice the change. Note how the time for the indicator to change is much faster. Disconnection of accessories is nearly instantaneous because there is no real handshaking that must occur. You simply remove the accessory.

6. Connect and reconnect a couple of times to note the change in the app. Good applications, in fact all Apple approved applications, will not be affected (crash) when connecting or disconnecting an accessory.

NOTE: In general, any accessory should function as described in the preceding exercise.

To create the actual hardware accessory to work with the iPhone and its software and applications requires the ability to design and develop commercial electronics circuits that are small, consume low power, and have a purpose. Let me restate that last one—the device you are creating must have a purpose.

When I was growing up, one of my coveted gifts for Christmas was a 101 Electronics Experimenter's Kit from Heathkit hobby electronics shop. I remember repeatedly tripping the breakers in the room where I had set up my laboratory.

Nowadays I don't see too many kids with electronic kits and, for that matter, I don't see them for sale much either. But they are out there and so is the kind of talent to actually make these nifty little iPhone add-ons.

Truthfully, it's much easier now than ever before for an amateur hobbyist to create the circuits that will contain the brains of tomorrow's million selling accessories. The guts of everything can be programmed in an off-the-shelf chip, smaller than a pea, and is more powerful than personal computers of just two decades ago.

The software to develop the circuit boards comes for free from rapid prototyping houses that will turn around your board in just a few days for as little as one hundred dollars. You can see the area where I developed my first iPhone accessory in Figure 1–4.

Figure 1–4. *A madman's iPhone lair. Note the use of PCs in the accessory development process*

Logic design, soldering, programming, and mechanical design are just some of the skills required to make a legitimate iPhone accessory. Fortunately, there are thousands of resources available instantly via online search engines to help you find the resource that you need to make your dream a reality.

To get a better idea of what it takes to develop an iPhone hardware accessory, let's take a look at the insides of one.

Credit Card Reader

Rather than focus now on our game controller, let's take a closer look at another typical accessory for an iPhone.

iPhone PoS terminal applications allow the small business to enter a customer's purchase, connect to an online merchant services account, and charge the card for the amount of purchase. The merchant no longer has to worry about bad checks or credit card transactions that won't get approved.

Up until now, these PoS applications were just that—applications that ran on the iPhone and nothing else. The merchant manually entered the card number, expiration date, card code, and other information required for the transaction. Mistakes were easily made.

Further, because the complete card stripe data was not sent to the merchant services account, the transaction was processed as if the card was not present. This results in higher fees for each transaction than if the card was swiped and the actual data transmitted.

By attaching a credit card reader to the iPhone PoS application, the actual data from the card's magnetic stripe is sent, requiring much less manual data entry, and allowing the merchant lower fees for each transaction (see Figure 1–5).

Figure 1–5. *iPhone Point of Sale Terminal*

Breaking down the PoS terminal determines that it is composed of two primary components. The card reader subassembly provides a slot for the card to slide through which aligns it up to the proper area of the read head, and the logic board connects the wires from the read head to the 30-pin connector of the iPhone.

Figures 1–6 and 1–7 show the heart of the pPoS accessory, the logic board containing all the processing hardware. Note that there are two primary integrated circuits (ICs) that make up the function on the logic board. The chip on the left, the controller, contains all the processing logic of the accessory and is where the firmware resides. The chip on the right contains all the security mechanisms to assure that this is an authorized accessory.

The board is roughly 1mm thick and contains four layers of interconnections between the ICs and the other components. Plainly visible at the top is the 30-pin iPhone mating connector. In the lower right of the board's top view, you can plainly see the orange socket that connects via cable to the card reader subassembly.

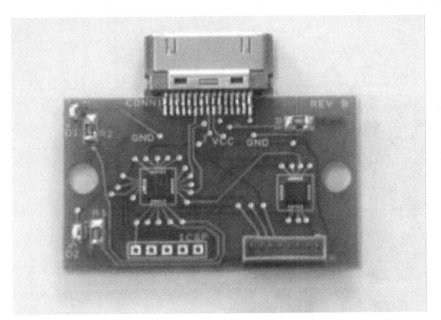

Figure 1–6. *Credit Card Reader (pPos) logic board (top view). The two black squares are the ICs that do most of the accessory's heavy lifting. The silver connector at the top attaches the board to the iPhone and the orange connector at the lower right goes to the card reader subassembly.*

The key point to take away from this discussion of the PoS accessory is how simple the actual accessory really is. Think of it this way: the iPhone is a computer, to which you wish to attach *something* to do *something*. With an external accessory, you make this connection happen.

You attach a *card reader* to do point of *sale processing*.

You attach a *thermocouple* (temperature sensor) to *monitor heating and cooling*.

You attach a *knob and a button* to *play a game*—your game controller.

> **NOTE:** The distinction between what an accessory may be used for and the portion of the accessory that acts as merely an interface will not always be this clear. In some cases, the processor shown in the PoS terminal may act as both an interface and the accessory itself, only if the processor has been tasked to perform some special processing that cannot be done by the iPhone hardware alone.

Figure 1–7. *Credit Card Reader Logic Board (bottom view)*

But I'm a Programmer

Now that you've been *under the hood* of an iPhone accessory, let's get back on track. Because this is a book about software, additional discussions of the hardware development issues surrounding accessories are going be deferred to the last section of this book. In Part 3, I provide an overview of all the other parts of accessory development. I will start off with basic information about Apple's Made For iPod/Works With iPhone program (MFi/WWi). To learn about the specs surrounding the iPhone interfaces or to be able to buy the iPhone parts you need to build your accessory, you must join this program.

Next, I'll describe the basics of hardware design for your accessory. You'll need a processor of some sort in order to execute the software on the accessory side of things. A schematic editor and PC Board design tool puts all the parts together for you so that it can be manufactured. Once you've got a board designed, you'll need to test it and then enclose it inside some type of case. It will need to be tested; not once, but several times. After all that, you will have to come up with some type of packaging if you intend to sell your accessory.

Did you notice that a processor was included in the accessory? Because it must identify itself to the iPhone's operating system, as well as your own application, the accessory needs to have some intelligence. The ability to identify, authenticate, perform functions, and communicate back and forth to the iPhone will all be performed by *firmware* that resides in your accessory.

What is firmware? Essentially, firmware is software that doesn't go away. The processor typically contains onboard memory that will hold the functional software. This memory is *non-volatile*, meaning that its contents do not disappear when power is removed. Another name for this memory is ROM—read-only memory. You may also hear it referred to as *flash* memory.

NOTE: I refer to the software stored inside your accessory as **firmware** because it stays in the processor's memory even when power is removed.

Inside your accessory, there will be a processor, very similar to the processor in the iPhone itself or the CPU that runs your computer. Because the needs of the accessory are small—it may only do a couple functions—the processor will be small. More specifically, the processor will have minimal functionality. It may operate at much slower speeds than typical CPUs. It will have fewer connections to the outside world. It will be physically small. It will draw very little power. Most importantly, it will be inexpensive in order to keep the accessory's manufacturing costs reasonable.

Part 3 concludes with a section outlining the other issues surrounding the development of your accessory. Here, the appearance of your product is discussed, where and how to get the tools needed for development, parts sources, business issues, and all the other things you might need or want to know.

The Software Approach

Before I got off on a tangent about building your own accessory, I stated that this is a book about software. But, if you are developing software for an accessory, don't you have to build an accessory so you can develop the software you will use for that accessory? Confusing?

Because I want my readers to get started immediately on developing software for accessories, I've developed an accessory game controller for use with this book. See the appendix for information about obtaining the accessory.

The game controller (GC) accessory gives you a simple device that includes both input and output for your software. The GC uses a knob to incrementally adjust an input value to your app. There is a pushbutton to give your app an immediate on/off state. I've thrown in a couple light-emitting diodes (LEDs) to provide indication from your app back to your accessory.

In Part 2, I walk you through the development of a simple *pong* style game that uses the External Accessory framework and GC to build upon the theoretical foundations I cover in the text.

As stated in the preface, the reader should have some knowledge of developing iPhone applications. In addition to having downloaded the software development kit (SDK) from Apple's iPhone developer site, you need to have joined the iPhone developer program as either an individual or a company or be part of an iPhone development team. This enables you to download your app to execute on iPhone hardware.

Because any accessory, including our GC, connects to an iPhone, you need to be able to download your app to the iPhone to use the External Accessory frameworks I will talk about in Chapter 2 and throughout this book.

In addition, having an understanding of the basic iPhone design patterns will be extremely helpful. Particularly useful would be to have the concept of delegates and view controllers already under your belt. In Chapter 3, I will cover the three basic design patterns used for the game: delegates, view controllers, and notifications.

The Pong Game

We're using the simple game of Pong as your frame of reference in working with iPhone accessories. OK, it's not glamorous but it works well for what we need to do (see Figure 1–8).

The concept is simple. Touch the serve button and a ball is sent towards your opponent, the computer. Simple collision detection is used to determine when the paddle hits the ball. The computer's primitive artificial intelligence (AI) tracks the paddle towards where the ball is headed at a predefined maximum rate that is set by a #define in the code. The player touches and moves left or right to control his paddle. The first player to reach five (5) wins. Pressing Serve starts the volley for each point. The ball is always served towards the computer's paddle.

You can add the sound of the ball hitting the paddle and some minor enhancements, but this is definitely a bare bones game that you will first build as a normal iPhone game app. This provides a basic introduction to the use of view controllers, sound, and the other bits that make up your version of Pong.

After getting to this point, you convert the controls over to use the game controller. The GC knob controls the position of your paddle. Turn the knob counter-clockwise and the paddle moves to the left. Turn it clockwise and it moves to the right. The game controller's pushbutton will take over the serve function.

It's a very simple game and interfacing exercise, but it covers all the various directions of input and output as well as discrete (on/off) and variable (position of the knob) values that can be sent. Any other form of I/O will just be a derivation of the basics that you build in your project.

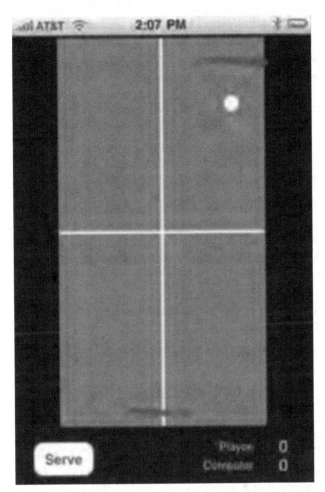

Figure 1–8. *The Pong Game*

Embedded Systems

To understand iPhone programming, you must understand embedded systems and the differences from what, I suppose, is still taught in every introductory programming course.

Most computer classes, at least the ones I took years ago, started teaching programming the same way. They first talk about input, processing, and output. While those three major steps work fine for just about any and all software out there, they always seem to sound a bit *linear*.

By linear I mean that it sounds like you always go through these three steps: input, processing, and output. For example, a checkbook program takes as input all the checks you've written this past month. The program works on the data and spits out the answer—your monthly statement. In addition, this program executes in parallel with a lot of other stuff happening on the computer on which it is executing.

An embedded system tends to run continuously in a *loop*. The loop is usually very fast, on the order of milliseconds or microseconds. To get input, one of two things happens. One way data is input is by *polling*. Somewhere in the loop, a subroutine goes out and, for example, checks a temperature reading. This capture routine doesn't necessarily worry about what to do with the information, it just captures it for use somewhere else.

Another option is via *interrupts*. The loop still executes very fast, but when that temperature gauge hits a certain point, let's say 100 degrees, it interrupts the loop to give it this information—that the temperature gauge is reading 100 degrees.

These explanations are somewhat over simplified, but, in general, this is how you want to think about things.

An iPhone uses this embedded system approach. It continually executes an event processing loop doing mundane housekeeping tasks until something happens—you press an icon on the springboard to start a program. You call this something that happens an *event*.

An event is something that happens outside the norm of the loop: the user presses a button or an internal timer counts down to zero.

As programmers, you normally use one of two methods to detect these events: polling and interrupts.

Polling is the continual, periodic checking of some value or event. An everyday example would be the normal mail delivery. The postman doesn't ring twice in this case, he doesn't even ring once. He just puts our mail in the box and moves on. Normally, you probably check the box, or *poll* its contents, once a day. If you're expecting something important, you might poll much more often.

The other form of event handling involves the use of interrupts. When an event occurs, the event itself notifies the processing loop that it has occurred. Usually, this involves some bit of hardware external to the processing loop. To imagine this, think of your telephone. You don't have to keep looking at your phone to see if someone is calling you; the phone rings to let you know when someone is on the line. It interrupts your normal activity to tell you to answer the phone.

I'll talk more about polling and interrupts when you start adding the game controller accessory to the Pong game, but, for now, the key idea is that this concept of polling and interrupts is how iPhone applications are designed.

The iPhone design orients itself heavily towards user interaction. A user touches or interrupts whatever is going on to start an application. Or maybe you're playing a game and moving your piece from one position on the game board to another. The iPhone internal software may continually look to see (or poll) where your finger is and move the piece to that location.

Building an Accessory

As mentioned in the opening of this book, the purpose here is to give the software engineer a quick insight into learning how to interface hardware accessories to the iPhone. Therefore, I won't be covering in any detail everything needed to build your own hardware accessory.

That said, Part 3 covers some of the information you would need to get started. The main thing you need to understand is that, in order to build an authorized hardware accessory, you will need to join Apple's Made For iPod/Works With iPhone (MFi/WWi) program. This program costs nothing to join and it provides the developer with a huge amount of specifications to further understand the internal workings of the iPhone. This is all that information you wonder about when looking at the iPhone as an (non-Apple) outsider.

In addition, the MFi/WWi program allows the developer to purchase key components that are otherwise not available to the general public. Apple maintains strict controls on the 30-pin connector needed to connect to an iPhone and this program provides the only way to get it.

I will also talk about the elementary pieces of an iPhone accessory and offer some suggestions on all varieties of things such as the processors you might choose for your accessory and what compiler to use to create the accessory's firmware. Also touched on are the more mundane subjects of business and financial organization and record keeping. Apple's MFi/WWi program requires developers to keep very close track of the day-to-day operation of their accessory projects.

Creating an iPhone accessory requires a lot of work, planning, and more than likely, several setbacks. What I hope to do in Part 3 is to provide you with a heads-up to what you might expect.

Summary

In this opening chapter, I've covered a broad set of material ranging from what an accessory is and why you might what to program one to the broader aspect of business planning for your accessory creation endeavors.

A hardware accessory provides an exciting avenue for the iPhone software developer to create something new and different to set them apart from the pack. Remember, at the time of this writing there were more than 100,000 apps in the App Store. It's hard to stand out among that crowd. At the same time, there very few iPhone accessories on the market and that really opens the playing field for the rest of us. This kind of opportunity comes along very rarely.

Both our accessory as well as the iPhone software itself uses interrupts or polling mechanisms as part of an embedded systems approach to software design. An embedded systems approach differs from conventional programming in that a continual loop is used to take care of general housekeeping while important events interrupt that loop to be serviced.

The next chapter begins with an in-depth look at the software tools Apple provides to permit our app to communicate with external hardware accessories.

KEY POINTS

- Apple's iPhone accessory program represents a new frontier in software development.

- Opportunities for accessories exist in many areas such as education, finance, health, and entertainment.

- For the purposes of this book, the iPhone can be divided into processing, communications, and interface sections.

- An iPhone accessory contains a processor of its own that executes firmware in order to communicate with the iPhone and app.

- I use the term Embedded System to describe the processing that occurs in an iPhone or iPhone accessory.

- Providing input to the iPhone is usually done via polling or interrupts.

- To create your own hardware accessory, you must be part of Apple's MFi/WWi program.

Chapter 2

EAAccessory Framework

iPhone OS 3.0, released in June 2009, included the External Accessory Framework allowing, for the first time, an iPhone application to communicate with a user defined piece of hardware. The first thing you're likely to notice is that Apple uses **EAAccessory**, which seems to mean "External Accessory Accessory," and thus double booking the Accessory term, but it's just something we have to live with.

Frameworks

When I first started programming in Mac OS X, for a long time the term framework confused me. Even though it was made clear that a framework was basically a library, I couldn't seem to get around the difference in terminology. Why did they call it framework and not just library?

The main thing to remember is that a framework is more than a library. A framework is actually a directory; a hierarchical directory that contains shared resources such as a library. In addition to a library, a framework may contain nib files, images, strings, header files, and even documentation. Think of it as the all-encompassing package one level above a library.

A framework, by means of its included libraries, provides a set of routines that can be used by the application to perform specific tasks. For example, UIKit provides the mechanisms for your application to communicate with the user via the iPhone's touchscreen. The Audio Toolbox framework provides the tools needed to allow the application to use sound.

Figure 2–1 illustrates the general structure of a framework. Note that a framework includes much more than the shared library that we tend to think of as being the framework itself.

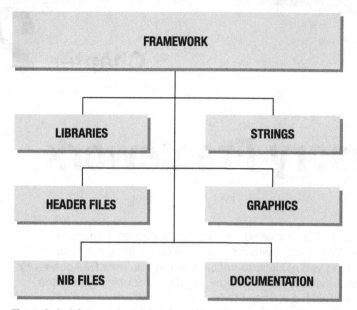

Figure 2–1. *A framework contains shared libraries as well as other elements in a directory structure.*

This book addresses one specific framework: the External Accessory Framework. Typically, though I'm not exactly sure why, Apple uses "EAAccessory" to represent the term External Accessory. In their documentation you will see terms like EAAccessoryManager or EAAccessory Class Reference.

Apple's External Accessory framework provides the iPhone software developer necessary support for communicating with external hardware. Support is provided for both the 30-pin dock connector and wireless communication via Bluetooth.

For the example using the Pong game, you will focus on connectivity using the 30-pin dock connector because that is how the game controller design works. The careful reader will note that the software never explicitly chooses the dock connector to work with. The mechanism that determines whether to use the dock connector or to connect via Bluetooth is part of the iPhone OS. We, as app developers, never see it.

So what do we see? In a nutshell, we see two streams: an input stream and an output stream. Developers who have used streams programming previously will be right at home with sending data to and receiving data from an external hardware accessory.

Streams

A fundamental programming abstraction, a stream provides a sequence of bits transmitted serially from one point to another. Streams are unidirectional. They go from point A to point B. So, for bi-directional data flow, you need two streams: input and output.

Streams provide a device-independent way of moving data. You need not worry about whether the device is your Pong game controller or a server on the other side of the globe. The stream simply provides the communications path.

Cocoa, Apple's name for the complete collection of frameworks, APIs and all the stuff that makes up Mac OS and iPhone OS, defines three classes of streams.

NSStream defines the interface and properties for all stream objects. It is the abstract class from which the other stream objects derive. NSInputStream and NSOutputStream are subclassed from NSStream and define a basic input and output behavior, respectively.

If the concept of streams seems new, it shouldn't. If you've ever programmed "Hello, World" in C, then you've already been using streams: stdin, stdout, and stderr are examples of streams. The statement printf by default outputs data to stdout and unless redirected, appears on the text terminal. In iPhone OS, you use NSLog to output test messages to the console much as printf is used in standard Unix C programming.

Protocols

Before digging into the details of the EA framework, one thing you must come to grips with is the concept of protocols. Now, as an experienced iPhone programmer, you're probably thinking that you already understand protocols. Protocols establish a set of required and/or optional protocols that an object must implement. And that is correct.

The problem is that the EA framework uses another definition of protocol. What's worse is that the EA framework actually uses *both* definitions of protocol.

First, let's make sure you understand Cocoa's use of protocols. Protocols provide a mechanism for objects to communicate with each other. This *interprocess communication* comes about through the use of Objective-C messages.

The UIApplication Delegate protocol fits the bill as the most common and frequently used protocol. It's one you see in almost any app you build. This protocol declares methods that are implemented by the delegate of the UIApplication. You see this in just about any app you create in the form of applicationDidFinishLaunching and all the other methods found in your app delegate.

Table 2-1. *UIApplicationDelegate protocol instance methods*

UIApplication Instance Methods
applicationDidFinishLaunching:
applicationDidFinishLaunchingWithOptions:
applicationDidBecomeActive:
applicationWillTerminate:
applicationDidReceiveMemoryWarning:
applicationWillResignActive
application:handleOpenURL:
application:didReceiveRemoteNotification:

Any iPhone software developer who has ever created an application should understand delegation. For these purposes, let's say you have this application that you're working on. There is only one application, which is a singleton. A singleton means that there is only one of this object, in this case just one UIApplication, in existence.

Instead of subclassing UIApplication, you normally create two files, a .c and a .h, that end in AppDelegate. This object will act as the delegate of the UIApplication. In other words, your app delegate implements the stuff that the application normally calls.

The code below shows part of the header file for your app delegate. The @interface says that you are defining the interface to the OurAppDelegate object. The elements defined within the curly brackets are the public properties of your object and include the window and navigationController.

```
@interface OurAppDelegate : NSObject <UIApplicationDelegate> {

    UIWindow *window;
    UINavigationController *navigationController;
}
```

What makes this unique is <UIApplicationDelegate> found in the definition. This statement tells you that the OurAppDelegate object will implement the required and possibly some methods of the UIApplicationDelegate protocol. You would expect to see methods such as applicationDidFinishLaunching performing setup functions in your code.

An object is not limited to only one protocol. Additional protocols can be added by using separating commas within the single set of brackets. For example, see the following code:

```
@interface OurAppDelegate : NSObject <UIApplicationDelegate, SecondProtcol> {

    UIWindow *window;
```

```
        UINavigationController *navigationController;
}
```

To define your own protocol, you might use the following:

```
@protocol OurProtocol
- (BOOL)send:(id)data;
- (id)receive; @optional
- (int)status;
@end
```

This protocol would require send: and status to be implemented, leaving receive as an option whether to include or to leave out.

OK, so you've spent some time on the first definition of protocols. This should already be familiar to most iPhone software developers. Now you need to understand a new, slightly different and slightly the same version of the term protocol.

Why did Apple choose to use the same name twice for different things? Well, they didn't. The second use of the term protocol is something that has been around for longer than even Apple.

In the early days of computing, instead of the sleek look of an aluminum iMac, you might have had a big black box that housed your processor and a separate, monochrome terminal. The standard terminal used, back in the day, was typically a VT100 attached to your processor enclosure with a serial, or RS-232, cable.

To communicate with the VT100 terminal, the processor's operating system used an established set of rules for how and what was to be transmitted over the serial cable. For example, the seven-bit ASCII code 0x13 represented a carriage return and a 0x10 represented a line-feed. So, if the user pressed the enter key on the VT100 terminal, a sequence of 0x13 followed by 0x10 would be sent to the processor and its operating system.

This is all fine and good, but what would happen if the processor decided to send something to the terminal at the same time that the terminal sent data to the processor? What was needed was a higher-level set of rules, or a traffic cop, to manage who sent data and when.

This higher-level set of rules is what is known as a protocol. We call the set of rules by which computers manage communications a protocol. Note that this is not too different from the earlier use of protocol. There, you had a set of rules that control the exchange of data between objects, using Objective-C messages, which may reside on the same processor and memory space.

So, to clarify, in this book I will use the term protocol in two different situations. In all situations, a protocol means a set of rules that we have to follow. In the first case, I use protocols to mean the way we send messages back and forth within Cocoa, in other words, the rules that we adhere to for message passing. The second use of protocol, which I will shortly describe in more detail, refers to the rules that govern communications between the iPhone OS and the firmware residing within the external accessory.

More on Protocols

Now let's look at some examples of protocols that govern communications between the iPhone and external accessories. Let's start with a real-world example of a credit card reader.

In Figure 2–2, you see the bi-directional link between the iPhone and your credit card reader. In normal operation, the user starts the application and selects the items that his customer is interested in purchasing. Once the total of all the items is determined, he attaches the card reader to the 30-pin dock connector of the iPhone.

For the moment, let's disregard all the setup that is performed between the iPhone and the card reader so you can focus on the nominal operation of the card reader.

Normally, most of the information will travel from the card reader to the iPhone, and contains all the data from one or both tracks of the magnetic stripe on the customer's card. Let's make this a little bit clearer and say that you are sending the card number, the cardholder's name, and the expiration date of the card. The app needs this information to complete the transaction.

Additionally, the application can normally start diagnostics on the card reader to determine if it is functioning correctly. Finally, the card reader may contain diagnostic indicators such as LEDs that can be controlled from the iPhone to verify an operational connection.

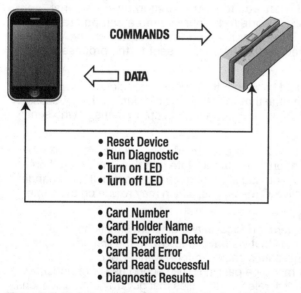

Figure 2–2. *Typical communications flow for the Card Reader Accessory*

So, in general, commands are sent from the iPhone to the card reader accessory with data (card information) being sent in the reverse direction. Looking at this closely, you see that there are two different types of data streams. First, there is the transaction information that is sent during normal operation. But a second mode of operation would include the diagnostic commands sent to the accessory and the status sent back.

The set of commands and status information used to communicate between the iPhone and card reader form your protocol. Specifically, each command and status chunk of information fits within a structured format that you define to be your protocol. Figure 2–3 depicts the generic format of commands and status transactions.

Commands and status are sent in fixed or variable sized data packets or groups of bytes. Generally, the packets are ordered by decreasing importance of information. For example, the command that you are telling the accessory to execute, arguably the most important part of the transfer, is the first part of the packet. It would therefore reside at byte position 0 in an n-byte length packet.

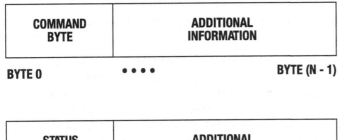

Figure 2–3. *Generic command and status byte structure*

In the case of the card reader, there exists only a small set of commands. So you permit each command to be one byte in length. At eight bits per byte this gives you 256 possible commands; plenty more than the handful you need.

So what is the additional information? Let's consider the command to turn on an LED. In actuality, you need to be able to turn the LED on or off. You could have a command for each or you could have a single command with a parameter to say whether you want the LED to turn on or off. Similarly, if you had multiple LEDs on the accessory, you might have an additional information field that tells you which LED to command.

So your LED command would contain three fields. First, the LED command itself, then the LED to operate upon, and, finally, whether you are turning it on or off. Figure 2–4 depicts the case where you have three LEDs in your accessory.

COMMAND BYTE	LED SELECT BYTE	ON/OFF BYTE
BYTE 0	BYTE 1	BYTE 2
0x01	LED #1 - 0x01	ON - 0x01
	LED #2 - 0x02	OFF - 0x02
	LED #3 - 0x03	

Figure 2–4. *The LED command packet structure*

For example, to turn off LED #2, you send the sequence 0x010202 from the iPhone to the accessory.

Status information works basically the same, but in the opposite direction. Instead of a command byte, you might have a status byte that indicates one of several conditions. For the results of a start diagnostics command, you might have 0x01 to mean that the tests completed successfully, 0x02 to mean that the tests completed but something failed, or 0x03 to mean that the tests hung up and did not complete. Additional information might include the duration of the diagnostic in milliseconds, the test that failed, or the last test that completed before the diagnostic routine hung.

What does all this have to do with protocols? The set of structures that you define to handle the communications between the iPhone and the accessory in both directions forms your protocol. So you might have some number of command structures like Figure 2–4 and another similar set for status as well as possibly other information that you transfer.

However many of these sets of transfer structures you create, when placed all together, they form the External Accessory protocol.

You might be asking, "What's the big deal? I always define some structure to my messaging."

The big deal in this case is that the protocol has to be named and defined in the properties list of your project. In addition, Apple requires a specific naming convention, reverse-DNS, using your company's Internet address or a name that you are authorized to use.

For example, if your company's name was fsda357 and you owned the domain fsda357.com, you might name your first protocol com.fsda357.p1, where p1 indicates this is your first protocol. You could just as easily call it com.fsda357.protocol1, or com.fsda357.protocolthx1138, or com. fsda357.ihatenamingprotocols. The key point to naming the protocol is that it must be unique and typically Apple likes to do that using reverse-DNS. Check out the preferences files on your Mac if you don't believe it.

With the June 2009 release of the iPhone SDK 3.0, support was added to include the protocol in your app's info-plist file. Figure 2–5 shows an example of a plist where you use the protocol COM.MACMEDX.P1.

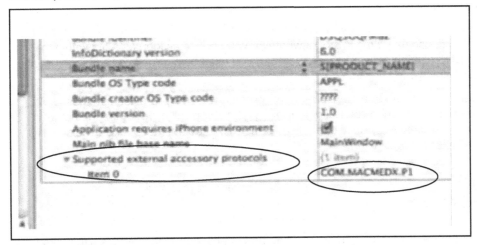

Figure 2–5. *iPhone SDK 3.0 protocol support in the info-plist file*

NOW, YOU TRY IT

Setting the External Accessory Protocol

You're going to use XCode to create a protocol and name it in an iPhone project.

1. Open XCode.

2. Select File➤New Project.

3. Select iPhone Application on the left and View-Based Application on the right.

4. Save as TestProtocol on your desktop.

5. Open the resources folder on the left and click on the testProtocol-Info.plist (if you used a different file name, select the appropriate plist file).

6. In the editor window, control (or right-) click on the first column bottom row. It may say Main Nib File Base Name, but it doesn't matter.

7. Select Add Row and from the drop-down select Supported External Accessory Protocol. Note that you see a disclosure arrow to the left of the name.

8. Open the disclosure triangle and you should see Item 0. You can set as many protocols as you need by clicking the + sign at the rightmost part of the row.

9. Click in the empty cell to the right of Supported External Accessory Protocol and type: com.yourcompany.p1, then hit enter. Congratulations, you have now created your first iPhone external accessory protocol name.

Choosing the name for your external accessory protocol may appear to be a totally arbitrary exercise. It is not. Because the protocol is the agreement made between the iPhone application and the external accessory firmware, the accessory also has a say in what name to use.

Basically, it works like this. If you are developing both the app and accessory yourself, or your team, can name the protocol whatever you choose as long as it fits within the reverse-DNS naming convention. Remember, you must own or have a license to use the com.company name chosen.

However, if you are an app developer and intending to use a pre-existing accessory, such as is the case when you build your pong game, you will have to use the name defined by the accessory developer. That name will, of course, also follow the same reverse-DNS naming convention.

> **NOTE:** The protocol name is case sensitive. Be careful to match exactly the name used in the app and accessory.

So, what happens if the names are mismatched? Let's look at the various situations.

First, consider the case of attaching an accessory to your iPhone for which there is no associated application. How is it determined that there is no associated application? This is what the protocol is for. If you have no apps on your iPhone that contain the protocol used by the accessory, you will see something like the screen in Figure 2–6.

Figure 2–6. *Missing app with accessory protocol*

This screen lets you know that there is no app on your iPhone containing the protocol used by the accessory you just attached. Why show this screen? If you select "Yes," you are taken to the App store and shown the app (or apps) that work with this accessory. This is kind of neat. So you can sell your accessory by mail order, from your store, or door-to-door...it doesn't matter. What you can't sell directly to your customer is an Apple approved iPhone application.

With this screen, your customer doesn't have to search the iTunes App Store, they're taken right to your app.

At the time of this writing, there are no commercially available iPhone accessories using the EA Framework, so this is somewhat subject to change. But I believe that hardware accessories will be sold and the application given away for free, or really, as part of the purchase price of the accessory.

However, since a lot of work likely went into the app that goes with the accessory, I suspect these apps won't be listed as free in order to keep everyone from downloading and possibly dissecting them.

What I think will be the most likely scenario, is that a code will be provided with each accessory sold to permit the accessory owner to get the app for free. You simply go to the front page of iTunes and select redeem coupon. This takes you right to the correct app associated with the application.

Programmers with significant experience programming apps may wonder about the bundle identifier. The bundle identifier is a random looking set of letters and numbers that create a unique key and is created in the iPhone developer program portal. Normally, you let Apple come up with a random identifier and you include this as part of the provisioning information when building your app.

The accessory developer must also include a bundle identifier in the accessory's firmware. Though not seen by the app developer, this accessory bundle identifier is passed to the iPhone OS when the accessory is first connected.

The accessory bundle identifier is used to limit apps that can communicate with the accessory. While one app can talk to many accessories as well as one accessory talking to many apps, they all have to have the same bundle identifier. A bundle identifier is associated with a single developer, which means that no matter which app an accessory works with, all those apps will generally be from the same developer.

The interesting thing is that, at the time of this writing, the bundle identifier doesn't seem to matter. That is, I've written apps that use one bundle identifier with an accessory programmed with a different bundle identifier. However, when Apple tests your accessory and the app that goes with it, you will fail the test should the bundle identifiers differ. I suspect that Apple may open up accessories to multiple apps from different vendors at some time in the future. It just seems like good business, but that is purely conjecture.

In summary, the protocol must be the same on the app and accessory or there will be no communications between the two, as well as, according to Apple requirements, both app and accessory must use the same bundle identifier.

Okay, that was a lot of talk about protocols. Mainly, I wanted you to understand there are two slightly different uses of the term protocol and when developing software for external accessories, we are concerned with both definitions. Now, let's get into the details of the EA framework.

The EA Framework

Let's begin the discussions of the External Accessory framework by getting a handle on the structure of the framework as well as some terminology.

> **NOTE:** The reader should go to the iPhone Developer site and download the External Accessory Framework Reference. This document contains information on the three important classes: EAAccessory Class, EAAccessory Manager Class, and EASession Class. It also discusses the EAAccessoryDelegate Protocol (the first of our two uses for the term protocol).

The EA Framework contains three classes: the EAAccessory class, the EAAccessoryManager class, and the EASession class.

Briefly, the EAAccessory class represents a single hardware accessory, while the EAAccessoryManager class manages any and all accessories that may be attached to your iPhone. At the time of this writing, Apple allows only a single attached accessory, but within the EAAccessoryManager, accessories are presented as a list. For future compatibility with new releases, applications dealing with accessories should always deal with them as an array.

Finally, EASession defines the connection or channel between the iPhone app and the external accessory. This logical entity, once established, gives the application the ability to use the properties and methods of the EAAccessory framework to handle all the communications between the app and the accessory.

EAAccessory Class Properties

As stated previously, the EAAccessory class provides the iPhone application with everything it needs to know about a single hardware accessory. Even before opening a session, properties within this class provide your app with everything it needs to get started.

Your app first needs to know if there is an accessory connected to the iPhone. The **connected** property's Boolean value provides a YES/NO indicator as to whether the accessory is currently connected to the iPhone OS-based device. The application uses this read-only property to decide whether or not to try and open a session with the accessory.

```
@property (nonatomic,readonly,getter=isConnected) BOOL connected
```

While the **connected** property might seem to be highly useful, apps tend to use a different method altogether when querying whether or not an accessory is available. In general, your apps tend to use the notification center to be alerted as to when an accessory is connected or disconnected. I will discuss this in much greater detail when talking about design patterns as well as when you build the Pong application.

The **connectionID** property's read-only value uniquely defines the accessory to the device. Again, because the framework provides a list of available accessories, each accessory must be uniquely identified. Although Apple only currently supports a single accessory per iPhone at this time, this requirement may change in the near future. As an iPhone app developer you should always design your application to handle accessories presented in an NSArray.

```
@property (nonatomic, readonly) NSUInteger connectionID
```

As an example of considering accessories delivered in an NSArray, consider the following code snippet.

```
for(EAAccessory *accessory in _accessoryList) {
        if ([disconnectedAccessory connectionID] == [accessory connectionID]) {
            break;
        }
        disconnectedAccessoryIndex++;
    }
```

This for statement would be typically found in a method called upon receipt of a notification of an accessory being disconnected. Assume that we have set up an NSMutableArray _accessoryList, and that when the accessory was first connected we added it to the array. This statement loops through each element of the _accessoryList array (which is just one element) and compares its connectionID to the connectionID of the accessory with which we are working:

```
[accessory connectionID]
```

If any additional processing were needed to handle the disconnected accessory, that code would be placed within the brackets before the **break** statement. All that this code segment does is to increment your index of disconnected accessories, which would be 1.

Because delegation is a central design pattern in most iPhone apps, the accessory's **delegate** property defines the object to receive notifications about changes to the status of the accessory object through implementing the methods of the EAAccessory delegate protocol. First, let's look at the interface definition of a sample accessory delegate object:

```
@interface accController : NSObject <EAAccessoryDelegate>{

    EAAccessory *_accessory;
    EASession *_session;
    NSString *_protocolString;
}
(void)accessoryDidDisconnect:(EAAccessory *)accessory;
@end
```

In this code snippet we define the object accController, subclassed from NSObject, to be your delegate for the accessory object. The <EAAccessoryDelegate> portion of the @interface statement requires that the object implement the accessoryDidDisconnect method as defined by the protocol, which I'll talk about later.

The class also defines the three public properties: _accessory, _session, and _protocolString. I will discuss these more in-depth later in this chapter when we talk about EASession.

Let's pause for a moment here to discuss delegates just a bit. Having previously written at least a couple iPhone apps, you've certainly come across delegation. When you read about delegation, the sentences all seem to make sense on their own, but a lot of people come away with an uneasy feeling that they just haven't gotten it completely.

Starting from the top, you build your program by creating a set of objects with properties and methods. We all get that; it's basic object-oriented programming. And, as discussed before, since you're doing embedded systems programming, your objects will generally respond to outside stimulus; either a loop within your code polls something until it changes, or maybe an external interrupt changes and calls a method of your object.

A delegate is nothing more than one of those objects within the set of objects that make up your program, or, specifically, your application. You might have view-controller objects, tab-bar controller objects, and even special, unique objects that you've made up. Because we tend, as developers, to get caught up in the details, it is easy to forget that your set of objects is also an object in itself. Together they form a UIApplication object.

Now, it's easy to see that this higher-level object, the UIApplication, also contains properties and methods. For example, there is a method called applicationDidFinishLaunching that is called when the application has, well, finished launching. But you never defined or subclassed a UIApplication object, correct? What you did was declare one of your objects to be the application delegate. Typically, most iPhone programming tutorials will create something that ends in AppDelegate and implements this ApplicationDelegate protocol and is where you find such good stuff as applicationDidFinishLaunching.

In essence, you create an application delegate to handle all the stuff that centers on your application: the starting, the stopping, the memory warnings, etc. A delegate is, therefore, the object you create (or code) that handles the work of some other object such as UIApplication, or, as is the subject of this book, the EAAccessory.

You create an object, the delegate object, to handle all the work that is created by your all-encompassing UIApplication or your accessory object, UIAccessory. Think of the delegate as the clerk you talk to when you go to the DMV to renew your license. You don't directly interface with the DMV system, but instead with a delegate of that system.

Continuing with our discussion of the properties associated with accessories, several of these provide specific details of the actual hardware itself.

The read-only **firmwareRevision** property provides an NSString that represents what version of firmware resides in the processor that controls the accessory. Remember, the accessory must handle identification and authentication with the iPhone's OS even before it can talk to your application.

```
@property (nonatomic, readonly) NSString *firmwareRevision
```

Prudence suggests that a cautious app developer be aware of the firmwareRevision and other detailed properties of the accessory to assure continued compatibility between app and accessory. For example, a newer firmware revision may indicate support within the accessory's protocol structure, for additional commands or status fields. That is, a newer, higher firmware revision may provide more details than an initial release of an accessory.

Similar to firmwareRevision, the **hardwareRevision** property gives the app developer important, up-to-date information about the hardware accessory attached to the iPhone. As the development of iPhone accessories is currently in its infancy, these attached devices may change frequently in the early stages of the program. Bugs will be fixed, features added, and changes may be made to accommodate revisions in the specifications from Apple.

```
@property (nonatomic, readonly) NSString *hardwareRevision
```

The **manufacturer** property, as its name implies, states the name of the company responsible for the iPhone accessory. While likely included in Apple's specification for completeness, I suspect this is one of those properties that developers will rarely use.

```
@property (nonatomic, readonly) NSString *manufacturer
```

Another property available to uniquely characterize the attached accessory is **modelNumber**. This property should be used by application software to define which model in the line is currently connected. Model numbers will likely differ to indicate different features present on the accessory. Consider a credit card reader attachment. One model might only read and process the swiped card information while another model may add a capability to support the customer's signature.

```
@property (nonatomic, readonly) NSString *modelNumber
```

In this case the iPhone app software needs to differentiate models of the card reader to determine if it will process the signature. Similarly, another model of the card reader might contain a bar code reader to scan the customer's merchandise. Here, the app would use the modelNumber property to differentiate which method would add items to the shopping cart.

The **name** property returns the descriptive name of the accessory. Most likely, use of this property would be as decoration. Decoration means that you might include the name of the property somewhere in your app, such as on a setup view, to provide visual feedback to the user that he has connected the correct accessory.

```
@property (nonatomic, readonly) NSString *name
```

I talked about protocols in depth earlier in this chapter. Now I come to the part where you actually use the **protocolStrings** property of the accessory.

```
@property (nonatomic, readonly) NSArray *protocolStrings
```

As seen earlier, Apple has taken the position that accessories will be presented in an array, but that, for the time being, only one accessory will be supported. You see this in the property definition above. The protocolStrings property is actually an NSArray of NSStrings.

For an example of how you use protocolStrings, take a look at the following code snippet.

```
- (void)setupAccessoryController:(EAAccessory *)accessory withProtocolString:(NSString *)protocolString
{
    [_accessory release];
    _accessory = [accessory retain];
    [_protocolString release];
    _protocolString = [protocolString copy];
}
```

Assuming you have created a separate object within your application to deal with the accessory, i.e., an accessory controller, you might use this bit of code within that object to deal with the setup when an accessory is first connected. Let's restate that just to be clear. When an accessory is first attached to the iPhone, somewhere within your app you will be notified of this event. One thing your app needs to do is set up the accessory controller object; you do this by calling the **setupAccessoryController** method shown previously.

I'll talk more about your accessory controller later, but, for the more curious reader, all you are doing here is releasing the old accessory and protocolString references and getting the new ones. You do it this way so that any previous references are flushed and new ones are re-referenced, in case you disconnected one accessory and reconnected another, possibly different, accessory.

Since I am still talking about the protocolStrings property, note that, in the header of this method, you use the NSString reference *protocolString as the property passed in. The statement below shows how you would actually call this method using the NSArray of protocolStrings property.

```
[accessoryController setupAccessoryController:_selectedAccessory
withProtocolString:[[_selectedAccessory protocolStrings] objectAtIndex:0]];
```

Since your setupAccessoryController method resides in the accessoryController object, you message that object using the method name. In the call, you pull out the first value of the NSArray protocolStrings using objectAtIndex with a value of zero to reference the first NSString in the array. Should Apple ever change things so that we could connect two accessories to one iPhone, you would, of course, use a different index.

When might you ever connect two accessories? Since accessories can be attached via Bluetooth as well as the 30-pin dock connector, Apple may eventually grant us the ability to use both communications paths to connect a single accessory. For the credit card reader example, you might have the reader itself attached via the 30-pin dock connector and a separate, wireless device to read a customer's signature.

The last property, **serialNumber**, provides detail about the connected accessory similar to hardwareRevision and modelNumber, but uniquely identifies this particular unit provided that the accessory manufacturer has uniquely serialized each unit. The serial number of a particular unit would likely be stored in EEPROM or similar non-volatile memory on the accessory.

```
@property (nonatomic, readonly) NSString *serialNumber
```

NOTE: EEPROM stands for Electrically Erasable Programmable Read-Only Memory. Non-Volatile memory retains its data even when power is removed from the device. Flash memory is a type of non-volatile memory.

Programming a unique serial number into each unit would likely be a major labor expense for a small business. Because Apple's specifications, at this time, do not seem to require individual serial numbers, only provide the capability for them, application developers should carefully check accessory documentation to determine if serial numbers are provided (the vendor might just use all zeroes for this field) and if they are unique.

Table 2–2 provides a concise look at each of the 10 EAAccessory class properties.

Table 2–2. *Properties for the EAAccessory Class*

Property Name	Format	Usage
Connected	BOOL	This indicates whether or not an accessory is connected to the iPhone.
connectionID	NSUInteger	The unique identification of the accessory to the device.
delegate	id<EAAccessoryDelegate>	This object is what will receive the notifications about the accessory such as when it's connected.
firmwareRevision	NSString	The version of the firmware that controls the accessory.
hardwareRevision	NSString	The version of the accessory.
manufacturer	NSString	The name of the company that manufactured the accessory.
modelNumber	NSString	The model number of the connected accessory.
name	NSString	The, usually decorative, name of the device attached to the iPhone.
protocolStrings	NSArray	An array of protocol names used by the accessory.
serialNumber	NSString	A number that uniquely identifies the specific unit. May or may not be available depending on manufacturer

EAAccessory Class Constants

The EAAccessory class also provides the constant **EAConnectionIDNone**; a constant to be used when identifying an unconnected accessory. EAConnectionIDNone is defined as an ENUM equated to 0. You use this constant to compare against the property **connectionID**. If the two values equate, meaning the connectionID returned was zero, then you have an invalid connection and need to execute some form of recovery such as retrying the connection or possibly notifying the user to try disconnecting and reconnecting the accessory.

EAAccessoryManager Class

The EAAccessoryManager handles the coordination between the accessory connections and the iPhone. This is the class you would use to retrieve the NSArray of accessories to which your application might attach. As stated before, Apple only currently allows a single attached accessory at any one time, but this may change in the future.

One thing that immediately confuses some accessory developers is the difference between the accessory controller you create in your application and the EAAccessoryManager object. You use the EAAccessoryManager singleton object to get the notifications you need in order to access attached accessories.

> **NOTE:** The term *singleton* is used to denote an object accessible from your iPhone application but is not something that you create or subclass. Think of it as an object you get for free. You generally access a singleton using a method that begins with the prefix "shared". For example, to access the EAAccessoryManager, you use the method sharedAccessoryManager.

You use your accessory controller object, within your app, to handle all the specific processing functions needed to deal with the accessory to which you are connecting. Another way to think of it is that the EAAccessoryManager doesn't know any details about any specific accessory, whereas, your accessory controller knows everything about the specific accessory for which it is designed.

Your code asks the EAAccessoryManager object to let you know when an accessory is available and when you can start using your own accessory controller.

Shared Accessory Manager

After your preliminary application setup has completed, the first thing you need to do when dealing with accessories is to access the shared accessory manager. The EAAccessoryManager class provides the following function in order for you to use the shared accessory manager:

```
+ sharedAccessoryManager
```

Note that this method uses the + symbol; this means that the method is a class method versus an instance method. What's the difference? Normally, when you create methods for your objects, you use a – symbol in front of the name. This means that the method name which follows works for any instance of the class. That is, when you send the object (the instance of the object) this message (method), the function declared works on that particular instance. You might have multiple instances of, say, a view controller object and you would differentiate by sending the message to the instance in which you are interested.

With the class method example shown above, however, you send the message to the class itself. Notice in the following code snippet how you might register to get accessory notifications.

```
    [[NSNotificationCenter defaultCenter] addObserver:self
selector:@selector(readerConnected:) name:EAAccessoryDidConnectNotification object:nil];

   [[NSNotificationCenter defaultCenter] addObserver:self
selector:@selector(readerDisconnected:)
name:EAAccessoryDidDisconnectNotification object:nil];

    [[EAAccessoryManager sharedAccessoryManager] registerForLocalNotifications];
```

You will dig further into this code later in the chapter on design patterns as well as when you get into interfacing the game controller for your Pong game. But, for now, the first two statements add the object in which this code is contained as observers for the EAAccessoryDidConnectNotification and EAAccessoryDidDisconnectNotification notifications. Simply put, this lets you know when an accessory is attached or disconnected from your iPhone and the appropriate method (either readerConnected or readerDisconnected) gets called. Though you use the specific notification names for EAAccessories, the two statements follow the standard way you use the notification center, i.e., other than the names of the notifications, this is standard notification center usage syntax.

The last statement registers you with the EAAccessoryManager to receive these notifications. The important point to take from this is that, in order to access the current shared accessory manager, you use:

```
[EAAccessoryManager sharedAccessoryManager]
```

This statement returns the instance of the EAAccessoryManager that you can access. So, if you are getting back an instance, then the methods you use on that instance should use the – symbol and not the +, correct? That's absolutely right, as you'll see next.

Accessory Manager Notification

Now you understand that the EAAccessoryManager's purpose in life is to inform of when an accessory is connected or disconnected. And, you know that this information is provided to you via the Notification center. Let's again look at the code from the previous section.

```
[[NSNotificationCenter defaultCenter] addObserver:self
selector:@selector(readerConnected:) name:EAAccessoryDidConnectNotification object:nil];
```

```
    [[NSNotificationCenter defaultCenter] addObserver:self
selector:@selector(readerDisconnected:)
name:EAAccessoryDidDisconnectNotification object:nil];

    [[EAAccessoryManager sharedAccessoryManager] registerForLocalNotifications];
```

As a quick reminder, the first two statements in this code snippet direct all the notifications for when an accessory is connected or disconnected to kick off two methods (readerConnected and readerDisconnected) within the object that contains the code.

In the last statement, you see that you must register with the EAAccessoryManager instance for the accessory connected notifications. The EAAccessory Framework's EAAccessoryManager class provides the following two methods to start and stop receiving notifications:

```
- registerForLocalNotifications
- unregisterForLocalNotifications
```

Our app calls the **registerForLocalNotifications** method to be notified when an accessory is connected or disconnected. The reason you need to use this is that the notification system does not send EAAccessory notifications (connected or disconnected) automatically. So, in the code segment above, if you didn't include the third line of code, you would not receive the connected or disconnected notifications.

Call this statement (registerForLocalNotifications) once, usually within the viewDidLoad of our primary view controller. The notification observers (the first two statements of the code segment) can be called either before (as is shown) or after calling registerForLocalNotifications.

Call the method **unregisterForLocalNotifications** when your application is ready to terminate (applicationDidTerminate) or if you are no longer interested in receiving accessory-related notifications.

Available Accessories from Accessory Manager

The last topic in this section discussing the EAAccessoryManager shows how you actually get the list of connected accessories. This is done by using the **connectedAccessories** property.

In the following code snippet, you see one way to use this property.

```
        EAAccessory *connectedAccessory =
        [[[EAAccessoryManager    sharedAccessoryManager]
        connectedAccessories] objectAtIndex:0];
```

In fact, this statement provides a nice little overview of several of the subjects I've just covered. First, to the left of the = assignment, you declare a pointer to an EAAccessory object that you call connectedAccessory. This will be the reference to the accessory you will work with in your code.

Next, fresh from the previous section, you see that you have returned the instance of the accessory manager to which you query the property connectedAccessories. This complex statement returns the NSArray of accessories. Finally, you return the 1st object located at index zero (remember that there is likely only one object in the array) to be assigned to the connectedAccessory reference.

In the Pong game that you will build later, you may find that you use the connectedAccessories property in a couple of different ways. In one such case, you might use the following statement to simply assign the list of connected accessories to our own NSArray object.

```
NSArray accessoryList   = [[NSMutableArray alloc] initWithArray:[[EAAccessoryManager
sharedAccessoryManager] connectedAccessories]];
```

You may use this form within your code if you wish to maintain a reference to the list of accessories returned from the shared accessory manager. This format will be more useful when Apple begins permitting multiple accessory connections.

You see another use for the connectedAccessories property in the following conditional statement. Here, if there are any accessories connected no matter what they are, you log a message to the console saying as much. A good time to use this format might be when you load your view controller that interacts with the accessory.

```
    if ([[EAAccessoryManager        sharedAccessoryManager] connectedAccessories])
            NSLog(@"there is already a connected accessory");
```

You will explore these structures in more depth in the following chapter when I discuss design patterns.

EASession

As I stated earlier, the EASession class creates the communications channel between the app and the accessory. So what is a session? Basically, a session abstractly represents the fact that we have an accessory attached and that you can talk to it using a protocol. And by protocol here, I mean the second definition I talked about earlier—the rules governing the message structure between the app and the accessory.

Your app generally references the session at three major times: (1) when you create the session, (2) when you open the session, and (3) when you close the session. You generally close the session in our dealloc routine in the accessory controller object.

The EASession object includes four properties: accessory, inputStream, outputStream, and protocolString. The astute observer will note that the protocolString property here is singular whereas for the EAAccessory object it was an NSArray and therefore plural. This reinforces the fact that while an accessory may be able to use several different protocols, a session uses a specific protocol. Thus, you could have, say, a diagnostic session using one protocol and an operations session that uses a different protocol.

```
@property (nonatomic, readonly) EAAccessory *accessory
```

The **accessory** property returns the reference to the accessory currently associated or attached to this session. This will, of course, in most instances, be the accessory currently connected to the iPhone. There may exist conditions where the accessory returned by session differs from the actual accessory attached to the iPhone. The two conditions that come to mind are: (1) an accessory is changed without having dropped the original session reference and (2) when Apple allows multiple accessories to be connected to the same iPhone.

Let's skip over streams for a moment and talk about the **protocolString** property of the EASession object.

```
@property (nonatomic, readonly) NSString *protocolString
```

This property returns the NSString containing the protocol associated with the session. When you create a session, you set the protocolString value as shown in the following statement:

```
EASession *session = [[EASession alloc] initWithAccessory:accessory
                      forProtocol:protocolString];
```

Here, you create a reference to an EASession object called session using the standard alloc-init methods. Remember, when using alloc-init, you must release the object somewhere else in the code. For a session, you typically use openSession and closeSession methods within your accessory controller object.

One other thing to note about this line of code is that, while you declared the EASession object explicitly (EASession *session) at the start of the statement, you may (and probably normally) want the EASession to be public. In that case, you would declare it in the interface specification for the accessory controller along with any other elements you need to be public such as the reference to the accessory and possibly the protocol string.

```
@interface CCT01Controller : NSObject <EAAccessoryDelegate>{

    EAAccessory *_accessory;
    EASession *_session;
    NSString *_protocolString;
}
```

Normally, after you execute the statement above, the first thing to check is whether or not a session was created as in:

```
    if (session)
    {
// do something ...
        }
```

If for some reason a valid session was not created, you will need to verify that you have a valid accessory and are using the correct protocolString.

If, however, the statement is TRUE, then you need to create the input and output streams that you use to transfer data between your app and the accessory. But before you get to that, you first need to describe streams.

```
@property (nonatomic, readonly) NSInputStream *inputStream
@property (nonatomic, readonly) NSOutputStream *outputStream
```

Streams

Streams are basically what their name implies: a sequence of data that goes from one point to another. Like its watery namesake, your streams travel in one direction: downstream. Therefore, in order to support bi-direction traffic, two data streams are required.

From within your frame of reference inside the iPhone application, you create an input stream to handle data coming from the accessory and an output stream to handle the data you send to the accessory. You use the Cocoa classes NSInputStream and NSOutputStream, both of which are derived from NSStream.

Stream objects also have properties associated with them. Most properties have to do with network security and configuration, and as such will not be discussed here. Most importantly, a stream object has a delegate associated with it. The delegate object, which in your case will be the accessory controller object, must support the **stream:handleEvent:** method. Apple has provided a prototype implementation for dealing with events from streams.

Essentially, whenever something happens in regards to a stream, this method is called. Depending on what eventCode was received you take one of several actions. But first, you need to create the streams and that is done in three steps for each (input and output) stream. This is where you use the **if (session)** statement.

```
    if (session)
    {
        [[session inputStream] setDelegate:self];
        [[session inputStream] scheduleInRunLoop:[NSRunLoop currentRunLoop]
forMode:NSDefaultRunLoopMode];
        [[session inputStream] open];

        [[session outputStream] setDelegate:self];
        [[session outputStream] scheduleInRunLoop:[NSRunLoop currentRunLoop]
forMode:NSDefaultRunLoopMode];
        [[session outputStream] open];

    }
    else
    {
        NSLog(@"creating session failed");
    }
```

Most likely, you will include the preceding code within your method that handles the opening of the EASession. If you determine that you have a valid session, then you follow three steps for each stream:

- Set the stream delegate (usually to self).

- Schedule the stream to execute within a run loop.

- Open the stream.

Once these three steps are completed, you now begin to receive calls to the **stream:handleEvent:** method.

> **TIP:** Remember the rule: One session per EAAccessoryDelegate protocol per accessory.

The first step for each stream is to set the delegate to this object in which the code resides. This causes the delegate method calls generated by the input and output streams to be handled within this object.

The second line of code for both the input stream and output stream sets the events to happen within the current run loop. You have the ability to set this to a different run loop, which you might do if there were a lot of user interface interactions happening in the main run loop; you would set this up to happen in a different thread and a different run loop. To keep things simple, you will be using the default run loop.

> **NOTE:** For more detailed information on run loops see the **Threading Programming Guide** in the iPhone OS Reference Library.

Finally, you open the stream to begin sending and receiving data.

Once the streams have been opened, the **stream:handleEvent:** method shown below will handle events from both the input and output stream. Why does this statement handle both input and output streams? It does so because you set the delegate to be self for both the input and output streams in the previous code snippet.

When any event of interest happens in either stream, this method gets called. Note the **NSStreamEventOpenCompleted**, **NSStreamEventErrorOccurred**, and **NSStreamEventEndOccurred** cases; these would occur for both the input and output stream and should be handled accordingly.

The event codes of most interest to us, **NSStreamEventHasBytesAvailable** and **NSStreamEventHasSpaceAvailable** refer to the input and output streams respectively. As is mostly obvious, the first case means that the accessory has sent data to the iPhone and it is ready to be read. The second case means that there is space available in the stream to send data to the accessory.

To deal with these two cases, either the **_writeData** or **_readData** are called. I will cover more about what happens in these routines when I start discussing design patterns.

> **NOTE:** Apple uses the underscore syntax (_writeData, _readData) in their EA Accessory Reference material on occasion. In general, you put an underscore in front of a method name to refer to a local method where you might also have methods with the same name elsewhere. For example, Apple uses writeData as a public method name in their example accessory controller, but then use _writeData to refer to a different method within the object acting as the accessory controller. Does this mean you'll see two writeData methods in the accessory controller object? Yes! Both _writeData and writeData will be found. Though slightly more confusing, you will follow this trend in order to track more closely with Apple's reference material.

```
- (void)stream:(NSStream *)aStream handleEvent:(NSStreamEvent)eventCode
{
    switch (eventCode) {
        case NSStreamEventNone:
            NSLog(@"stream %@ event none", aStream);
            break;
        case NSStreamEventOpenCompleted:
            //  Do something for Open Completed event
                    break;
        case NSStreamEventHasBytesAvailable:
            NSLog(@"stream %@ event bytes available", aStream);
            [self _readData];
            break;
        case NSStreamEventHasSpaceAvailable:
            NSLog(@"stream %@ event space available", aStream);
            [self _writeData];
            break;
        case NSStreamEventErrorOccurred:
            //  Do something for Error event
            break;
        case NSStreamEventEndEncountered:
                        //  Do something for End event
            break;
        default:
            break;
    }
}
```

Summary

This chapter covered all the details needed to understand Apple's EAAccessory framework. The EAAccessory framework is a directory that contains the accessory runtime library and more. Apple uses **EAAccessory**, which seems to mean "External Accessory Accessory", even though it's double booking the Accessory term.

I also discussed the difference between the two uses of protocol. In creating EAAccessory programs, you used both the <EAAccessoryDelegate> protocol as well as the protocol (communications rules) that defines how data pass over the input and output streams between the iPhone and the accessory. You also broke down some sample protocols into their constituent parts such as command byte, status byte, and auxiliary data fields. Remember that protocol names used by the accessory that you will use in your code must be entered into the project's property list file.

Next, you dove down into the details of the three EAAccessory Framework components: the EAAccessory class, the EAAccessoryManager class, and the EASession class. The EAAccessory class references your attached accessory and provides ten properties about it, the most useful being the connected property, the delegate property, and the NSArray protocolStrings property.

The EAAccessoryManager provides the list of available accessories to which you can connect. Remember that, as of this writing, Apple permits only a single accessory per iPhone, but that it still must be dealt with as the element in the NSArray.

Finally, I covered the methods and properties associated with establishing an EASession which is the logical communications path between the accessory and your iPhone application.

KEY POINTS

- A Framework is a hierarchical directory containing shared resources such as a library, nib files, images, strings, header files, and even documentation.

- The overloaded term protocol refers both to the set of methods required to support communications between objects as well as the set of rules governing the communications over a logical connection.

- When developing code for external accessories, you will use both forms of protocols.

- The EAAccessory framework consists of the EAAccessory class, the EAAccessoryManager class, and the EASession class.

- You subclass EAAccessory to reference the accessory to which you are connecting.

- The most useful properties of the EAAccessory class are the connected property, the delegate property, and the NSArray protocolStrings property.

- The EAAccessoryManager provides the list of available accessories to which you can connect.

- NSStreams handle the communications between the iPhone application and the accessory. Both an NSInputStream and an NSOutputStream are required.

- Before you can use your accessory, an EASession must be established.

Chapter 3

EA Framework Design Patterns

Now that the guts of the EAAccessory framework have been covered, I want to look at some templates, or design patterns, for common functionality that you will be using. By working through several common design patterns now, you will be able to quickly grasp the finer points of what's going on in subsequent chapters and not get buried.

I will begin with the usual suspects: MVC, delegation, singletons, and notifications. You may be familiar with some or all of these from your previous iPhone application development. I'm going to focus on how they are used with the EAAccessory framework.

After reviewing these standard design patterns, I am going to describe what I have chosen to call the EA Pattern. The EA Pattern is really nothing more than the judicious use of the common Cocoa patterns in a structured format. Think of it like the difference between frameworks and libraries. Just as a framework is a hierarchical structure that includes libraries as well as other elements, our EA Pattern will include lower-level design patterns organized into a hierarchy of its own.

Object-Oriented Programming

No discussion of design patterns would be complete without paying allegiance to its predecessor, object-oriented programming (OOP). We all should understand what OOP is and how it differs from what we did in ancient times: functional programming.

In a nutshell, before OOP, we programmers looked at the problem, broke it down into its constituent parts, created a map of how those parts fit together, implemented the various pieces, and put them all together. Table 3–1 describes this process along with the common terminology.

Table 3–1. *Functional System Design*

What We Did	What We Called It
Looked at the problem	System Analysis
Broke down the problem into its constituent parts	Functional Decomposition
Created a map of how all the parts fit together	Systems Design or Systems Architecture
Implemented the various pieces	Unit Code and Test
Put them all back together	Systems Integration and Test

This process tended to work really well, in the beginning. The problems began as soon as whatever was designed needed to be changed.

Take the scenario where John, an experienced individual in the programming department of a printer manufacturer, is asked to design and implement a computerized system for moving completed printers from the assembly area to the shipping area.

John, along with his hardware engineering partner, go out to the manufacturing floor and observe, talk to people, ask questions, and so forth. They get an idea of what is going on. They decide what works, what doesn't, what can be added, what can be subtracted, what can change, and so on. They break the process down into the constituent parts and decide how all that should go back together.

They come up with a design that utilizes hardware consisting of computers, switches, conveyors, marking systems, and so on. John begins working on his software design while his hardware counterpart puts in all the hardware.

At night, when the floor is closed, John and the engineering team go out to the floor, install the software, and after a lot of trial and error achieve project completion. They're rewarded and productivity on the line improves and everything goes well.

Two years later, the success of the low-cost printer the company has been selling gives rise to several new models. Rather than making individual lines for each printer, the company wants to maximize use of its skill base. They want the power supply guy to do all the power supplies for all the printers and not hire three different power supply workers. In general, for each functional area of manufacturing, they want to reuse the skill set for the new printers.

Another problem surfaces in that these new printers are laser printers whereas the old printer was a line printer. So, the company adds a section of the assembly area for laser subassembly.

They ask Chris, a new programmer who took over John's position, to make the changes to the software for the new lines.

This is where the problems start. First, the original system design that John implemented was for one particular printer, and while it would have been nice to design and implement it thinking forward to the likely scenario that other printer designs might come along, there was no budget for that so it was not done.

Second, because John had only a short time to perform integration testing, and this was done at night under severe time constraints, John failed to completely document the last minute fixes to get things working.

When Chris reviews the code to see what's going on, things don't seem to line up. While the documentation and comments say one thing, the code appears to do something else. So Chris has to dissect the code and basically rebuild it from what John has left behind. The comments, because they don't accurately reflect the actual software build, actually cause more work to be done. Chris has to pretty much verify or disprove each comment. In essence, it becomes better for him to completely toss the comments and reconstruct everything directly from the code.

> **NOTE:** A software build is a released version of the operational program being used by its intended customers. For example, you can see the software build of your Mac by clicking on the apple and selecting **About This Mac**. Then select **More Info** and click **software**. You will see something like: Mac OS X 10.6.1 (10B504) where the numbers/letters in parentheses represent the build number.

Chris can select from two options: try to modify the original code to work with the new system or create a new set of software from scratch, this time avoiding the problems that his predecessor left behind, which is unlikely.

Experienced programmers from "back in the day" know the rest of the story here. You never get the money to redesign the system the "right way." Your marching orders are "just make it work and we'll get the money to fix things next year." Think that money will actually come next year?

Without reliving some of my own past nightmares, I think we can all see where this is going.

So what do you do?

This is where the miracle of OOP comes in to save us functional programming heathens. We pray at the church of OOP, say twenty "Hail reuse" and we're cleansed of our functional filth. Well, not exactly.

The Basics of OOP

Through OOP you can create systems that consist of objects. Each object has properties and methods and they interact. And basically, that's it.

Sure, there are things like information hiding, polymorphism, inheritance, modularity, encapsulation, and data abstraction, but those are just details about the objects, the properties, and methods.

Think about the real world...you and me and everyone else. Within the definition of OOP, each individual is an object. We have properties like sex, hair color, height, and so on. We also have things we do, or methods, eating, sleeping, working, and so on. We also interact. A person might call the "eat dinner" method on the members of her family: her spouse and children as well as herself.

Take a step back and instead of saying that each person is an object, let's say that an object is a human being. We list all the common properties of humans as well as their methods...the things they can do.

So what is Jane? Jane is an instance of the human object, just as is Adam, Paul, Julie, and every single individual that ever lived or ever will live; one of the properties could be "isAlive".

Enough with the abstraction already, you see that the OOP model works at large, but how about for a particular problem? Let's go back to the printer product line. You have objects such as printer, conveyor, switch (to move from one line to another), workstation, and so on. You could also have object instances that come and go: worker ID #1334, worker ID #2227, and so on.

This will get really ugly quickly if continued, so let's conclude with looking at a specific object example, the workstation object (see Figure 3–1).

Figure 3–1. *The workstation object*

To maintain familiarity with the purpose of this book, I will describe the object using objective-C. First, let's see what the object's interface (what goes into the .h file) might look like.

```
@interface WorkStation : NSObject  {

    NSString *purpose;
    NSString *department;
    BOOL     *isOccupied;
    BOOL     *isOperational;
    BOOL     *hasParts;

 // and more stuff

}
- (void) stockParts:(id)partType;
- (void) setOperationMode:(id)modeType
- (void) addOperator;
- (void) removeOperator;
@end
```

Obviously this code snippet doesn't contain everything needed to define the actual workstation, but it definitely gives an idea of how to connect a real world object with the software environment.

First, note that by defining the class of object as WorkStation it is subclassed, or derived, from the general NSObject class. This means that it inherits all the properties and methods of that most general of all classes, but it does not mean that you have to use all of them. In fact, you may hardly use any. Note the capitalization of WorkStation. When you define a class, common practice is to capitalize the first letter and all first letters of each word that you concatenate to form your object name. You will see later, when naming object instances, that you leave the first letter lowercase.

Next, within the brackets, define the properties that you want to be made public, that is, which other objects can be seen. For example, you might have a supervisor object that needs to see if the workstation is occupied, if it is running (operational) and if it has parts. The supervisor might not care about purpose or department because it may be that the supervisor is for all power supply operations. Thus the workstation's purpose would be power supply installation and it would be in the power supply installation department.

So why include them? Suppose there is an object that oversees all manufacturing. That object will need to differentiate workstations by both department and purpose to determine and predict any bottlenecks that might occur. There would likely be plenty more properties listed here. While there is no general rule of thumb as to how many properties to include, try to keep it contained. You don't want pages and pages of properties to have to go through whenever you look at your code. Remember, properties themselves can be objects.

Instead of the individual Boolean values:

```
    BOOL     *isOccupied;
    BOOL     *isOperational;
    BOOL     *hasParts;
```

You might instead define a status object that contains all three:

```
@interface WorkStation : NSObject  {
```

```
NSString           *purpose;
NSString           *department
StatusObject       *workstationStatus;

// and more stuff

}
```

> **NOTE:** You may also use the @private keyword before you declare a variable that you do not want to be public. Some OO programmers use the underscore '_' before a variable to indicate that it is private. Apple discourages this practice.

After you define the properties of the workstation, you need to know what functions the workstation object is capable of performing. Some items that come to mind are stocking parts into the station, changing modes (assembling, testing, restocking, etc.), and adding or removing an operator to the station. The status of this action will, in turn, define other properties as well as methods that become available or unavailable. For example, unless the workstation has an operator as set by the **addOperator** method, it wouldn't be able to change to assembling or testing modes as those are likely to need someone to actually do the work.

You could go on and on about the example workstation object and all that it encompasses, but that's a discussion for an OOP text. What you want to do is discover how the object-oriented paradigm applies to interfacing iPhone accessories and to the example project.

To start with the obvious, the accessory hardware that you are concerned with is an object. It will have properties such as a BOOL isConnected that is either YES or NO depending on, well, whether it is connected or not. Other characteristic properties might be: protocolUsed, sessionEstablished, sessionID, outputStreamID, inputStreamID, etc. You may or may not use these particular properties in your implementation—there is no definitive set of methods or properties for any project's object definition. This is all up to the designer.

The accessory controller gives you the first is-clearly-an-object object. But what else should you include? Is it the screen or maybe the program itself? First, think about the overall top-level object. What is it? It's your game program. It's not just the iPhone, but the program, the controller, and to some extent, even the player. After all, the player will have properties such as score or isServing, as well as properties such as movePaddle and pressButton.

Even the objects within other objects need to be considered here. I talked about the game as a whole, but all the parts of the game—playersPaddle, computersPaddle, ballObject, and even bounds—need to be addressed. After all, you're going to move the paddles, which will move the balls, and each of those will have positions, and I think you're starting to see it now. In a sentence, every individual component of the system (the game program, controller, and iPhone) that contains properties and is capable of doing something can be considered an individually defined object.

Figure 3–2 shows the game program's screen. Are these all the objects for the game? No, of course not. Beside any consideration of the accessory game controller or the iPhone itself, you're missing **state** objects. State objects are those objects that represent something about the system that may or may not stand on its own. Weird sentence, huh? But what I mean here is really the status of something, particularly the game itself. Is the ball on the player's side or the computer's side; whose turn is it to serve; are you at a game point; and various others.

Why do you need to concern yourself with these particular state variables or *state objects*? Again, you don't really, at least not these particular ones and not in all cases. More than likely, however, you will need some state information about the game that changes during the course of the game. It could be something as simple as an object that reflects whether a player can win on the next point or not. In such a case, you might provide a method for that object to take the individual players' scores and compute YES or NO.

The needs of the particular design will determine not only which state objects you need to create in your game object, but any tangible (ball, paddle, etc.) objects as well. In addition to all the objects that you create and can "see," there is one more class that you must consider.

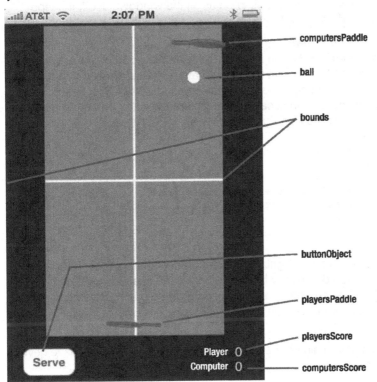

Figure 3–2. *Tangible game objects*

The UIApplication Class

The one other issue to consider is the UIApplication Class. It's one of those things in iPhone programming that tends to hang around in the periphery and, as programmers, we avoid it for as long as we can. In general, through the use of delegation which I will talk about very soon, you can avoid dealing with the application class and where it fits into the big (or even the medium-sized) picture.

Most of us understand that there is only one instance of the UIApplication class, possibly but usually not subclassed. But where does it come from? I mean, I never created an object that subclassed UIApplication. And what does it do anyway? Don't we already handle everything in the code that needs to be done? Taking, the last question first: NO, not even close to it.

The UIApplication handles all the routing of user events. When you touch the screen, for example, UIApplication deals with all of that. Normally, you have very standard things you want to do—touch gestures, button presses, swipes, and so forth; UIApplication keeps you from dealing with those at the kind of low-level programming you would have needed to do a decade or so ago.

UIApplication dispatches messages from control objects (UIControl) to the target objects responsible for implementing the results of those actions. UIApplication also knows about all the stuff going on in your app such as all the windows used; it keeps track of all open windows and, through those, any interactions with UIView objects.

So where does it come from? It's created for you anytime you use an XCode template. Look in the *Other Sources* folder and open the main.m file. In the good ol' days, when we wrote programs in C, everyone had a main function. That's what gets called first anytime we wrote a C program. Same thing goes here. Just as in standard C, Objective-C doesn't really differ—the main function is called first. Difference is, it doesn't do much. Take a look at the main.m file for the Pong game.

```
#import <UIKit/UIKit.h>

int main(int argc, char *argv[]) {

    NSAutoreleasePool * pool = [[NSAutoreleasePool alloc] init];
    int retVal = UIApplicationMain(argc, argv, nil, nil);
    [pool release];
    return retVal;
}
```

If you've written in standard C, you recognize the function declaration: main returns an int and is passed in (which would normally be by the command line when the program is called) two arguments. The first argument **argc** is a count of the parameters passed in, using the second argument, a character array **argv[]**.

The header and the following four lines of code comprise the entire main function and are generated by XCode and you almost never change anything. I personally have never needed to change main.m.

The NSAutoreleasePool is used to set up Cocoa's reference-counting system for keeping track of objects in the system. As you probably know, memory is very tight in an iPhone and any variables that aren't being used, probably shouldn't be hanging around. Cocoa for the Mac provides an automated service called garbage collection that periodically cleans up the garbage and handles this for you. Again, because of the limited memory in an iPhone there isn't enough space to have something as sophisticated as garbage collection.

First of all, iPhone apps tend to be small, again due mostly to limited memory, and as such, simpler. Because of the simplicity of the app, it isn't too difficult to keep track of the variables and make them come and go as needed. Having a well-designed and well-partitioned application can help a lot with this management.

When you create an object, usually something derived from NSObject, you generally will allocate and initialize the object. In the code below from your credit card reader example, you create an instance of the NSString to hold the credit card number that you will read from the card's magnetic stripe. Notice that you first allocate an instance of the NSString object, and initialize with **num** (the name from the card) and set other parameters such as the encoding scheme you wish to use.

```
NSString *card = [[NSString alloc] initWithData:num
encoding:NSUTF8StringEncoding];
```

When you are done using the instance of the NSString object you call **card**, you get rid of it by deallocating it, most often done in the viewcontroller's (or whatever object which contains **card**) **dealloc** routine. That's a pretty simple solution and helps to keep a standard way of doing things. Is that how it was done in the card reader app? Not at all.

Just because it's easy to put all your dealloc statements in a single place, doesn't make it good programming. First of all, if you have a lot of these hanging around, you could start running out of memory. And unless you've implemented the memory shortage methods—meaning you really haven't done any memory management—your app will more than likely be terminated by the OS.

```
[card  release];
```

If you are allocating objects for short-term use, as I did with the data being read off of a credit card, you can get rid of it (release it) as soon as you're done. That's the way the card reader app works. You get the data off the card in some raw format such as unsigned integers, create an object with it, and pass that object to where it needs to be, say, the web site for the merchant services. Since you don't need it anymore, there's no reason to keep it around. Likely, the transaction will complete and all you need to know is whether it was successful or not.

There is another very good reason for doing it this way. When dealing with personal information, and the iPhone is certainly a personal device, it's best not to keep personal information around at all, if you don't need it. The Payment Card Industry (PCI) provides requirements that secure apps must meet in this regards. Some credit card companies won't allow their cards to even be processed on systems that don't follow the rules. Nulling out (erasing) an object and releasing it when it is no longer needed is one of the methods to implement the PCI's requirements.

Getting back to the UIApplication object, check out the statement below. This is where our UIApplication object is created.

```
int retVal = UIApplicationMain(argc, argv, nil, nil);
```

Note that the first two parameters are the same as in the old standard C, main function. The third and fourth functions are usually nil. The third function is name of the UIApplication class or subclass. By specifying nil, UIApplication is assumed. The fourth parameter is the name of the class from which the application delegate is instantiated. Normally nil is specified if you intend to load the delegate object from your application's main nib file, which is what you usually do.

Now that I've talked about where the UIApplication object comes from, let's talk about what it does for you. Below is a list of the tasks, which you can think of as methods, that UIApplication does.

Getting the Application Instance

+ sharedApplication

Getting Application Windows

keyWindow   property

windows   property

Controlling and Handling Events

- sendEvent:

- sendAction:to:from:forEvent:

- beginIgnoringInteractionEvents

- endIgnoringInteractionEvents

- isIgnoringInteractionEvents

applicationSupportsShakeToEdit   property

proximitySensingEnabled   property

Opening a URL Resource

- openURL:

- canOpenURL:

Registering for Remote Notifications

- registerForRemoteNotificationTypes:

- unregisterForRemoteNotifications

- enabledRemoteNotificationTypes

Managing Application Activity

      `idleTimerDisabled` `property`

Managing Status Bar Orientation

    `- setStatusBarOrientation:animated:`

    `statusBarOrientation` `property`

    `statusBarOrientationAnimationDuration` `property`

Controlling Application Appearance

    `- setStatusBarHidden:animated:`

    `statusBarHidden` `property`

    `- setStatusBarStyle:animated:`

    `statusBarStyle` `property`

    `statusBarFrame` `property`

    `networkActivityIndicatorVisible` `property`

    `applicationIconBadgeNumber` `property`

Setting and Getting the Delegate

      `delegate` `property`

Now do you see why it's not a good idea to subclass UIApplication? Imagine having to deal with all of this yourself, when delegation is a much better option.

Delegation

I live in a house with my wife. For better or worse, we each *own* the house. From time to time the house needs to be cleaned up and we each have some responsibility for doing so. However, because I am so devoted to writing this book, I can't get to my housework. So what do I do? I delegate it to my wife.

Let's say for simplicity that I'm only responsible for doing the laundry and mowing the lawn. But, because of time crunch, deadlines, and the occasional nap, I can't get to those things and still write this book. I choose to—and I won't talk about the repercussions of this—delegate those tasks to my wife. This means that she gets them taken care of for me. Note that I didn't say she *does* them for me, I said taken care of.

Let's say she's okay with doing the laundry—I don't have that much to do anyway, she just throws it in the machine—but she just doesn't want to deal with mowing the lawn. How does the lawn get done? She delegates that to the kid down the road. She gives him a message (phone call) to say come do the lawn. He comes down, cuts the lawn, and polls her (knocks on the door) to get paid. That's really all there is to delegation; one object does something for another.

From the last chapter, you will remember that the delegate protocol mechanism establishes the rules as to what the delegate needs to do. Below is the interface definition for the Pong game's application delegate. Again, notice the <UIApplicationDelegate> in the @interface statement. This says that the pongViewController class will implement the UIApplicationDelegate protocol.

```
@class pongViewController;

@interface pongAppDelegate : NSObject <UIApplicationDelegate> {
    UIWindow *window;
    pongViewController *viewController;
}

@property (nonatomic, retain) IBOutlet UIWindow *window;
@property (nonatomic, retain) IBOutlet pongViewController *viewController;

@end
```

Okay, you say. You've seen what the UIApplication does (or can do) in the previous list and you understand what you need to know about delegation in regard to the UIApplicationDelegate protocol. But, if you look closely, you might say to yourself, "Wait, what's going on? I don't see the delegate methods I have to implement in the list of tasks that UIApplication does for us." That's because they're not there.

Confusing? Maybe, but check out the following two lists of UIApplication notifications and UIApplicationDelegate methods. The first list comes from the UIApplication class reference and specifies all the notifications that the UIApplication singleton (you get this by using the sharedApplication method) can post. The second list provides the methods the UIApplication delegate can handle according to the UIApplication delegate protocol.

- UIApplicationDidBecomeActiveNotification
- UIApplicationDidChangeStatusBarFrameNotification
- UIApplicationDidFinishLaunchingNotification
- UIApplicationDidReceiveMemoryWarningNotification
- UIApplicationSignificantTimeChangeNotification
- UIApplicationWillChangeStatusBarOrientationNotification
- UIApplicationDidChangeStatusBarOrientationNotification
- UIApplicationWillChangeStatusBarFrameNotification
- UIApplicationWillResignActiveNotification
- UIApplicationWillTerminateNotification
- application:didChangeStatusBarFrame:
- application:didChangeStatusBarOrientation:

- `application:didFailToRegisterForRemoteNotificationsWithError:`
- `application:didFinishLaunchingWithOptions:`
- `application:didReceiveRemoteNotification:`
- `application:didRegisterForRemoteNotificationsWithDeviceToken:`
- `application:handleOpenURL:`
- `application:willChangeStatusBarFrame:`
- `application:willChangeStatusBarOrientation:duration:`
- `applicationDidBecomeActive:`
- `applicationDidFinishLaunching:`
- `applicationDidReceiveMemoryWarning:`
- `applicationSignificantTimeChange:`
- `applicationWillResignActive:`
- `applicationWillTerminate:`

Initially, you might think that both lists should be the same. After all, if the `UIApplication` object (the singleton) is posting notifications, then you might expect that they get posted to the delegate, the object that handles them for the application object. But looking at the first list you see ten notifications and in the delegate list there are 15 delegate methods. What's going on?

Let's start by breaking it all down into categories. Each delegate method belongs to one of the following six categories:

- Controlling Application Behavior
- Opening a URL Resource
- Managing Status Bar Orientation
- Responding to a Change in Active Status
- Controlling Application Appearance
- Handling Remote Notifications

Assigning the 15 delegate methods to the above six categories provides the following:

Controlling Application Behavior

- `applicationDidFinishLaunching:`

- `application:didFinishLaunchingWithOptions:`

- `applicationWillTerminate:`

- `applicationDidReceiveMemoryWarning:`

- `applicationSignificantTimeChange:`

Opening a URL Resource

    - application:handleOpenURL:

Managing Status Bar Orientation

    - application:willChangeStatusBarOrientation:duration:

    - application:didChangeStatusBarOrientation:

Responding to a Change in Active Status

    - applicationWillResignActive:

    - applicationDidBecomeActive:

Controlling Application Appearance

    - application:willChangeStatusBarFrame:

    - application:didChangeStatusBarFrame:

Handling Remote Notifications

    - application:didReceiveRemoteNotification:

    - application:didRegisterForRemoteNotificationsWithDeviceToken:

    - application:didFailToRegisterForRemoteNotificationsWithError

Ah, that's nice. There's starting to be some order to things. But what about the list of ten UIApplication notifications? Where do they come in? If you look carefully, you can match up all ten UIApplication notifications to ten similar items in the UIApplicationDelegate methods. That leaves five methods defined by the delegate protocol that are not in the set of UIApplication notifications. They are the following:

- applicationDidFinishLaunching:

- application:handleOpenURL:

- application:didReceivedRemoteNotification:

- application:didRegisterForRemoteNotificationsWithDeviceToken:

- application:didFailToRegisterForRemoteNotificationsWithError:

I could talk about this for several more pages and I'm not sure the complication level would get much better. The key thing to note is this: subclassing UIApplication would require you to deal with not only the ten notifications that the UIApplication singleton sends out (you'd have to manage that in your code), you'd also need to take care of thirteen instance methods from the UIApplication class.

Isn't it much simpler to create an application delegate object that conforms to the UIApplicationDelegate protocol and implement your selected methods from the delegate list? Many times in object-oriented programming, the standard procedure is to subclass. What I've tried to show here, admittedly in a roundabout way, are reasons to use delegation instead.

In summary then, delegation provides a method for dealing with complicated objects such as the single application instance much more simply than by subclassing the more complicated object. You set up a simpler object that implements a mere handful of delegate methods that you are likely to need.

Take a look at the pong game's application delegate:

```objc
#import "pongAppDelegate.h"
#import "pongViewController.h"

@implementation pongAppDelegate

@synthesize window;
@synthesize viewController;


- (void)applicationDidFinishLaunching:(UIApplication *)application {

    // Override point for customization after app launch
    [window addSubview:viewController.view];
    [window makeKeyAndVisible];
}


- (void)dealloc {
    [viewController release];
    [window release];
    [super dealloc];
}

@end
```

Do you see how many delegate methods there are? One! That's right, your application delegate only needs to implement the applicationDidFinishLaunching:application: method. You usually implement the applicationDidFinishLaunching: delegate method because this is where you load views or restore old settings and preferences. I think we can all agree that delegation offers a much simpler solution for dealing with the application itself.

OOP and Delegation

Before I got off on a tangent about the virtues of delegation, I was discussing design patterns—common, reusable templates to help quickly implement the project. So far, I've discussed one design pattern (delegation) and the general concept of OOP. We could call OOP a design pattern if we wanted to—after all, it does define a common way to implement this system using objects. But historically, OOP refers more to the strategy used to solve the problem. Generally, you either solve a problem using functional decomposition or object-oriented analysis (OOA). As discussed earlier, functional decomposition breaks the problem down by what it does and OOA breaks down the problem into its constituent parts and how they interact.

Before I go on and talk about more design patterns, let's see where we are. I defined the Pong game problem earlier and broke it up into objects. I talked a little bit about their properties and how they use methods to communicate and interact, so you have the basic object model.

To add delegation, let's think about where it would come into play. You've already seen that you're going to implement the UIApplicationDelegate protocol and at least the applicationDidFinishLaunching: method to get things rolling.

You're also going to use the EAAccessory delegate protocol in order to be informed about when an accessory is connected or disconnected.

If you incorporate the OOP model and delegation for UIApplication and EAAccessory, Figure 3–3 provides a basic, diagrammatical representation of where you are so far.

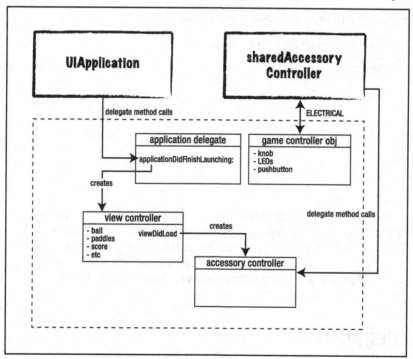

Figure 3–3. *Game architecture using OOP and delegation*

This program consists of the application delegate that handles all the method calls initiated by the sharedApplication. In general, this is mainly the notification that the application has finished launching.

When the applicationDidFinishLaunching delegate method is called, the app delegate creates the root view controller, which in turn puts something to display onto the iPhone screen. You've also added a game controller object and an accessory controller object.

The game controller object represents the actual hardware controller accessory in your system. You don't do anything with the actual game controller; it's just a piece of hardware hanging off the iPhone. You could have left the block for it out of the illustration completely, but that might lead to some confusion as to where the sharedAccessoryController gets its information.

This is where delegation becomes pretty clear. You have the actual controller object (the hardware) that communicates with the iPhone's OS and the sharedAccessoryController that gets created when you run your app. You created the Accessory delegate—the part of the system that you program. Because you receive notifications from the sharedAccessory controller, you use your accessory controller delegate as the gateway to communicate with the actual game controller hardware.

If you redraw Figure 3–3 as is shown in Figure 3–4 with the hardware now outside your system box, then everything within the dotted rectangle represents the system (program or app) that was created.

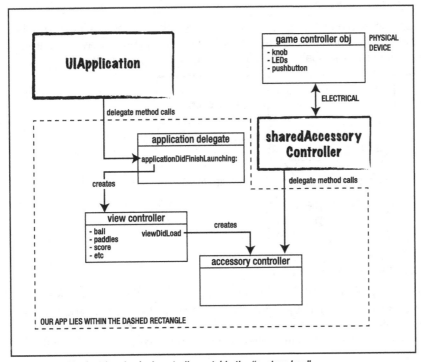

Figure 3–4. *Moving the physical controller outside the "system box"*

Figure 3–4 much more clearly delineates the parts of the system. The physical hardware connects through iPhone OS to the sharedAccessory controller once you create it.

Similarly, the shared UIApplication singleton also exists outside your system boundary. Both of those shared controllers communicate with the code via delegation.

The picture, however, is not complete. In addition to the Model-View-Controller (MVC) organization of the system that I will talk about next, the accessory controller delegate must pass data to and from the hardware accessory. While delegation does some of the work, specifically dealing with when an accessory is connected or disconnected, most of the heavy lifting (passing data back and forth) uses notifications. Notifications represent the final design pattern that I talk about in this chapter.

Model-View-Controller

As if things haven't gotten messy enough, now you come to the basic organizational structure of the app. Let's say this at the start; MVC represents a great way to partition your system. The thing is, for very small applications, it's not really needed, and, in fact, can complicate your project more than it needs to.

So what is MVC? Very simply, MVC divides your system into three parts: the view which is what the user sees, the model which represents all the data and states of your system, and the controller, in essence, the connection between the model and the view.

Since you are operating within OOP, each of the elements—the model, the view, and the controller—are all objects. In addition to defining what roles the objects play, MVC also defines how the objects communicate. Figure 3–5 presents the basic view of MVC.

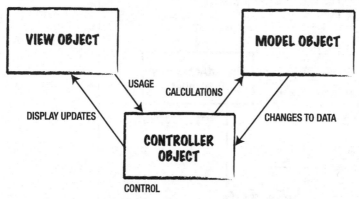

Figure 3–5. *Basic Model-View-Controller organization*

As mentioned previously, the view is not just what the user sees, but the object with which he or she interacts. It contains the controls as well as all the images, labels, icons, and so forth. A user interacts with the view object not just by sight, but by touch (for control) as well as sound. Yes, as counter-intuitive as it might seem, sound emanates from the view object.

Going to the other end, you see the model object contains the state of the system. In the Pong game, the model object knows the score, where the paddles and balls are, and so forth. By separating the model this way, so that it is its own entity, the model as well as the view controller can be reused.

Reuse means that you don't have to reinvent the wheel, or, in this case, a particular object such as the model object. Reuse was one of the great sales pitches for object-oriented design way back when. The problem was, MVC came a little bit after OOA/OOP. So everyone just plunged into OOP, and wound up in the same boat as they had with functional programming. Personally, I believe this is the very reason why OOP took as long as it did to catch on. What was missing was a good way to architect the objects in a system. This is what MVC brings to the table.

OK, you want an example. Here's a very simple, very practical example based on the project that you are concerned with in this book. Suppose you want an Air Hockey game instead of a Pong game. I can see the lights going off in some of your heads already.

The model object could stay completely intact. You change the view object from a table tennis table to an air hockey table, change the puck object, change the paddles, and change the sound the impact between objects make.

You might, of course, want to change the scoring and serving mechanism to conform to whatever rules you want to implement in the Air Hockey game versus the Pong game, but that doesn't affect how the basic mechanics of the game function.

The controller object provides the glue between the view object and the model object. In most scenarios, the controller object provides the uniqueness to each system. It is the least likely object to provide substantial reuse. The controller object provides the customized part of your system.

You do not use a strict interpretation of MVC in the design of your Pong application. Because the actual game is so simple, separating out the model, view, and controller for the game would result in much more code to maintain. If you were developing a production-level game with all the bells and whistles, then you probably would take that approach. But, for the prototyping case, choose to tweak the design pattern slightly.

Taking a step back for a moment, think about what the user sees when he plays the Pong game. He sees a screen with a table, controls, and various feedback elements. How does he see it? He sees it all on a single screen. The app doesn't page to another spot in the room. It doesn't flip or twist or any number of other possibilities. What the user always sees is a **screenful of information**.

If you wander the hallowed halls of 1 Infinite Loop in Cupertino (Apple Headquarters) you're likely to hear that term, screenful of information, more than once. Remember what the iPhone is. It is a small, infrequently used, short period of usage device. A user pulls the phone out, usually in response to a particular stimulus—she wants to check the time of the next bus or is bored waiting and needs a distraction. In such cases, the user's request is likely to be in the form of a screenful of information—a bus schedule or the view from the Pong game.

When the screenful of information is very small and manageable, such as with your Pong game, a whole MVC might be represented within a single set of code. By set of code, I mean the combination of the interface (.h) file and the implementation (.m) file.

Does this violate the rule of MVC? Not if you consider the rule to be more of a guideline. When in doubt you need to consider the overall goals of your project as bounded by your resources. Most of the time, no matter whether you divide your source code into distinct model, view, and controller files, or if you put something all into a single object file, you still need to design your system conforming to MVC.

Only by looking at your system before you start coding can you really see what you need to do. If you have a huge model object with dozens of status fields and calculations, then it's easy to see that it makes sense to separate along the lines of MVC. On the other hand, as in the Pong game, you've got less than a handful of data elements and only three things moving on the screen—two paddles and a ball—then packaging everything in one set of code may be the way to go.

Looking at this game system for a moment, I clearly talked about the game, the paddles, board, ball, scoring, and so on, but what about the controller? How does it fit in?

Think about it this way—does the game work without the controller? It absolutely does. In fact, when you build the first iteration, you will not even consider the accessory game controller. You'll build your game as if it is a basic, touch-the-screen-to-play game application.

The addition of a hardware accessory controller to the already developed game app depicts one of the strengths of OOP. You change the basic system by adding a real-world piece of hardware, and represent it as a delegate object that you add to the system. Remember when I talked about upgrading the system that ran the manufacturing floor. The simple change of adding a new printer line created havoc and necessitated the complete redesign of a system.

I will demonstrate that, through the use of delegation and notification, you can very easily expand your system—your game—to use a hardware accessory controller with minimal modifications.

> **NOTE:** Every system designed contains some form of the MVC design pattern. While you will often choose to put everything in one file, the more clearly the lines are drawn between M, V, and C, the easier you will find it to reuse the parts of the system. The need or desire to reuse parts of your system always arises more than you anticipate. A corollary to that is the ability to reuse parts of a system always turns out to be work that you anticipate.

Notification

Of all the design patterns discussed in this book, notifications are far and away my favorite. They are also one of the most overused tools in Cocoa/Objective-C with the possible exception of Dictionaries, because notifications are so easy to use.

Start with a simple program containing several objects. Each object contains its own set of properties and methods. You build the system and use method calls to pass information between objects. For example, in the Pong game, you move the ball by a certain amount each time period. When an interval timer expires, say with a period of 10 milliseconds, you might call a moveBall method that multiplies the 10ms times the speed of the ball. That method erases the old ball and displays it at the new position.

What I've just described is the goal of the development process. In an ideal world, you'd always use method calls to pass data to objects and get those objects to do something. Unfortunately, a system like this is rarely achievable.

One of the reasons for this inability to adhere to a strict OOP philosophy comes from the fact that systems evolve. Even before the initial release of the system, you more than likely will find the need to autonomously pass data between objects. By autonomously, I mean that one object needs to send data somewhere, but the originating object doesn't know where to send it. This is where notifications come in.

Notifications allow objects to post information to a notification center that then resends that information to all interested objects. In general object-oriented programming, we refer to capability this as *message passing*.

Some documentation refers to the similarities between notification and delegation; mainly because delegation also uses notification. While I personally don't see too much similarity between the two patterns, a lot of people may, therefore let's define the three key areas where they differ.

First, delegation permits only one delegate object to receive a notification, in comparison to using the notification center, where many objects can be addressed. That seems great, but there's one thing to consider; using delegation with just one object being notified permits that receiver to provide a return value. Using notifications to multiple addresses prohibits the use of return values.

Second, using delegation, you pass only predefined delegate methods. With notification you can send any message you like through the notification center including user data.

Finally, using delegation, the receiving object understands something about the sender object. The receiver knows that the sender exited. There's a connection between the two. Using notification, that connection becomes decoupled. The receiver processes notifications that it has registered for, but doesn't have to understand anything about the sender. It only needs to know how to process the notification that may come from anywhere.

While delegation provides a tight coupling between sender and receiver, notifications are termed *loosely coupled*. Figure 3–6 shows the differences in data flow between delegation and notification.

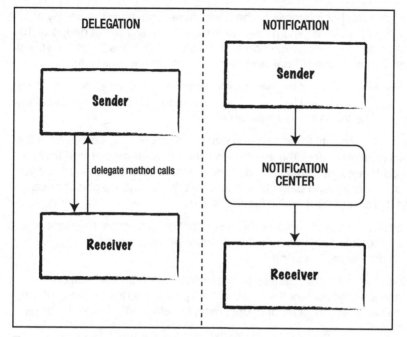

Figure 3–6. *Message flow differences between delegation and notification*

Immediately, you see that the two-way connection of delegation on the left of Figure 3–6 results in a visible *closeness* between the sender and receiver. Inserting the notification center between the sender and receiver, as well as providing only one-way communication, as shown on the right, creates an immediate decoupling between the objects.

Taking things a step further, you see in Figure 3–7 the multi-cast capability of the notification center to take in one notification from the sender and pass it off to many receivers. Also of note is that, in order to get notifications, receivers must register with the notification center first.

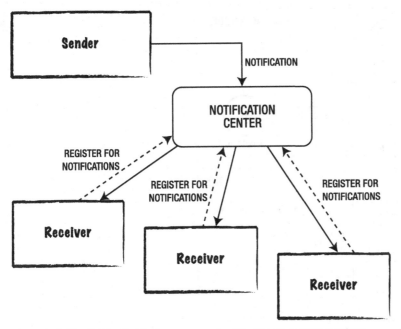

Figure 3-7. *The Notification Center can resend notifications to multiple receivers*

When might it be a good time to use notification? For the Pong game, anytime something changes on the accessory game controller, you're going to send a notification. When the user presses (or releases) the pushbutton on the game controller, a notification will be posted. When the user rotates the knob in order to move the paddle, notifications will be posted.

The pushbutton seems pretty straightforward. It is either engaged or released (pushed or not pushed). But, because the knob's position is variable—all the way counter-clockwise to all the way clockwise and anywhere in between—you need more information.

Before I go on, let's take a look at how the knob works on your accessory controller. Take a look at Figure 3-8 for the general flow of data originating with the movement of the knob, to the point inside the app where the player's paddle is actually moved.

Within the game controller, the software executes a fast timing loop, on the order of a few milliseconds per iteration. On every cycle of that loop, the software reads the position of the knob. If the knob's position is the same—it hasn't been turned since the last time it was checked—nothing happens. However, if the position read by the loop this time is different than the last time it checked, the new value is sent over the 30-pin dock connector to the iPhone.

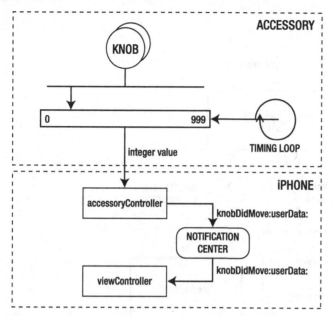

Figure 3–8. *Data flow for the Accessory Controller's knob*

Our app's `accessoryController` receives the new position and has the option of either passing the raw data onto where it can be used, or doing some calculations based on the position and sending that refined bit of information. In either case, information related to the position moves to the view controller that will reposition the player's paddle.

The `accessoryController` must handle a non-predictable and possibly high rate of data from the controller, especially in a game application where the knob is likely to be constantly moving. Because of this, unless the calculations it performs on the incoming data can be done quickly, it might be better for the `accessoryController` just to send the raw data where it needs to go. This would likely be the view controller object where the raw position data would be converted to the new position of the player's paddle.

Similarly, consider the credit card reader accessory I've talked about. Just as the accessory controller initiates the data transfer of the knob's new position whenever the knob is turned, the credit card reader operates very similarly. When the business owner swipes the customer's card, software inside the reader sends that number across the 30-pin connector to the iPhone application. Similarly, the `accessoryController` in the card reader app would pass the cardholder's information to the view controller object as well as the code responsible for completing the transaction. Here's a case where the data is multi-cast.

Take a look at the following line of code:

```
[[NSNotificationCenter defaultCenter] addObserver:self
    selector:@selector(cardRead:) name:kCardSwiped object:nil];
```

This is how an observer within the credit card reader application would register to receive notifications.

The first part of the statement returns the default NSNotificationCenter, which, much like the UIApplication or sharedAccessoryController, is a singleton object, i.e., there is only one of them and it's not something to subclass.

The rest of the line of code adds this object (self) as the observer. This means the notification center knows that to send certain notifications to this object. The **selector** statement defines the method within this object that gets called when we get the notification. The notification to which this refers is set by the **name** parameter, kCardSwiped. The **object** parameter sets the sender of the notification. By entering in nil for this value, you process any kCardSwiped notifications regardless of where they come from.

To see how the data is sent from the card reader's controller, note the following code segment:

```
NSMutableDictionary *dict = [[ NSMutableDictionary alloc] init];

[ dict   setObject:num forKey:@"cardNumber"];
[ dict   setObject:name forKey:@"cardName"];
[ dict   setObject:year forKey:@"cardExpYear"];
[ dict   setObject:month forKey:@"cardExpMonth"];


        [[NSNotificationCenter  defaultCenter]
    postNotificationName:kCardSwiped object:self userInfo:dict];
  [dict release];
```

When the card reader controller object receives the card data (number, name, expiration month, and expiration year, for example) from the reader over the 30-pin connector (remember that this would work the same if the accessory was connected by Bluetooth), convert the raw data into objects, prior to this code.

First create a dictionary object into which you can insert key-value pairs. Key-value pairing combines a name with a value. Think of an actual dictionary where the word you are looking up would be the key and the value would be the set of definitions. You can easily find the word because the dictionary is indexed alphabetically. Similarly, when using NSDictionary (or NSMutableDictionary) objects, the Key is the quick index to get to the value.

One other thing to note is that you use NSMutableDictionary. This allows you to create the object first, then change it as you add the individual pieces of data.

The next four lines of code add each of the four pieces of information to the dictionary object. The values **num**, **name**, **year**, **month** are added using the respective keys **cardNumber**, **cardName**, **cardExpYear**, and **cardExpMonth**.

After this setup, all you need to do is post the notification as can be seen in the statement:

```
[[NSNotificationCenter  defaultCenter]
        postNotificationName:kCardSwiped object:self userInfo:dict];
```

You retrieve the default notification center as before; tell it the object that is sending the notification, **self**; and add the dictionary (dict) you created as the supplemental userInfo parameter. In keeping with good memory management practices, because you created this object (the dict) using alloc and init, you release it to free memory space.

You've now addressed two out of the three steps for using notifications: registering an object to receive notifications and posting a notification containing userInfo. For the final piece of the pie, your receiver object, after being notified, needs to act on the notification and, in this case, get the userInfo dictionary that was sent with the notification.

In an earlier code segment, you saw that, when your object received the notification, the cardRead method was selected.

> **NOTE:** Most statements in Cocoa that need to reference a particular method, use the selector field. As with the term protocol, selectors also have two meanings in Cocoa. First, a selector can be the name of a method when it is referred to in source code. Second, selector refers to the unique identifier that replaces the method name when the source code is compiled. Using @selector( ) in a statement refers to the compiled selector that represents the method at runtime.

To pull the credit card information from the dictionary, use the following four statements—one for each data object. The first portion of each statement accesses the userInfo field of the notification. Then, using simple Key-Value retrieval, pull out each of the data objects for use in completing the credit card transaction.

```
NSData *num = [[notification userInfo]
                          objectForKey:@"cardNumber"];

NSData  *name   = [[notification        userInfo]
    objectForKey:@"cardName"];

NSData  *year   = [[notification        userInfo]
    objectForKey:@"cardExpYear"];
NSData  *month  = [[notification        userInfo]
    objectForKey:@"cardExpMonth"];
```

EA Pattern

Before describing the EA Pattern, you should understand that what I have described so far represents a small set of the available patterns.

Other fundamental design patterns include two-stage creation, templates, dynamic allocation and creation, and enumerators. Patterns like the singleton that were discussed, as well as hierarchies, outlet-target-actions, and responder chains provide support for keeping your system loosely coupled.

For different system designs, I believe that there is a superset of these patterns that may form the "best architecture." Think of it like a house. A house contains bedrooms, bathrooms, living rooms, sleeping rooms, utility rooms, and so on. Each of those rooms has a basic design, or you could say pattern.

Designing a house for an urban dweller differs greatly from what you would do for someone who wants to build a farm. A house for a surfer will differ greatly from that for a mountain man. But they are all created from the same basic parts.

For any system where an external accessory will be used, you must use certain patterns. Delegation deals with handing the application overhead as well as being responsible for the actual hardware accessory. Notification tells you when an accessory is connected or removed.

Another system, a productivity app such as a to-do list for example, probably wouldn't have need for notification. On the other hand, because a to-do list is a set of items, the pattern of enumeration might come in very handy.

Table 3–1 lists the four basic patterns that comprise the higher-level EA Pattern and how they are used.

Table 3–1. *The EA Pattern*

Pattern	Usage
OOP	Representation of each of the objects in the system: the ball, the paddle, the table, the players' scores, and the controller
MVC	Separation of system functions into (possibly) reusable elements
Delegation	UIApplication and controller connect/disconnect method calls
Notification	Pass controller specific data to the objects that need it

Summary

Before getting into specific design patterns, I first addressed the overall way to construct iPhone programs—as object-oriented programs. OOP differs significantly in the way problems are addressed versus functional design. In OOP, we represent the system as the individual objects that make up the system. Each object has properties that describe it and methods that define what the object actions. Like a neighborhood comprised of people, houses, cars, streets, and so on, an OOP system is the composition of all its objects and their interactions.

You built a preliminary description of the objects with the Pong game that includes the paddles, the ball, the boundary, the score, and the serve button.

I described the UIApplication class and its purpose. The UIApplication, a singleton object in the application, handles all of the routing of user events in your system. Usually UIApplication is not subclassed, but instead handled through a delegate that conforms to the UIApplicationDelegate protocol.

Delegation allows one object to act on behalf of another, usually complex, object, so that you don't have to subclass the complex object. The most common example is the UIApplicationDelegate whose protocol includes the often-used applicationDidFinishLaunching: method call. The EAAccessory sharedAccessoryController works much like the shared UIApplication singleton. It sends notification when an accessory is physically connected or removed from the iPhone.

The Model-View-Controller design pattern delineates a system into reusable parts. The model contains the system state information and usually only interacts with the controller. The View provides the user interface including controls and display information and also interacts with the controller. With this separation, pieces such as the model might be easily reusable in another similar system. Take the model for the Pong game. While not exactly the same as the rules of play, Pong's model could be easily reused in another similar game such as Air Hockey. The Air Hockey view would differ significantly, but the model would stay much the same.

While MVC provides the ideal way to partition a system, sometimes practicality dictates combining functions together. In very small applications such as the prototype Pong game, it becomes simpler to combine MVC into a concept called a screenful of information. A screenful of information is just that, the part of the code that manages pretty much everything that a user sees on a single screen. For Pong, this might mean putting the ball movement, the collision detection, sounds, the scoring, and so forth, all inside a single view controller. Inside of the view controller itself, you may still logically partition things according to MVC guidelines.

Notification provides a means to loosely couple objects. Where delegation provides means for objects to communicate, those communication paths are one-to-one and very specifically defined. Notification works by sending information to a central dispatcher, the notification center, which then forwards the message to whoever is interested.

Notification consists of three parts: (1) an object must register for notifications with the notification center; (2) an object sends a notification to the notification center which may include the userInfo field which a dictionary of Key-Value pairs; (3) a receiver object must have a method, defined by using @selector( ) when registering to act upon the notification and retrieve any userInfo data passed with the notification.

KEY POINTS

- We develop software for the iPhone using an object-oriented method. OOA (object-oriented analysis) breaks the system problem into its constituent parts, while OOP (object-oriented programming) builds the system through software.

- Design patterns are common templates used to build the system.

- The Model-View-Controller (MVC) design pattern separates the user interaction with a system from the model that represents the system, providing a better chance of reuse of the various parts of the system.

- In MVC, the controller element separates the view from the model and is generally the most specific (non-reusable) part of the system.

- Delegation reduces the programmer's work by permitting one object to do the work required by another, usually more complex, object. The alternative to implementing delegation would be to subclass the more complex object.

- We commonly use delegation when creating the application delegate that handles such methods as `applicationDidFinishLaunching`.

- Notification provides the system with the means to send messages from one object to many others. The sending object doesn't need to know who is receiving the message and the receivers do not have to know who sent the message.

- In addition to the specific message, notifications can include a `userInfo` field to pass other information between objects using a Key-Value dictionary.

- Lower-level patterns such as delegation, MVC, and notification combine to form more complex patterns such as the EA pattern to address specific, complex problems.

Part **II**

Project Walkthrough

Chapter 4

The Game Controller

This chapter digs into the game controller that you'll be using to interface to the sample application, the Pong game. Your understanding of the controller will be developed from the inside-out, meaning that I will discuss the initial design and show the various stages of development from logic diagrams to the completed unit.

However, before getting started on the game controller, it might help to take a detailed look at another sample accessory that is currently in production at the time of writing.

The Griffin iTrip

For a long while now, Griffin has been making accessories for every popular MP3 player on the market including the iPod and iPhone. One of their most popular devices, the FM transmitter, takes the output of various music players and converts it to a radio frequency (RF) frequency modulated (FM) signal. This weak signal can then be transmitted a short range to an FM radio and picked up on an unused station, typically on your car's radio.

Recently, as part of Apple's MFi/WWi program, Griffin released the iTrip for the iPhone and iPod, shown in Figure 4–1. The iTrip works exactly as an Apple accessory is supposed to—when you first attach the iTrip to your iPhone or iPod Touch, it will detect that the iTrip application is not present and ask if you would like to retrieve it from the App Store. Selecting yes takes you there where you can immediately download and start using the app.

In addition to the iPhone and iPod Touch, the iTrip works with other iPods sending music to a nearby FM radio. These other iPod generations do not require any app to operate correctly. The iTrip exchanges data with Apple products via the 30-pin connector the same as your Game Controller.

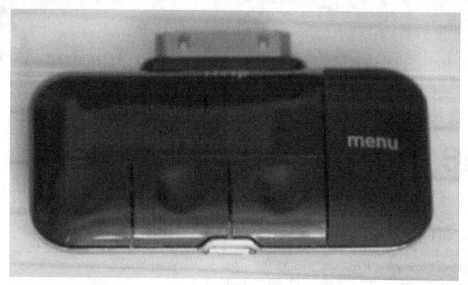

Figure 4–1. *The Griffin iTrip*

Figure 4–2 shows the iTrip application icon on the iPhone springboard. Prior to starting the app, you attach the iTrip to the iPhone at the 30-pin dock connector, as shown in Figure 4–3. You can then tune the RF transmitter to an open FM station as well as selecting various presets that can be accessed by a single touch of either the App screen or the iTrip buttons.

If you attempt to start the iTrip app without the iTrip accessory attached, or remove the accessory while the application is running, you will see the screen in Figure 4–4 telling you to reattach the iTrip accessory.

NOTE: Information on Griffin's complete line of products can be found at their web site http://www.griffintechnology.com.

Figure 4–2. *The iTrip Application icon*

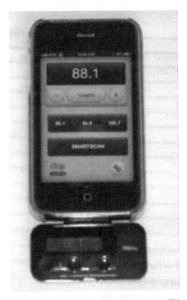

Figure 4–3. *An iTrip attached to an iPhone with the app executing*

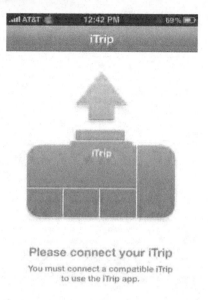

Figure 4-4. *The iTrip app requests that you connect your iTrip*

iTrip Dissected

Now that you've seen the Griffin iTrip as a customer who would be using one, let's take a closer look at the insides. You're not going to reverse engineer the device or anything so sinister, but, as thorough developers, it is always good practice to see how our peers do their job.

> **NOTE:** If you are planning to develop your own hardware accessories, definitely try to obtain any currently available accessories to use as reference material in your work. At times, you may become frustrated at some part of the Apple Interface Specification that doesn't seem to make sense. By examining a working, commercially available accessory, you will see that someone else "has done it" and if they can, then so can you.

Pulling off the top cover of the iTrip with a hobbyist's knife reveals the insides, as you can see in Figure 4-5. You see the three preset buttons at the bottom of the logic board, the menu button to the right side, the left-middle black rectangle is the small LCD which shows the station number to which the iTrip is tuned, and at the top is the 30-pin dock connector.

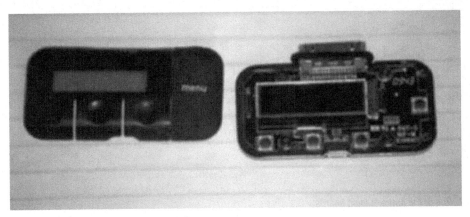

Figure 4–5. *The iTrip top cover removed*

Figure 4–6. *The bottom of the iTrip logic board*

I removed the logic board by unscrewing it from the case and then flipped it over in Figure 4–6. You can see several ICs and surface mount components on this fairly dense board. The chip on the right side of the board in Figure 4–6 with a spot of white paint is the primary processor of the iTrip. At the bottom of the logic board, there is another micro-USB connector. A separately available charging adapter can be connected through this port to charge the iPhone or iPod while the iTrip is being used. Apple does not permit commercial use of the receptacle (iPod/iPhone) end of the dock connector. Therefore, devices that need to passthrough-charge the Apple device must add a different type of connector such as this micro-USB.

A quick comparison of the iTrip logic board with one of the author's early boards shown in Figure 4–7 reveals the similarity in board size and the much greater differences in complexity. The author's board, because it has much less work to do, is far less complex.

Figure 4–7. *One of the author's logic boards*

Game Controller Design

Now that you've had a look at a typical accessory, let's consider what needs to be done for your game controller accessory. First of all, there's the usual chicken-and-egg problem. That is, do you first create your application and then design the accessory to work with it, or, do you develop your accessory and build an app that works with it? Unlike most chicken-and-egg scenarios, this one is easy.

As iPhone application developers, you create a solution for a problem. This means that, in a large percentage of cases where you are presented with a problem to solve, you design the system that meets your requirements. And, as a software developer, that means you pretty much develop the software solution first. Then, if needed, you develop any additional accessory hardware to meet requirements that the software doesn't handle by itself.

There will be some specific cases where you need to build a hardware accessory to handle unique I/O and you will likely know those requirements from the start. Other applications, such as games, may not even need an accessory controller at all. Adding an accessory might be done just to make your app stand out from the rest.

In this exercise, you're actually taking this latter approach. The Pong game certainly works well enough with the player using his finger on the touch screen to control paddle movement and other operations such as serving the ball. Having already developed some iPhone applications, I can certainly understand view controllers and accessing touches to understand how it all works.

Building the accessory game controller to take over those functions which you already know how to handle presents an incremental approach to the design. The game controller only takes things a step or two beyond what you already understand. By not *jumping into the frying pan* so to speak, you limit the amount of new territory to cover in developing your accessory. So let's get started.

The Game Controller's Functions

First you need to set the parameters of your design. What will the controller do? In thinking about the game of Pong, you obviously will want the controller to handle the movement of your paddle.

The Potentiometer for Paddle Movement

You could have a two-axis controller meaning that you can move the paddle along the up-down axis, or the left-right axis. This would require a control such as a joystick to be part of the controller. Because two-axis control is really no more than two one-axis controls, for now, you'll stick with simply being able to move the paddle left or right, i.e., along only one axis. For this, all you need is a potentiometer or knob.

A potentiometer is basically a resistor with a third tap that moves along the length of the resistance. Measuring from this center tap to one of the ends will return a resistance measurement that depends on the position of that center tap.

Let's say the total resistance of the potentiometer, from the outer ends, is 10k Ohms.

> **NOTE:** Ohms is the unit of measurement for resistance. Similarly, a volt is the unit of measurement for voltage, and an amp is the unit of measurement for current. Typically, most systems that you are working with will operate in the milliamps (thousandths of an amp), millivolts (thousandths of a volt) and killiohms (thousands of ohms). Ohms is an inverse relationship to volts and amps, i.e., as the current (amps) or voltage (volts) gets smaller, the resistance (ohms) gets larger.

If you put the probes of a multimeter across these leads, and set the function to Ohms, you will indeed measure 10k Ohms. If you move one of the probes to the middle, then what will you measure? It depends on the position of the tap, which is determined by the position to which you turn the knob of the potentiometer.

Before going on, a quick couple of analogies might help. If you think of your electrical system as if it were water in a set of pipes, then voltage would be the amount of pressure of the water through those pipes. Think of it as how far on you have set the knob. The more open, the more pressure. The more closed, the less pressure. All the way off, no pressure.

Current can be thought of as how fast the water moves through those pipes. Though it seems similar to pressure, it isn't. Imagine you turn your garden hose all the way on and you get a good stream of water coming out of the end at some speed, then, imagine your hose grows to the size of a hose on a fire truck. You can imagine that the water would not come out as fast. Similarly, imagine you have your same hose and place your thumb partially over the opening—what happens? The water speeds up and comes out faster. Note that at no time did you change the pressure into the hose.

What you did do was change the resistance. When you changed from a small hose to a larger one, you decreased the resistance so that for the same amount of pressure (start thinking voltage) you got a lower flow (or current). The inverse happened when you decreased the size of the hose (increased the resistance); you got more flow (or a higher current).

Figure 4–8 depicts three cases of electrical flow in your system. The zig-zag line represents the resistance of the potentiometer, with the lines at the top and bottom being the end taps. The center tap with the arrow is where you are going to take your measurement.

The three cases are: (1) you measure before the current gets to the resistance, (2) you measure when the current has gone part way through the resistance, and (3) you measure after the current has travelled through all the resistance.

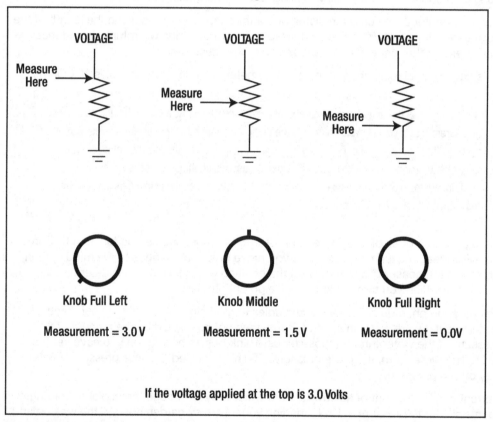

Figure 4–8. *Readings from a potentiometer*

If you take your measurement before the current has seen any resistance, then you are simply measuring the full value. You might want to ask, "The full value of what?" Do you measure current or voltage? Without going into too many details, you measure **voltage**. This is what the electronic device that you are using measures, so that's what you have to use as well. If you assume that the total voltage is 3.0 volts, then in the leftmost case, you would measure 3.0 volts at the center tap.

Skipping the rightmost case, your measurement takes place at the bottom, or far end, of the potentiometer's total resistance. As can be seen in Figure 4–8, you measure 0.0 volts because the current has passed through the total resistance of the circuit.

Finally, if the knob were set exactly at the middle position, then you would be measuring at exactly the half resistance point, and expect to get half the total voltage, or 1.5 volts, which is exactly (to the certainty of the measuring equipment) what you see.

Now all you need do is take these measurements with your accessory board, and when they change (the knob rotates) you send the updated reading to your iPhone application. The iPhone app can then determine where it wants to place the paddle. A simple scenario would be to position the paddle all the way to the left if the reading is 3.0 volts and all the way right if the reading is 0.0 volts. Then the app extrapolates an in-between position for any other readings.

The Pushbutton to Serve

Let's add a pushbutton to your controller that causes a ball to be served. Sure, you could easily do this by tapping the screen, but that wouldn't serve your learning function very much, would it?

At first glance, it seems like you're going to measure a value as you did in the previous section with the potentiometer, and return it to the app. Then, depending on that value, the app will either serve or not serve a ball.

The problem here is that doing it the same way means that you have to constantly measure the switch value like you did with the knob. It might be simple, but it just seems like a lot of unnecessary work considering that the pushbutton will be pressed a lot more infrequently than the rate at which the knob will be rotated. There must be a better way.

There is, and you've talked about it already. The solution is to allow the pushbutton to *interrupt* your process whenever it is pressed. As an alternative to continually checking the value of an object, or *polling*, using interrupts allows the application to continue on with its business, then handle the interrupt whenever it occurs. By assigning a priority to the interrupt such that it takes precedence over all or most other functions when it occurs, the interrupt will be handled first. Appropriately, you call the function that deals with servicing the interrupt, an *interrupt handler*.

Our accessory processor, therefore, must have the capability to handle external interrupts. As you'll see later, the processor of choice will be the Microchip PIC16LF1936 controller that supports externally triggered interrupts for your pushbutton. In addition, the PIC16LF1936 contains an analog-to-digital converter to read the measurements from the potentiometer discussed in the previous section and convert them to a format (digital) suitable for the iPhone application.

Electrical and Physical Design

You're also going to add some feedback on your controller in the form of light- emitting diodes (LEDs) that you can control from the iPhone app. You could go on about how this might provide a source of visual feedback for something. Perhaps you might want to flash a red LED when your opponent's paddle strikes the ball and green when yours hits it. What's really important, though, is that you demonstrate that you can send data not only from the accessory controller, but to it as well.

So what's your controller going to look like? First, it's probably going to be not much wider than the iPhone itself and will be connected at the bottom 30-pin connector. A rough idea of your controller's beginnings would look something like Figure 4–9.

Figure 4–9. *Prototyping the game controller*

Here, I've taken a small rectangular piece of copper used for creating a circuit board and cut it to about the width of an iPhone. I've placed a 10k Ohm potentiometer on the right that will be used to control the paddle. The three leads I talked about earlier poke through the board at the bottom of the potentiometer. To the left is the pushbutton switch. I've made it roughly the size of an adult thumb so it can be easily accessed.

I'll extend the design to include the 30-pin connector at the top of the board, roughly in the middle. The red and green LEDs will stand between the pushbutton and the potentiometer, roughly in the center of the board.

Your board will also require a processor, the Microchip PIC16LF1936 as mentioned earlier, as well as a few other components. I'll talk more about parts selection in general in the hardware design section. Because of the small size of the board, you will use more than just the top surface of the board to route your connections. In fact, you're going to create a 4–layer board, where the connections between components will route over four separate connection layers. There are some other specific requirements for the board that I'll talk about later when I get into board design, but for now, the fabricated boards are shown in Figure 4–10.

Figure 4–10. *Prototype versus fabricated circuit board*

On the green fabricated board at the bottom are the outlines for the pushbutton switch on the left and the potentiometer on the right. At the top, the row of small silver rectangles provides the placement for your 30-pin connector. There are 15 pins on top and 15 pins on the bottom of the board. To the left, the black square near the top is the PIC16LF1936 controller, the brains of the accessory. To the upper right is a special-purpose chip that handles the authorization between the accessory and the iPhone.

Near the center of the board you can see the outlines for LED1 and LED2 where your green and red LEDs will be soldered. To the right of the LEDs you can see four pairs of silver squares, solder pads, used for mounting surface mount chip resistors. Finally, the five small holes arranged horizontally at the bottom provide a mount point for a five-pin connector that will be used to program the PIC controller once the board is assembled.

Figure 4–11 shows the completed board once all the components are soldered onto the board, along with a knob for the potentiometer.

Figure 4–11. *Assembled logic board for the game controller*

Test Software

Your completed board needs to be put through its paces (tested) before you jump into the complexities of an iPhone game application. Generally, in any development process, it's always best to make small, incremental steps, proceeding from known circumstances, into the unknown. Ideally, you'd like to have a proven piece of software to test your, as yet, unknown logic board. Fortunately, Apple has provided it.

If you are a member of the Apple iPhone development program, you have access to a very valuable suite of example code. What you need for your test is the EADemo code. Apple provided this as part of the 2009 World Wide Developer's Conference and hopefully by the time this book comes to press it will be available as part of the standard set of sample code.

The sample application consists of four parts: the application delegate, the root view controller (a navigation controller), the accessory controller, and the view controller. I discussed much of this architecture in the chapter on the External Accessory Framework and will cover it again when I describe how to build the Pong application. For now, only the key differences will be addressed.

The application delegate is straightforward and does nothing more than add the navigation controller to the window.

Within the viewDidLoad method of the navigation controller the first two lines of code add observers of the accessory connect and disconnect notifications and the third line starts their delivery. The fifth line of code in the viewDidLoad method gets the list of connected accessories from the shared accessory manager object, as shown in Figure 4–12.

```
- (void)viewDidLoad {
[[NSNotificationCenter defaultCenter] addObserver:self
            selector:@selector(accessoryConnected:)
                    name:EAAccessoryDidConnectNotification
                    object:nil];
[[NSNotificationCenter defaultCenter] addObserver:self
            selector:@selector(accessoryDisconnected:)
                    name:EAAccessoryDidDisconnectNotification object:nil];
[[EAAccessoryManager sharedAccessoryManager]
        registerForLocalNotifications];

accessoryController = [EADAccessoryController sharedController];
accessoryList = [[NSMutableArray alloc]
        initWithArray:[[EAAccessoryManager sharedAccessoryManager]
        connectedAccessories]];

    [self setTitle:@"Accessories"];
    [super viewDidLoad];
}
```

Figure 4–12. *The navigation controller's table view of accessories*

The table view lists only one accessory, the game controller (GAMCON). Pressing the info icon on the right side of the table cell provides more detailed information on the accessory and can be seen in Figure 4–13.

Figure 4–13. *Pressing the info icon reveals more details about the attached accessory.*

You can see that the accessory is connected and has a name of GAMCON. The manufacturer is MACMEDX and the model is SLIMLINE. Other information includes the serial number of the unit, the firmware revision, hardware revision, and the protocols that the accessory supports. There is nothing magic about this information. All these elements are programmed into the accessory and passed to the iPhone when the accessory is connected. Typically, all this information would be programmed in data EEPROM when the accessory is assembled. An incrementing field would be used to program incrementing serial numbers to uniquely identify each unit.

NOTE: EEPROM is electronically (or electrically) erasable programmable read only memory. This memory can store information even when the power is removed, unlike typical RAM, and is used for holding data that must persist across power outages.

Selecting the accessory cell causes the modal dialog to appear allowing the user to select the protocol to be used with the accessory (Figure 4–14).

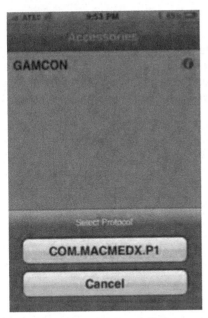

Figure 4–14. *Modal dialog to select accessory protocol*

As discussed earlier, the protocol button on the modal dialog in Figure 4–14 refers to the organization of the communications messages that move between the iPhone application and the controller's firmware. This would include control packets to perform such actions as turning on or off LEDs, as well as sending the position information of the potentiometer and the pushbutton to the iPhone app. Pressing this button on the action sheet modal dialog results in execution of the following method.

```
- (void)actionSheet:(UIActionSheet *)actionSheet
        clickedButtonAtIndex:(NSInteger)buttonIndex {
    if (selectedAccessory && (buttonIndex >= 0) &&
        (buttonIndex < [[selectedAccessory protocolStrings] count])) {

[accessoryController
                    setupControllerForAccessory:selectedAccessory
            withProtocolString:[[selectedAccessory protocolStrings]
                    objectAtIndex:buttonIndex]];

EADAccessoryDetailsViewContoller *accessoryDetailsViewController =
            [[EADAccessoryDetailsViewContoller alloc]
                    initWithNibName:@"EADAccessoryDetails" bundle:nil];

[[self navigationController]
            pushViewController:accessoryDetailsViewController animated:YES];

[accessoryDetailsViewController release];
    } // end if

[selectedAccessory release];
selectedAccessory = nil;
[protocolSelectionActionSheet release];
```

```
protocolSelectionActionSheet = nil;
}
```

The two key things that happen in this code are: (1) the `setupControllerForAccessory` method in the controller object is called, passing in the protocol used by the accessory, and (2) the detail view controller for the accessory is loaded using `initWithNibName`. In essence, this code starts the accessory controller so your app can exchange information and brings up the window in Figure 4–15.

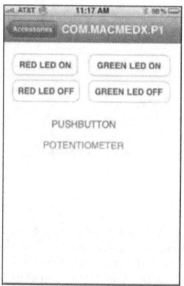

Figure 4–15. *The accessoryDetailsViewController Xib file*

Using Interface Builder, you've created the nib (xib) file that allows you to test the accessory board functionality. You can turn on or off either of the LEDs using one of the four pushbuttons. In addition, the two labels PUSHBUTTON and POTENTIOMETER provide a way to see information when either one of those two controls is used.

To test the LEDs, you create a method for each of the four basic functions—red on, red off, green on, green off—and control-drag from the button to the first responder in Interface Builder to make the connection. The four functions should obviously be located in the detailed view controller file and are shown in the following code.

```
- (IBAction)turnOnRedLED:(id)sender
{
    const uint8_t buf[2] = {0x98, 0x01};
    [[EADAccessoryController sharedController] writeData:[NSData dataWithBytes:buf
length:2]];
}

- (IBAction)turnOffRedLED:(id)sender
{
    const uint8_t buf[2] = {0x98, 0x02};
    [[EADAccessoryController sharedController] writeData:[NSData dataWithBytes:buf
length:2]];
```

```
}
- (IBAction)turnOnGreenLED:(id)sender
{
    const uint8_t buf[2] = {0x98, 0x03};
    [[EADAccessoryController sharedController] writeData:[NSData dataWithBytes:buf
length:2]];
}

- (IBAction)turnOffGreenLED:(id)sender
{
    const uint8_t buf[2] = {0x98, 0x04};
    [[EADAccessoryController sharedController] writeData:[NSData dataWithBytes:buf
length:2]];
}
```

From the discussion of protocols earlier, you see that each function sends a two-byte packet to the accessory—each packet containing a control byte and a parameter byte. The control byte 0x98 tells the accessory that this is a command to be executed and the parameter byte (either 0x01, 0x02, 0x03, or 0x04) tells the accessory which specific LED to turn on or off.

But how do you actually send the data to the accessory? Look at the second line of each method. The first part of each statement returns the shared accessory controller and to that controller you pass the writeData method with two parameters: the buffer containing the command packet and the length (two bytes) to be sent.

> **NOTE:** At the time of this writing, the source code for Apple's External Accessory Demo was only available when you purchased the 2009 WWDC proceedings. Copyright restrictions prevent its duplication in this book. Check with Apple for more information.

Now that you're able to send data to the accessory, you need to consider how to get data from the accessory to the iPhone and the iPhone application. As mentioned earlier, the accessory sends two different data types to the iPhone.

The first data type sent to the iPhone tells the application when the button is pressed by the user. The button press *interrupts* the normal programming loop executing on the firmware in the accessory. As can be seen in Figure 4–16, as soon as the accessory has initialized, it enters a loop that does nothing.

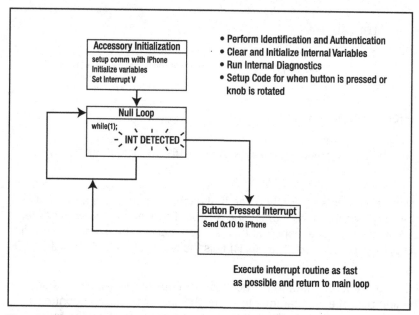

Figure 4–16. *Interrupt routine for pushbutton*

This *null loop* continually loops on itself until it is interrupted by an external event. In Figure 4–16, that event would be when the user presses the pushbutton. Internal to the accessory game controller, the normal 3.0 volts is reduced to 0 volts. This negative transition (3 to 0) is interpreted as an interrupt by the PIC16LF1936 processor. Within the PIC processor, the code jumps to a table of interrupt vectors (addresses of specific routines) determined by the base address of the table plus an offset indicated by the type of interrupt that occurred.

As shown in Figure 4–17, when the PIC controller powers on, it first jumps over tables that include the addresses of interrupt routines to the start of the main code. Doing it this way provides a known set of addresses that the programmer sets up for the interrupt routines.

If a pushbutton interrupt occurs while executing the null loop, after saving state, the address at the start of the interrupt table offset by the number of the interrupt is loaded into the program counter. This code executes, and, in your case, sends the 0x10 value over the serial connection to the iPhone telling the iPhone app that the button was pressed.

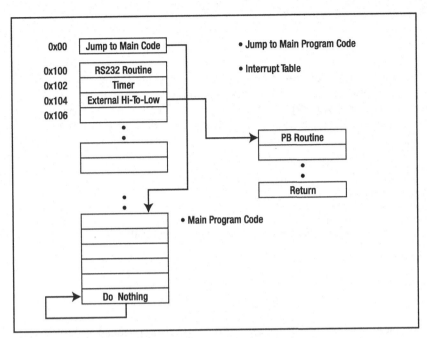

Figure 4-17. *Accessory firmware interrupt vector table concept*

On the iPhone side, the application sees any incoming data as an NSStream, which I discussed earlier. Both the input (to iPhone from accessory) and output streams are set up when you open the session to your accessory.

The openSession routine sets the delegate to itself and attempts to open the session for the indicated protocol. If successful, meaning the session variable is not null, the routine opens the input and output streams.

```
- (BOOL)openSession
{
    [accessory setDelegate:self];
    session = [[EASession alloc] initWithAccessory:_accessory
forProtocol:_protocolString];

    if (session)
    {
        [[session inputStream] setDelegate:self];
        [[session inputStream] scheduleInRunLoop:[NSRunLoop currentRunLoop]
forMode:NSDefaultRunLoopMode];
        [[session inputStream] open];

        [[session outputStream] setDelegate:self];
        [[session outputStream] scheduleInRunLoop:[NSRunLoop currentRunLoop]
forMode:NSDefaultRunLoopMode];
        [[session outputStream] open];
    }
    else
    {
        // handle failed open session
```

```
    }
    return (session != nil);
}
```

For each direction (input and output) the stream delegate is first set to this object, and next scheduled in the default run loop. Afterwards the stream is opened and ready for processing. When you're done working with the accessory, the streams are closed in the reverse order from above. In addition, you must release and clear the session variable.

```
- (void)closeSession
{
    [[session inputStream] close];
    [[session inputStream] removeFromRunLoop:[NSRunLoop currentRunLoop]
forMode:NSDefaultRunLoopMode];
    [[session inputStream] setDelegate:nil];
    [[session outputStream] close];
    [[session outputStream] removeFromRunLoop:[NSRunLoop currentRunLoop]
forMode:NSDefaultRunLoopMode];
    [[session outputStream] setDelegate:nil];

    [session release];
    session = nil;
}
```

This sets up communications with the accessory, but how do you process incoming and outgoing data? The answer should be familiar. Remember setting delegate to self in the above code? You set the stream delegate to self because in this file you create a routine stream:handleEven:eventCode that processes stream events.

```
- (void)stream:(NSStream *)aStream handleEvent:(NSStreamEvent)eventCode
{
    switch (eventCode) {
        case NSStreamEventNone:
                        break;
        case NSStreamEventOpenCompleted:
                break;
        case NSStreamEventHasBytesAvailable:
            [self readData];
            break;
        case NSStreamEventHasSpaceAvailable:
            [self writeData];
            break;
        case NSStreamEventErrorOccurred:
            break;
        case NSStreamEventEndEncountered:
            break;
        default:
            break;
    }
}
```

While all events should be taken into account in any released code, here you are only interested in reading and writing. The event NSStreamEventHasBytesAvailable: lets you know that there is data from the accessory that needs to be read and you call the readData method. The event NSStreamEventHasSpaceAvailable: lets the code know that the outgoing stream has space for writing data and you call the writeData method.

Note that the first event means that you have data that needs to be read and processed while the second event only indicates that you have space to write any data that is waiting to be written. The writeData routine very simply checks if the stream still has space available and if there is something to be written (_writeData length is greater than zero). If everything is a go, then you call the NSStream write:maxLength: method to actually send out the data.

```
- (void)writeData {
    while (((([session outputStream] hasSpaceAvailable]) && ([_writeData length] > 0))
    {
        NSInteger bytesWritten = [[session outputStream] write:[_writeData bytes]
maxLength:[_writeData length]];
        if (bytesWritten == -1)
        {
                        // handle write error
            break;
        }
        else if (bytesWritten > 0)
        {
            [_writeData replaceBytesInRange:NSMakeRange(0, bytesWritten) withBytes:NULL
length:0];
        }
    }
}
```

If an NSStream has data to be read from the accessory by the iPhone application, then the readData method is called.

```
- (void)readData {
    uint8_t buf[EAD_INPUT_BUFFER_SIZE];

    while ([[_session inputStream] hasBytesAvailable])
    {
        NSInteger bytesRead = [[_session inputStream] read:buf
maxLength:EAD_INPUT_BUFFER_SIZE];
                if (buf[0] == 0x10) {
                        [[NSNotificationCenter  defaultCenter]
postNotificationName:@"PBPRESSED" object:self]; // no user data

                }
                if (buf[0] == 0x20) {
                        NSData *data = [[NSData alloc] initWithBytes:buf
        length:bytesRead];

                    unsigned char i = buf[1];
                    NSNumber *posInt = [[NSNumber alloc] initWithUnsignedChar:i];
                    NSLog(@"_readData position = %d",[posInt intValue]);

                    NSMutableDictionary *dict = [[ NSMutableDictionary alloc]
    // we use a dictionary to send it via notification center
                                                                init];
                    [ dict  setObject:posInt forKey:@"parameter"];
```

```
                        [[NSNotificationCenter  defaultCenter]
postNotificationName:@"POTTURNED" object:self userInfo:dict];
                        [dict release];
            }


    }
}
```

First, the method sets up an input buffer into which raw bytes are read. Then, within the while loop, after all the bytes are read, two checks are performed. The first check looks to see if this is a button press, i.e., you have received a 0x10 command byte from the accessory. The other option is if you've received knob position data from the accessory. In that case, you receive a 0x20 byte in the first position followed by a byte value from 0x00 to 0xFF indicating the position of rotation.

In either case—a button press or a knob rotation position—a notification informs all listeners of the situation. In the case of a button pressed, no additional information is needed other than to know that the event occurred. However, in the case of a knob rotation, additional userInfo includes a dictionary entry with the key parameter referencing the knob's position that is sent as an NSNumber.

All that remains to be done is for that application to use the information—a button press or a new knob position—as appropriate. Figure 4–17 shows the results of pressing the pushbutton several times and Figure 4–18 shows what happens when the knob is rotated to a new position.

Figure 4–18. *Pressing the game controller's pushbutton*

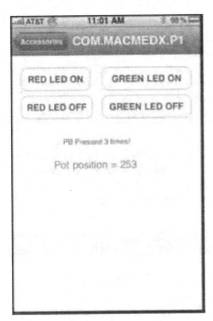

Figure 4–19. *Rotating the game controller's knob*

Summary

This chapter provided more detail on the specific functions of the game controller and how it interfaces to the iPhone.

First, I took a look at a similar iPhone accessory, the Griffin iTrip. The iTrip provides the means for connecting the audio output to a FM receiver. Using the iTrip as an example shows you what you can expect with your own accessory. Using a known, production-level accessory provides a fantastic baseline to use when comparing your own product development.

While an accessory developer would normally create an accessory as part of a solution to a problem, in this case, for the purposes of education, I took a different approach. The rationale was to look at typical communications that happen between an iPhone and any accessory. In general, you are either going to send information to the accessory from the iPhone or the reverse.

Starting with the Pong game concept, the most obvious control needed would be to set the position of the player's paddle. For this, you use a potentiometer whose electrical resistance varies as the position is changed. The processor and firmware within the controller reads the voltage from the center tap of the potientiometer and sends that to the iPhone.

Though not strictly needed, you add a second user control in the form of a pushbutton to tell the application to serve the ball. Because this function operates much more infrequently than the paddle position, you use an interrupt routine to service the pushbutton. The interrupt routine *fires* whenever the button is pressed causing whatever is currently happening to pause, and transfer control to the pushbutton routine. However, because all you need to do is inform the iPhone app that the button was pressed, only a single byte (0x10) of data is sent to the iPhone as opposed to when the knob is repositioned. In the latter case, not only does the app need to know that the event occurred (the knob turned) but it also needs to know the new position. In this case, you send two bytes; one indicates that the event occurred and the second byte contains the new position of the knob.

Input and output data between the iPhone and accessory are handled by streams, in particular, NSStreams. NSStream provides events that the delegate handles indicating when data is available from the accessory to be read, when the output stream is empty and data can be sent to the accessory, as well as various error conditions.

KEY POINTS

- Use existing accessories as reference when developing your own to provide valuable information on how a functioning system operates.

- Your game controller needs to send data to the iPhone to indicate the position of the player's paddle as well as an indication of when the serve button is pressed.

- Some functions such as serve operate infrequently and are suitable to the use of interrupts.

- An interrupt routine functions by pausing whatever is occurring in the main program, quickly executing the code to process the interrupt, then returning to where the main program left off.

- NSStreams handle the data transfer between the iPhone application and an accessory.

Chapter 5

Specifying a Pong Game

So far, I've talked about most of the tools you need to begin working on iPhone and iPod touch accessories. Now, let's get started with some actual programming and slowly bring all the pieces together.

Keeping It Simple

Although you could develop a very intricate game that you might possibly be able to put in the App store and sell, you're going to keep things very simple. The more complexity and coolness that you build into the game, the more time you'll spend writing and debugging code that doesn't pertain to the subject matter of the book. Remember, you're trying to learn about interfacing iPhone accessories, the undertapped market of the iPhone world. With over one hundred thousand games in the App store at the time of writing, and half of those being games, you can figure your chances on this Pong game being the next breakout star.

So let's talk about the game. What do you want it to do? In essence, you want to bounce an object that resembles a ball back and forth across the screen. The player should be able to move something that acts as a paddle to catch up with the ball when it is on his side. That brings up the notion of sides. You're going to declare that the top part of the screen—the side closest to the power button—is the opponent's space and the half of the screen near the bottom and the home button is the player's space. You could of course use the auto-rotate feature and play the game upside-down from those conditions, but to keep things simple, you won't.

Let's talk about player and opponent. Although it seems obvious that the player is the human that taps the icon to start the game and moves the paddle, you need to state these things up front in your specification for whatever system you are building.

Specification

I cannot over stress the importance of writing a system specification. A specification doesn't have to be a multipage document with droning on paragraphs containing *shalls*, *shoulds*, *musts*, *wills*, etc. For a large, multipart system, it may very well go into the tens or even hundreds of pages. There could be design reviews, teams working on different sections, code reviews, and all the other things associated with large companies.

How big should your specification for the Pong game be? The correct answer is "it depends." But that doesn't help you. I'm going to go out on a limb here and say that you want your specification to be two pages. Wow! You made a commitment. Two pages. So what's on those two pages?

Page One—Drawings

Let's make one page some sketches of our game: you'll have a rectangle to act as your playing surface—you'll probably want to make it a similar green color to a real table tennis game table. There should be lines on it like there are on a real table, as you can see in Figure 5–1.

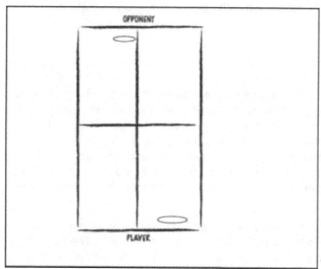

Figure 5–1. *Initial playing surface drawing*

Okay, you've got a good start. You've established your playing surface and it has the general look of a table tennis table. Your player and opponent sides have been defined.

> **NOTE:** Wonder why I call it table tennis and not Ping-Pong? The name Ping-Pong actually belongs to the game company Parker Brothers, whereas the term table tennis is the actual name of the game as defined by the International Table Tennis Federation (ITTF).

The approximate positions of the paddles are also set. Is this enough? For that you have to ask yourself some questions. First, how will you initiate game play? You could just tap the screen, but that's too easy. Saying that is like saying "Oh yeah, it's in there, I just didn't show it because it was obvious." Here's the thing. Nothing is obvious when you're buried in code, it's late, you're tired, and have deadlines to meet. There's a saying in playwriting: if it's not on the page, it's not on the stage. This means, if it's not written down, you won't be seeing it. The key point—write it down!

You also need to keep score and show it to the player. So you have to add the score somewhere, and, the labels indicating which score belongs to whom. How do the paddles move? You talked about this earlier, but you didn't show it. For simplicity you're going to have the paddles move only to the left and to the right to work with the potentiometer on your game controller.

There are also some less obvious things. Does the game table take up the whole screen or is it smaller? Here you need to think about how realistic you want your game to be. A regulation table is nine feet long by five feet wide or simply nine by five. The iPhone screen is 480 by 320, or reducing that, three by two. The dimensions don't match. They're close—if you multiply the iPhone screen dimensions by three, you get nine by six. But that's still not nine by five. This is where it becomes a judgment call.

Normally, I would take the safe route—the technically safe route—and make the playing surface match the iPhone's screen dimensions. You don't have to worry about what's outside the table bounds and can even choose to either let the ball continue out or have it bounce back into play as if the edges were a wall.

Like I said, that's normally what I'd do. For this exercise, I'm going to stick with a table that retains the nine by five dimensions and place it inside a virtual room. My feeling on this is that, when you play table tennis, you move far to the left and right of the table to make shots with significant angles.

This differs from a game like air hockey where you are constrained by the sides of the playing surface. The thing is, in air hockey, you're aiming for a small target and the reduced set of angles makes sense. Your opponent only has to guard a small, central area. But in your table tennis type of game, you open up the playing field with much wider margins. Like you, your opponent can move to extreme angles to win the point, so you're going to let that happen in your game.

Anything else? Hmmm, let's think about it. You've decided on the table dimensions, restricted the player's paddle movements to left and right, you added scoring. Is anything missing? It may sound overly detailed, but you need to add the ball to the drawing. Trust me. It's a very small thing to add and it makes your diagram complete. Now let's take a look at your revised drawing in Figure 5–2.

All the elements just described have been added to make things a little more clear. You added both the player's and computer's score along with labels to tell which is which. You added a serve button, the ball, and an example movement line. You added a separate rectangle around the playing surface to indicate that the table is within the iPhone screen bounds, and you added a ball.

Let's cheat and see what the final game is going to look like to see how close you need to be on your spec drawing. Looking at Figure 5–3 you can see that the drawing very closely represents what is in your final Pong game.

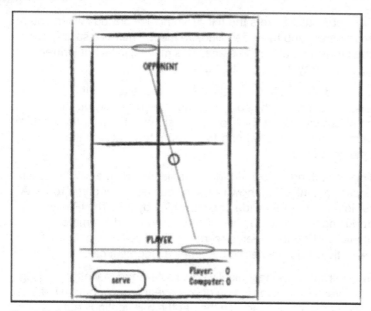

Figure 5-2. *The revised game drawing*

You've created your game table and placed it within the screen's boundaries. The area outside the playing surface is black, while you've made the table green with white lines to simulate a regulation table. There is another white line that runs along the edge of all four sides of the table that you decided not to add.

The table has been moved further in at the bottom of the screen to make room for the serve button and scoring. If it hadn't occurred to you yet, think about what would happen if you made the whole screen your playing surface. The serve button and scores would be covering your playing surface. Of course, you could dim them or hide them when in play, but that creates a more complex game scenario that you would need to manage. For your exercise, it's much easier just to give them an area outside your field of play.

So you've probably beaten the drawing to death and should move on to requirements. But you're not. You need to know about what happens in more complex systems.

The Pong game has only one screen. You could have added more—a setup screen perhaps or maybe a preferences screen. But you didn't add those in order to keep the game simple and focus on dealing with accessory interfacing. But, in the real world, most other apps will have multiple screens. Even the simplest games intended for the market will have more than one screen.

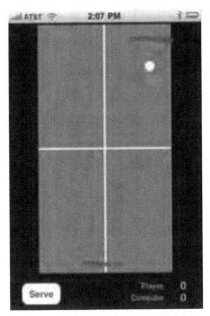

Figure 5–3. *The actual game screen*

If you're anxious to get moving on the game, feel free to skip ahead. However, I want to cover a couple more examples to stress the importance of good preparation work.

Let's take another game example and make it as simple as possible. You'll even make it simpler than your Pong game. How do you do that? You make it a one-player game. Let's use the example of a slot machine.

A slot machine has one player pressing a button. This causes three (or more) wheels to start spinning, and, when they stop, certain combinations pay out. Why didn't you use this for your accessory controller program if it's simpler than Pong? Your accessory needs to control something and, if you chose to make it a slot machine, all there would be to control would be the spin button and that wouldn't do much for your learning.

What's involved with a slot machine? Take a look at Figure 5–4 depicting the initial concept for a slot machine game.

As you can see, it's very simple. There is a single screen that contains controls, scoring, and visual feedback. The control set consists of two ways to place a bet and a button to initiate the spin. The spin button corresponds to the serve button on the Pong game. You give your player a limit that he can bet and allow him to wager from one unit (dollar) up to that maximum. By tapping the BET+1 button, he can wager in increments from one dollar to the maximum currently set as ten. You also can say that whatever his last bet was carries over to the next spin. So, if he wagers seven and loses, his next wager is again going to be seven.

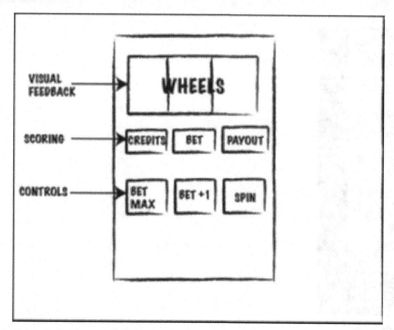

Figure 5–4. *Slot game initial concept*

Because there isn't any real money involved, most players will generally bet the largest amount most of the time. For this, you provide the BET MAX button. Finally, when the player is ready, he presses the SPIN button; the wheels turn, the lights flash, and the music plays. But wait? Are those on the drawing? No.

Before you get back to your pad and paper to make changes to the design, let's look for anything else you should add.

To get the mood of a casino you want flashing lights, sounds, the smell of cigarette smoke and sexy cocktail waitresses walking around. You can't get the last two, but you can certainly add the lights and sound. But what if a player doesn't want sounds? You need a way for him to change the mode of the game to be silent.

Anything else? Sure, what if the player wants to start over? For this, you want to add a reset button. Also, slot machines, depending on how they are set up, are notorious for long times between payouts—at least all the ones I've played. For this, let's give the player an option to increase the odds.

You'll stop there with your settings as you get the point. You've added three setting controls: a reset, a change odds option, and a sound setting. Where do you put these? Certainly, there is room on the main page, but that would defeat the style of the game. You want your player focused on playing the game, not tweaking settings. What you want to do is add a setup page. Remember how I said even small games could expand their number of pages quickly?

So you add three buttons to a second page. Immediately that begs the question: isn't that going to look empty? You could make them larger or fancy, but that would just look like you're trying to cover up your mistake.

Once again, let's think about how a slot machine works, or more specifically, how it pays out. A lot of people seem to think if you get three of a kind that's when you win. It is, but given the odds, that almost never happens. There are certain icons that win whenever they are shown on the payline. Typically, whenever you get a cherry (or the particular major symbol for the game) you win something. It may be your bet amount, or something less or more.

> **NOTE:** The payline on a slot machine is a real or suggested line that generally runs though the center of the slot symbols. For a symbol to register it should be centered on the payline. If a symbol is offset, or say, three-quarters of it is above the payline and one-quarter of it below, then it usually doesn't register. You may have three of a kind in the window and not get a payout—this is typically because all three symbols are not aligned and centered on the payline.

You need a scoring table. Most slot machines have them somewhere on them; I suspect they are probably required by certain local laws. You'll add one to your setup screen so your player can plan his strategy.

Taking all these things into consideration, let's look again at the slot machine design in Figure 5–5.

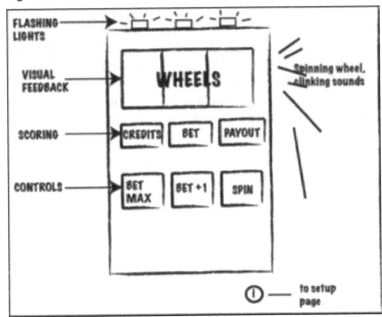

Figure 5–5. *Revised slot machine game design*

You've added three lights at the top that will flash when the game is active (wheels spinning), an indicator that you have sounds playing and a way to get to the settings. The circle with an 'i' inside at the bottom represents the standard way of getting to a setup page. A user taps on the symbol and you flip the image to your setup page.

Figure 5–6 shows what your setup page will look like.

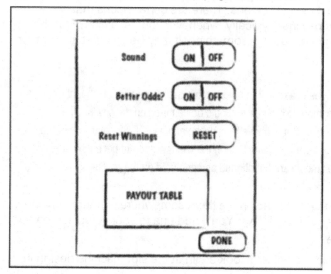

Figure 5–6. *Slot machine game setup page*

There are slider switches to turn on or off the sound and better odds settings. There's a pushbutton to reset the user's winnings back to the starting amount. At the bottom is the DONE button that ends the settings option and returns you to the game, and finally, the payout table to give the user an idea of his chances.

To wrap up this section on screen design, take a look at Figures 5–7 and 5–8 for a comparison of the slot game's screen designs and the actual final version.

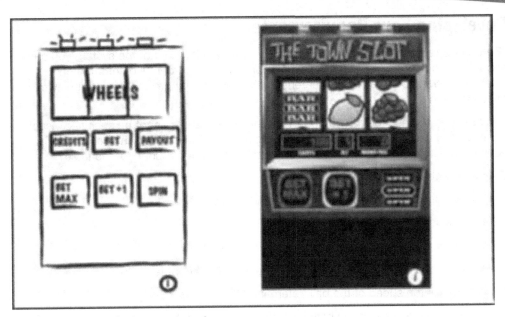

Figure 5–7. *Slot game front screen comparison*

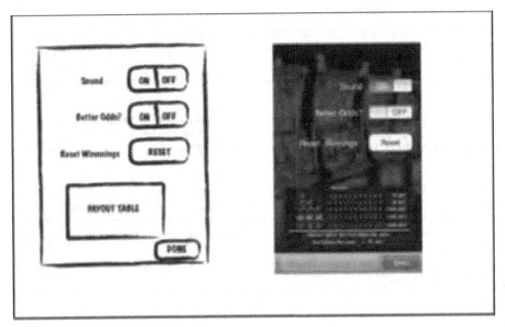

Figure 5–8. *Slot game back screen comparison*

Developing Your Requirements

The visual specifications already defined generally specify most of the system you are about to build. Keep in mind that an iPhone processes a screenful of information at a time and drawing pictures of the screens at the start of your project is a great way to describe them.

You still need to describe the other parts of the system that cannot be specified visually. For example, which direction do you want the serve button to send the ball initially? Or, how do you handle the boundary of the screen versus the boundary of the table?

Take a look at the following list:

- In which direction does the serve send the ball?

- Does the ball bounce off the walls of the room?

- Does the ball make a sound when it hits a paddle?

- Does the ball make a sound to simulate hitting the table?

- How is the speed of the ball determined?

- How is the angle of the ball after a hit or bounce determined?

- How do you keep score?

This represents a good list of questions that you need to answer for your very simple game. Remember, these are not your specification, but the questions you must answer to develop your specification. I can hear you say, "But aren't you really just pushing the work back a level? Making me answer questions is just a different way of writing specs, isn't it?"

Think of it as pitching a story idea. You are the producer and some schmuck is trying to sell you on his greatest screenplay. The screenwriter walks into your office and you ask him to tell you his idea. He says, "It's a story about an iPhone that is killing everyone at a high school." And then silence.

You wait, expecting to hear more, but nothing comes. In your mind, you visualize this iPhone that is more or less a rectangular version of Chucky from *Child's Play* only with a springboard full of icons for his face. Supposing you've had a really bad year with flops, this one, on the surface, doesn't seem too bad. It may even make it to the SciFi channel, since what bad movie doesn't?

But you need more. *You begin to ask questions*, just like you did previously. You are trying to find out more; is the iPhone possessed? Do the good guys or the iPhone win in the end? How does this iPhone have all this power?

As you start to ask the questions, you find out that it's not the iPhone killing people at all. There's an evil mastermind sending mind-controlling video messages to people that cause them to kill themselves. (And you wonder why Apple held off on multi-media SMS until 3.0.)

The point of the analogy is that, while you may have a good idea for a game or any software project, you need to ask the hard questions to flush out the details to create a specification. So let's get to it.

Let me stress again that you are concerned with the process of interfacing an iPhone accessory, your game controller, as a learning process. So you can lighten up on the strictness of your approach.

Take the direction issue. In a regulation table tennis game, players alternate service every two points. You could do that, but, since this is not regulation, let's make the service function easy; *activating the serve will always send the ball in the direction of the opponent, the computer's paddle.*

Issue number two: does the ball go outside the walls of the screen or bounce? If you allow the ball to go outside the walls, and thus end a point, then you have to add complex logic to deal with the direction of ball changes when hitting the paddles. Imagine the ball is served to the computer at a small angle so it hits the computer's paddle at an angle while the paddle is near, but not past the edge of the table. You have to know the exact position and invert the direction, so it bounces back into the table area.

If you are developing a production level game then of course you want to deal with all these complex scenarios. However, for you, *if the ball hits the left or right sides of the screen boundary, then it bounces back into play.*

This is much like the air hockey logic I talked about earlier. It's not perfect, but it makes the game a little less complicated while maintaining play at the same time.

Does the ball make a sound when it hits the paddle? You could easily justify not using any sound for your game under the same premise that this is a learning process. But sound is more than just a game enhancement in this situation; it also provides an intrinsic debugging tool. When the ball and the paddle are about to collide, you'll hear whatever sound you decide to use for the impact. So, *when the ball impacts either player's paddle a sound will be played.*

Much like a ball hitting one of the players' paddles, the ball also makes a sound when it hits the table. But this is a much more difficult problem to solve in a game such as yours. Sure, it would be nice to have it, but do you really need it for what you're trying to accomplish?

This dilemma represents something you'll see a lot of as you develop more and more complex systems. Some of the features you will want to put into your program will obviously need to be there or there will be a really good reason to not put them in. But then there will be those that land right in the middle, like your second sound issue.

You may see these things called "nice to haves," meaning, of course, that they would be nice to have in your system, but you could live without them. So let's put the sound of the ball hitting the table as a nice to have.

In regard to the speed of the ball and how you determine it, you first have to think about speed in general and what you even mean by it. Without getting overly complicated, let's just say that the speed of the ball is going to be related to the distance it travels over unit time.

In your game, you will create a game loop, meaning that on every iteration through the loop you update the game; you move the ball and the paddles to their new position. For the ball, you will define a set of constants, x_delta and y_delta, that determine the ball's initial speed in the x and y directions. In the loop, the new position is set to be the value of x times the x_delta value and y times y_delta.

This means that your ball always moves at the same speed. This will get dull really quickly. To alleviate the boredom at the expense of the human player losing some points, you're going to make an adjustment as the game progresses. Each time the computer hits the ball, you're going to bump up the speed in the y direction. You can experiment with how much or how often you bump up the speed, but let's at least make the game a bit interesting.

To summarize, *the ball's speed will be set to the same starting value and slightly increased each time the computer's paddle hits the ball*.

When the ball hits either player's paddle, it will bounce off at a new angle. Think of it as banking a shot when playing pool. Look at Figure 5–9 to see this illustrated.

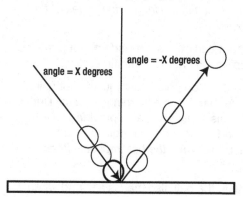

Figure 5–9. *Angle of ball on impact with a surface*

If a ball hits a wall at an angle of X degrees, then it will bounce off in the opposite direction at approximately –X degrees. This is pretty intuitive and I won't get into the nasty details of the mathematics involved, but will stick with this simple explanation for your game.

What happens in the case depicted in Figure 5–10 in your game?

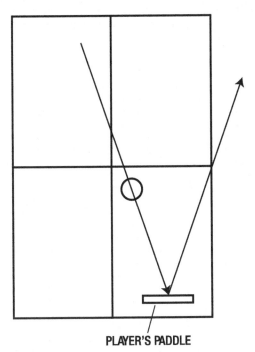

PLAYER'S PADDLE

Figure 5-10. *Ball hitting player's paddle at angle*

The ball hits the player's paddle and bounces away from the table causing the player to lose pretty much every time. You need a way to correct for this. What you want is something more like that depicted in Figure 5–11. You want the ball to be hit back towards the table to keep it in play.

Therefore, you will add the requirement to your system that, *when the ball is off to the side of the table, after it impacts a paddle, the x direction will be reversed*. This will tend to make it look a little more like a real game.

Finally, there's the issue of keeping score. Again, to keep things simple, you're going to define winning a point as when a player misses hitting the ball. Again, similar to an air hockey game, imagine that the whole back wall is your opponent's goal and, when you miss hitting the ball, your opponent wins the point. That being said, *when a player misses hitting the ball and the ball travels into the same player's end zone, the other player scores a point*.

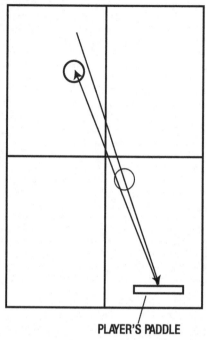

PLAYER'S PADDLE

Figure 5–11. *Ball kept in play by changing X direction*

So that about does it for your simple set of requirements. You might ask, "When does a player win the game?" That's going to be up to you. In a regulation table tennis game, the first player to eleven wins but he has to win by at least two points. So if the game is 10-10, the next point doesn't win, but the game continues until one player is ahead by two. This adds undue complication for what you are trying to accomplish, so you'll just let the game continue as long as you want. Remember, your real goal is learning how to interface accessories.

Summary

This relatively short chapter focused on developing a set of written requirements for your game. The purpose of the requirements, and writing them down, is to keep you focused when you get neck-deep into coding. Sticking them to a wall in front of where you are coding is not a bad idea. This way, they are always visible when you are working on your code. If you get lost, you can always look up and see what you are supposed to be doing.

A set of requirements for iPhone development should consist of two parts. You should construct a set of illustrations of your screens that you will be developing. Always keep in mind the concept of a screenful of information. That's what you are working with.

The second part of your set of requirements should be a list of things that your system needs to do. In the real world, this would be your list of "shalls"…the start button shall initiate processing; the score shall be displayed in at least 12 point font; and so on.

For small systems, it's okay just to keep them simple, but always try to make the requirement something that is tangible. Don't write a requirement like, "Make the game exciting," although that should be a goal, it's a requirement that cannot be quantified.

KEY POINTS

- Before starting the design of your system, develop a written set of requirements to use as a guide for everything that follows.

- Draw pictures of what your system's screens will look like and try to include as many of the elements of the system as possible so you don't forget anything.

- Write a quantifiable set of requirement statements about what your system needs to do.

Chapter **6**

Coding a Pong Game

You've designed and built your game controller and specified the basic operation of the Pong game. You know what the screens will look like and it's now time to start writing the application.

But hold on. Like me, you've probably been guilty of reading a book or an article on the web that described a cool iPhone program and, before you took the time to understand what was going on, you fired up Xcode and got it running on the simulator. I want to take the first part of this chapter to discuss what's going on under the hood when you write iPhone programs.

Architecture

The first thing you need to do before you open up Xcode is define the basic structure of the program. This is where those design patterns I talked about earlier start to become useful.

Read through any book on iPhone programming and you'll see the same basic architecture; you start with an application delegate, add some controllers to do the work at the lower levels, and add some views. But what's really going on?

The Application Life Cycle

Everyone working on iPhone applications should understand the basic life cycle of an iPhone app. The Apple documentation does an excellent job of throwing a lot of information at you. The problem is that you may try to read and understand it all early in your iPhone programming career. Then, as you start to get comfortable with using Interface Builder and are able to create simple apps in your sleep, you forget about all that Apple technical stuff until you've buried yourself in a coding problem late at night and think that there is no way out. So let's do a little review.

In essence, an application's life cycle is (1) the user taps the app icon to being, (2) it executes and you use it to do what you need to do, then (3) you press the home button to terminate the app. Notice that you don't terminate programmatically. I certainly remember the good old days where a program started, it ran, and then it ended. You usually would put in a catchy little "Good Bye" to let you know when it stopped. But Apple discourages ending an iPhone app programmatically. Look in the Apple Human Interface Guidelines and you'll see that Apple says that terminating an app programmatically will look like a crash to the user. I think that's good advice.

So what happens when the user taps an icon to being? The first thing that is called is the main() function. If you've programmed in C before, then you're more than likely familiar with main(). Every program (in standard C) must have one main() function. When you start the program, that's where the loader starts. Every other function is really just subroutines called from main().

What does main look like? The following is an example main() function taken from one of my applications that I have on the App store.

```
#import <UIKit/UIKit.h>

int main(int argc, char *argv[]) {

    NSAutoreleasePool * pool = [[NSAutoreleasePool alloc] init];
    int retVal = UIApplicationMain(argc, argv, nil, nil);
    [pool release];
    return retVal;
}
```

Here is a main() function generated from Xcode for the Pong game:

```
#import <UIKit/UIKit.h>

int main(int argc, char *argv[]) {

    NSAutoreleasePool * pool = [[NSAutoreleasePool alloc] init];
    int retVal = UIApplicationMain(argc, argv, nil, nil);
    [pool release];
    return retVal;
}
```

Notice anything? They're exactly the same. In fact, you will almost never have to do anything to main(). You can probably tell that main() does three things, but if not I'll point them out.

The first thing main() does is to create an autorelease pool. You're more than likely familiar with the autorelease pool; it sets up the memory management system so that objects don't have to be released in the same functional block of code where they are created. Sure, when you do an alloc-init in a method, you make sure to add a release before the method ends to avoid memory leaks. But that doesn't mean the object is released at that moment.

In the following code, you're pushing a view controller from your navigation controller.

```
MyViewController *vc = [[MyViewController alloc]
        initWithNibName:@"MyView" bundle:nil];
[self.navigationController    pushViewController:vc
                                    animated:YES];

[vc release];
```

This code fragment, likely the result of a user tapping on a cell in a tableView, does three things: it creates an instance of the type MyViewController, it pushes that view onto the navigation stack and then releases it. Because the viewController is being used—you are likely looking at it after it is pushed—it still has a positive retain count.

The retain count mechanism very simply adds one to or takes one away from an object. When the object is at zero, that's when that magical autorelease pool comes into play. In the previous segment of code, the alloc-init of the viewController gives it a plus one. When it is pushed onto the stack, the navigation controller takes some control over the viewController, and bumps its retain count so now it's at plus two. In the last statement in this segment, you release the viewController. This decrements the retain count so it's now at plus one.

When will it go away? Well, assuming the view is visible and under the control of the navigation controller, when the user is done with it, he will press the back button in the upper left of the navigation controller. That pops the view from the stack and also decrements the retain count so it becomes zero. At the next point in the current, run loop when the autorelease pool functionality is called, so the object is removed.

You'll get to step number two of main() in just a moment, but let's skip ahead to step three. The third and last thing done by main() is to release the autorelease pool. After that, the program terminates and control goes back to UIKit and you're typically taken back to the springboard, i.e., your home page.

In case you're still a little unclear on this autorelease thing, it may help to think of an autorelease pool as exactly what it is, a collection of objects. You should understand by now that if you alloc-init an object, somewhere you're going to have to release it or you get the dreaded memory leak. But all you're really doing when you release the objects, in a sense, is passing the control to actually get rid of the space they take up in memory to the autorelease pool function.

What main() does in steps one and two is exactly the same thing you do to your objects but for a much more complicated object, the autorelease pool. Make sense? It may help to look at a code snippet from a Cocoa program written for the Mac.

```
int main (int argc, const char * argv[]) {

    NSAutoreleasePool *pool = [[NSAutoreleasePool alloc] init];
//
// All the other programming stuff
[pool release];
return 0;
}
```

You can clearly see that steps one and three are the same for your iPhone app; you create an autorelease pool at the beginning of your main() and release it at the end. The iPhone SDK just happens to give it to you for free.

Steps one and three seem pretty much like system-level housekeeping, and that's exactly what they are. All the work is done when you call UIApplicationMain.

```
int retVal = UIApplicationMain(argc, argv, nil, nil);
```

Notice the four arguments that you pass along with the call to UIApplicationMain. The first two, argc and argc, are just copied from the initial main(). You've been showing the main() function as not having any parameters for brevity, but remember that it really looks like:

```
int main(int argc, char *argv[])
```

Historically, this is how you get command-line parameters into your program. In the old days, you would write programs that were called from the Unix command line. Imagine a program that sorts numbers into increasing order. You provide some numbers and are returned the same numbers but in ascending order.

```
unixPrompt> sortNums    5 2 7 3 10 1 99
sorted numbers = 1,2,3,5,7,10,99
```

I admit it's pretty basic, but this is just to illustrate what's going on in main(). So, in this example, what would be the values of argc and argv? Well, argc stands for argument count and represents the number of arguments that are passed to main contained in the argument vector **argv[]**. What would the value of argc be in the preceding example? The argc, which by the way is defined as an int, parameter would contain the value 8. However, there are only seven parameters. The thing is argv[0] contains the name of the program, i.e., "unixPrompt". So that argv[1] = 5, argv[2] = 2, and so on.

Therefore, whatever is passed into main when the program starts is passed through to UIApplicationMain. Good to know, but in reality, you're never likely to deal with these two parameters. What about the third and fourth parameters to UIApplicationMain?

Both the third and fourth parameters are strings with the third being the class name of the principal class, and the fourth being the class name of the application delegate. Could I have possibly said that in a more confusing way?

Let's take them one at a time. What is the principal class? First let's look at things on a Mac. Go to your Mac's application folder and single click on a program like Safari. It can be any program; I'm just using Safari because it's likely that everyone has it on her Mac. Control Click and then from the options select "Show Package Contents." You should see a Contents folder which you can open and see more stuff. This stuff is the program. Programs or applications on the Mac are packages or bundles of things like the executable, image files, property lists, and so on. These are generally termed your program's resources and this directory is called the bundle. In this bundle are stored all the classes of your program.

The *principal class* controls all the other classes in the bundle. Think of it as the highest level of authority in your program. In a Cocoa application on the Mac, the principal class is defined though the info.plist file, whereas on the iPhone it's defined in main() as the third parameter.

You've set the principal class to nil, but what does that mean? Setting the principal class to nil means that UIKit will use the UIApplication class by default. This is almost always what you want. Remember from before, the UIApplication is the singleton (only one per application) that provides the central point of control for an application. That sounds exactly like what you want. UIApplication's (or the application object's) main purpose is to handle events, typically touch events. You typically assign the application a delegate that informs the application of significant events. This, of course, is your application delegate.

The fourth parameter string sets the name of the class of the application delegate. You know what an application delegate is, but what do you put here?

```
int retVal = UIApplicationMain(argc, argv, nil, nil);
```

As you can see in the call to UIApplicationMain, you pass nil for the fourth parameter, the name of the application delegate. By passing nil, you tell UIKit to go and get the application delegate object from the program's main nib file.

Let's pause for a moment to investigate this. Fire up Xcode and go to File ➤ New Project. Create an iPhone OS View-Based Application and name it **deleteMe**, placing it on your desktop. In the Groups&Files section on the left, locate the MainWindow.xib file. It should be inside the Resources folder, as shown in Figure 6–1.

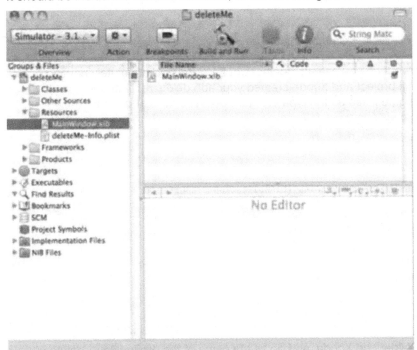

Figure 6–1. *Xcode example for deleteMe*

Double-click MainWindow.xib to open Interface Builder. Locate the window titled MainWindow.xib and single click on the application delegate. It will be titled **Delete Me App Delegate**, as shown in Figure 6–2.

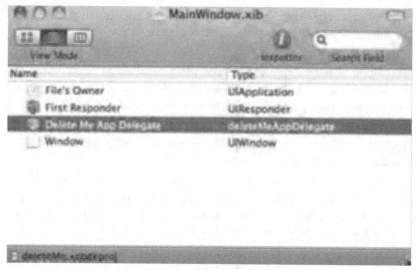

Figure 6–2. *Selecting the app delegate in Interface Builder*

That went by fast, but do you see the coolness of this? You did absolutely nothing other than create a blank project and Xcode created your app delegate. Note the deleteMeAppDelegate listed as the type in Figure 6–2. The familiar code for the application delegate is shown as follows:

```
@implementation deleteMeAppDelegate

@synthesize window;

- (void)applicationDidFinishLaunching:(UIApplication *)application {

    // Override point for customization after application launch
    [window makeKeyAndVisible];
}

- (void)dealloc {
    [window release];
    [super dealloc];
}

@end
```

Close Interface Builder and Xcode, and do as the name of the project says, delete it.

You've seen that Xcode is geared towards using an application delegate that it creates for you and is loaded by the main nib file.

You've now covered the third and fourth parameters in your call to UIApplicationMain and that set them to nil; more specifically, the main() program created by Xcode sets them to nil by default. What if you don't want to do it this way? A couple better questions to ask would be: (1) When would you not want to do it this way? and (2) How would you do it differently?

Have you ever subclassed the UIApplication class? Most likely, 99 times out of 100, the answer is no. Why? You normally use an application delegate. Why do you use an application delegate? It's much easier to use an application delegate—remember delegation is one of the principal design patterns in Cocoa and for the iPhone. But suppose you did need to subclass UIApplication?

I think this is one of those questions that those of us who are not Gurus in iPhone development kind of have on the tip of the tongue ready to ask, but are not sure how to phrase it. After all, a lot of us have done C++ programming and isn't subclassing the thing to do?

Look again at an application delegate. It handles the things defined by the protocol UIApplicationDelegateProtocol. The instance methods in the protocol such as applicationDidFinish are what you handle in your application delegate object. But what if you need to handle something that a UIApplication handles that isn't covered by the protocol? Let's make that a tad clearer and form it as a statement, and, oh what the heck, I'll even emphasize it.

Subclass UIApplication if you need to control a method that is not handled by the UIApplicationDelegateProtocol.

That's great and all, but when would this ever happen? Let's assume that you have an application that needs to count every time the user touches the screen while the app is running. This is not at the start of a game that counts touches, but every single touch while in the app. The user could tap to go to setup, tap to do something, or even tap to end the program. You need to capture every single touch. Maybe, you've deployed an app to a user group and you want to find out about the use of it. There are more simple ways of course, but this is just an example.

Each time the user touches the screen, the UIApplication sendEvent method is called. In order to find out about touches (or any event) in your example, you need to override sendEvent. The UIApplicationDelegateProtocol does not cover sendEvent but it is a method of the UIApplicationClass. Starting to come together? To override sendEvent, you need to subclass UIApplication.

Does this mean you create another object in your project? No. You simply have your application delegate subclass UIApplication and then in main() change the principal object to the application delegate. The call to UIApplicationMain then becomes:

```
int retVal = UIApplicationMain(argc, argv, @"AppDelegate", nil);
```

Some of you may never need this and that's fine. What I hope you have gotten from this is that the application process should not be a mystery. You may never need to subclass UIApplication or change the call to UIApplicationMain, but if you need to—and there are legitimate reasons for this as you've seen—then it's not all that hard to do so.

Pong Game Architecture

You've probably guessed by now that the Pong game architecture is fairly simple, and that would be correct. Your Pong game can be divided into three main parts: the application delegate, the game's view controller, and the accessory controller. Take a look at Figure 6–3 to see the functional relationship.

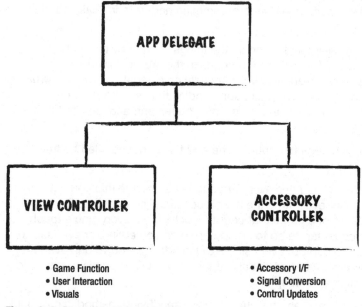

Figure 6–3. *Pong game high-level architecture*

The application delegate handles all the details of the main application. For Pong, this means three things: (1) setting up any start conditions once the app has finished loading, (2) loading the initial view/viewController, and (3) handling system cleanup when the app terminates.

So let's begin coding. Launch Xcode and go to File ➤ New Project. Under iPhone OS click Application and select View-based Application. You should see the window in Figure 6–4.

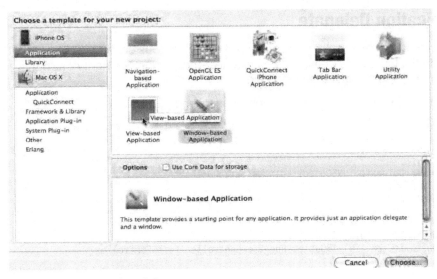

Figure 6–4. *Project creation window*

Name the project Pong and save it wherever you'd like. Xcode will provide you with the project window and open the Classes, Other Sources, and Resources folders on the left. Your project window should look like that shown in Figure 6–5.

While this all seems pretty straightforward, carefully check the list of files on the left side to make sure they match. Creating a different project type causes a different set of files to be produced.

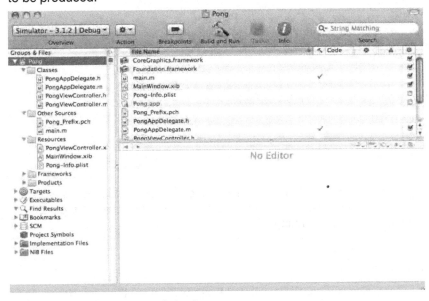

Figure 6–5. *Initial Xcode project window for pong game*

The Application Delegate

Xcode has created two of your three modules and all you did was create the project. You could add the third piece of the puzzle, your accessory controller, right now, but let's wait and get the basic game running first.

Take a look at the following code for the application delegate:

```
#import <UIKit/UIKit.h>

@class PongViewController;

@interface PongAppDelegate : NSObject <UIApplicationDelegate> {
    UIWindow *window;
    PongViewController *viewController;
}

@property (nonatomic, retain) IBOutlet UIWindow *window;
@property (nonatomic, retain) IBOutlet PongViewController *viewController;

@end

#import "PongAppDelegate.h"
#import "PongViewController.h"

@implementation PongAppDelegate

@synthesize window;
@synthesize viewController;


- (void)applicationDidFinishLaunching:(UIApplication *)application {

    // Override point for customization after app launch
    [window addSubview:viewController.view];
    [window makeKeyAndVisible];
}

- (void)dealloc {
    [viewController release];
    [window release];
    [super dealloc];
}

@end
```

The application delegate, immediately upon launch of the program, adds the view of our viewController object to the window and then makes that window visible. So far, so good; your view controller is now running the show.

The View Controller

Like all good iPhone developers, you start with the PongViewController's interface specification and then work on your nib file. Xcode gave the following interface file:

```
#import <UIKit/UIKit.h>

@interface PongViewController : UIViewController {

}
@end
```

Not much there—in fact, other than defining your PongVIewController to be a subclass of UIViewController, there is nothing there. First thing to do is add the IBOutlets for your actual view.

In case you don't already know about IBOutlet and IBAction, they are really just compiler directives to Xcode to provide hints as to what the properties or methods are being used for. You can see from the following Xcode definitions that IBOutlet actual equates to nothing and IBAction to void.

```
#ifndef IBOutlet
#define IBOutlet
#endif

#ifndef IBAction
#define IBAction void
#endif
```

If you are ever curious about the origin of a keyword, just place your cursor over the variable and CMD-Click to be taken to where the file is defined.

> **NOTE:** Don't confuse this with Option-Click-ing on a keyword that provides a look-up feature in Xcode.

You will need at least six elements on your screen: (1) the ball, (2) the player's paddle, (3) the computer's paddle, (4) the player's score, (5) the computer's score, and (6) a status label that you can use to inform the player whether he's won or lost. Therefore, add the following IBOutlets to your PongViewController.h file.

```
IBOutlet UIImageView *ball;
IBOutlet UIImageView *playerPaddle;
IBOutlet UIImageView *compPaddle;
IBOutlet UILabel      *playerScoreView;
IBOutlet UILabel      *compScoreView;
IBOutlet UILabel      *winOrLoseView;
```

Don't forget to add the property definitions as well.

```
@property (nonatomic,retain) IBOutlet UIImageView *ball;
@property (nonatomic,retain) IBOutlet UIImageView *playerPaddle;
@property (nonatomic,retain) IBOutlet UIImageView *compPaddle;
@property (nonatomic,retain) IBOutlet UILabel    *playerScoreView;
@property (nonatomic,retain) IBOutlet UILabel    *compScoreView;
@property (nonatomic,retain) IBOutlet UILabel    *winOrLoseView;
```

You use the @property keyword as a shortcut to defining properties in your application, as well as automatic synthesis of getter and setter methods, which you'll see later when you start writing the implementation code. In case you don't know, the keywords between the parentheses are the actual properties you want to assign to this variable. When you write retain inside the parentheses, you're saying that you want this variable to use the retain/release mechanisms talked about earlier for the getter and setter. A different option here might be to use copy in place of retain. As for nonatomic, you use this value generally because you are writing single threaded code and you want it to run faster. If you set the property to atomic (as opposed to nonatomic), which is the default if you don't specify either, the synthesized code locks the variable so that reads and writes from different threads are serialized and you don't wind up with partially written values that can crash your system.

Before moving on to the implementation file, add the following line:

```
-(IBAction) serveAction;
```

This creates the reference to which you will connect the serve button. Make sure you save the .h file either using Command-S or saving from the File menu. A lot of problems when using Interface Builder can be traced to not having saved the file where you want to make your connections.

Before moving on to IB, let's add the final third of your system. Click once on the Classes folder to select it and Control-Click and Add ➢ New File then create a UIViewController class. I called mine PongViewController. Make sure you add both the .m and .h files.

> **NOTE:** Ever wonder why some things are capitalized (like PongViewController) and some are not (pongViewController)? The standard convention is to capitalize the first letter of classes that you use to create instances. For example, PongViewController is a class. There really is no PongViewController until you create one. When you do create one, because it is an instance (something real), it will start with a lower case letter. Here's an example:
>
> ```
> PongViewController *pongViewController = [[PongViewController alloc]
> init];
> ```
>
> That is a lot of words to create a single variable, but the left side means that you're making pongViewController a type of PongViewController just like you would if you did "int I" where we make 'I' a type of int. On the right side, because the PongViewController is derived from an NSObject, you use alloc-init to create the instance, assigning the instance (just like you might assign 0 to i) to pongViewController.

The Nib

Still in Xcode, click once on the Resources folder to select it and Control-Click and Add ➢ New File and create a User Interface>View Xib file... I called mine pongViewController.xib since it will be associated with the PongViewController you will create shortly. But since it's not really a controller and more of a view, it might be better to leave off the controller from the name. On the other hand, as you work on more complex systems with lots of controllers and views, you need a good naming convention to keep things straight. Although the name I chose for the nib file isn't really accurate, I always know which view controller it belongs to. Whatever way you decide to go, try to develop a method that is consistent and works for you.

Because you should have had some experience programming in Xcode, using Interface Builder, and creating iPhone projects already, I'm not going to walk you step-by-step though creating the nib file. I'm going to show you critical screenshots and give a brief description of what was done to create it.

First, take a look at the completed pongViewController main window with all the directories open. You can see that you created, below the view since IB provided the view for you, four Image views representing the table, the ball, and the two paddles. Then you see the button that you use to serve the ball and a bunch of labels. There are five labels: a pair for the player's score, a pair for the computer's score, and one to indicate who won the game.

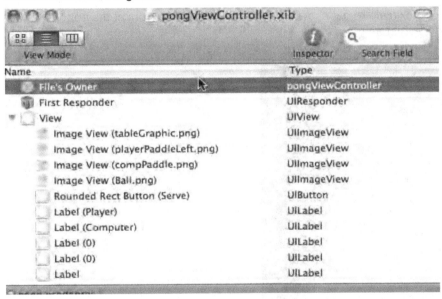

Figure 6–6. *The NIB's main window*

You can see that the first four image views have an associated graphics file. You should be able to download these files from the Apress web site. You should then import the files into your project's Resources folder by using the Command-Click then Add ➤ Existing Files. You then set each of the four image views to use one of the graphics files by clicking on the Image View name in the main window and on the property inspector, by selecting the name of the graphics file. An example for the tableGraphic.png file is shown in Figure 6–7.

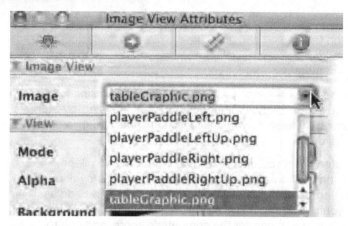

Figure 6–7. *Associating a graphics file to an ImageView*

Create the approximate layout shown in Figure 6–8 providing room at the bottom for the score and serve button.

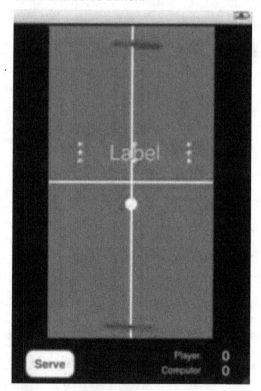

Figure 6–8. *General pong layout*

You've added the text "Label" to the win/lose label to make its position in the game clear. Before saving, make sure to remove the text so that the label is not visible during play.

Now it's time to go and make all the connections. I understand that it can be a little daunting. I said earlier that I'm not going to walk you through each connection and I'm sticking to that, but what I will do is show you some screenshots that should help.

First, you should understand that the File's Owner is directly related to the view you just created. What should its class be set to? This one should be easy and you should immediately shout out "PongViewController" class. Click on the File's Owner to select it and then go to the Identity Inspector and set its class to pongViewController, adjusting the name as necessary for your naming convention (see Figure 6–9).

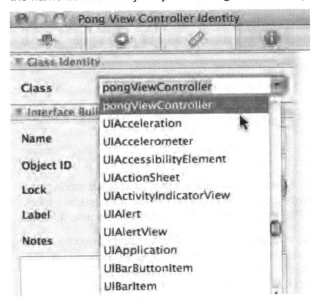

Figure 6–9. *Setting the File's Owner class*

I hope you're feeling comfortable with what you're doing in IB. Figure 6–10 should be the icing on the cake as it shows everything you need to know about finishing up.

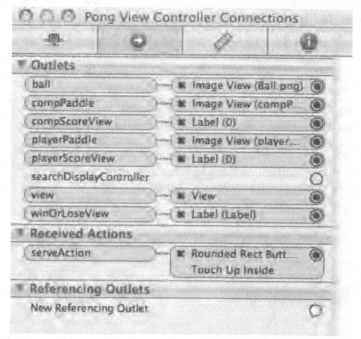

Figure 6–10. *The remaining connections*

From Figure 6–10, you can see all the necessary connections that need to be made from most of the objects that you added. Note that you don't need to connect the labels that tell you whose score you are seeing ("Player" or "Computer") because they never change.

Be careful of the direction with which you make the connections. There are some things about IB you need to be aware of. It seems that when you make a connection from the File's Owner to one of the imageViews, the popup only shows imageViews. But if you make a connection to one of the UILabels, it will only show UILabels. I assume it works that way to prevent errors, but it could be confusing for a user that didn't understand what's going on...just something to take note of.

Back to Figure 6–10, all the connections shown should be obvious to an experienced IB user such as yourself. The outlets you created are all matched up with either a label or an imageView of a game object. You connected the button to the serveAction method. The view is connected to the view outlet of the File's Owner, which, as you remember, is the pongViewController. Save your work and let's go back to Xcode to finish the game.

The Pong game operates as an autonomous loop, similar to the general operation of the iPhone itself. You're going to create this loop by creating an interval timer that periodically calls the gameLoop function. The gameLoop function updates everything about the game for each interval. To set the loop, you use the following method call:

```
[NSTimer scheduledTimerWithTimeInterval:0.05
            target:self
            selector:@selector(gameLoop)
            userInfo:nil repeats: YES];
```

The function of this code segment should be obvious to even the casual iPhone developer. I'll cover it here for clarity, but be warned, speed is picking up so I won't be examining every line of code.

This single line of code creates a timer from the NSTimer class that fires (sends a message) every 0.05 seconds. The message is sent to this object (target:self) causing the gameLoop method (selector:@(selector(gameLoop)) to fire. No extra information is passed to gameLoop (userInfo:nil) and this loop runs continuously (repeats:YES).

The gameLoop function performs all the necessary functions to make the game update, the primary ones being:

- See if anyone scored.
    - Player scored?
    - Computer scored?
- Has the ball hit the edge of the room?
- Did the player's paddle hit the ball?
- Did the computer's paddle hit the ball?
- Is the game over?

Much more detail goes into the gameLoop method as you will see shortly, but let's quickly cover the other support methods you'll need to make the game work. The methods I'm going to list are not the only way to define the program. In fact, I suspect there are many better ways of doing things. In fact, in many cases I purposefully did some things counter to the way they should be done, just to see what happens and make things more interesting.

> **NOTE:** While I included sections of the code for discussions here, the complete code with comments can be found at the end of the chapter.

I included the method setServePosition to position the ball after a point has been scored. The ball is placed at roughly the center of the table so it can be served towards the computer. A fairly obvious upgrade to this would be to set the ball's starting position back near the server's paddle. This would also require keeping track of the scores so that the serve can be alternated every two points.

```
-(void) setServePosition {
    ball.center    = CGPointMake(BALL_STARTING_X, BALL_STARTING_Y);
    ballSpeed = CGPointMake(BALL_DELTA_X, -BALL_DELTA_Y);
}
```

The compPlay method is the basic artificial intelligence of the whole program. It does nothing more than move the computer's paddle towards the ball along the horizontal axis, i.e., no Y-axis movement. There are two speeds (reaction time) of the computer; it moves slower when the ball is on the player's side of the table and faster when the ball is on the computer's side. The constant (#define) COMP_REACTION_TIME sets the computer's performance. A higher number provides a faster response and therefore a better player.

```
-(void) compPlay {

    if(ball.center.y <= self.view.center.y + COMP_SETUP_TIME)    {
        if(ball.center.x < compPaddle.center.x) {
            CGPoint compLocation =
                CGPointMake(compPaddle.center.x -
                COMP_REACTION_TIME, compPaddle.center.y);
        compPaddle.center = compLocation;
        }
        if(ball.center.x > compPaddle.center.x) {
            CGPoint compLocation = CGPointMake(compPaddle.center.x +
            COMP_REACTION_TIME, compPaddle.center.y);
            compPaddle.center = compLocation;
        }
    }
}
```

Interestingly enough, with all the code and things that even this simple game does, the player (user) only interacts with the game (exclusive of starting or stopping) at two different times. When he presses the SERVE button, you know that the serveAction method fires. This is what you set up with IB. What about the second condition when he moves his paddle?

When a user touches the iPhone screen, the sendEvent method of the UIApplication gets called, which is transparent to you (unless you've overridden it which requires subclassing UIApplication). What you do see is the touchesBegan:withEvent: method that is part of the UIResponder class. This provides objects (your code) the interface needed to handle user touches.

> **NOTE:** Although you can handle multiple touch events as well, you're going to assume that all touches are single touch events.

For the Pong game, you use the touchesBegan as a gateway. This version of the method does two things: (1) it checks to see if the game status is IN_PLAY, and if it is, then (2) it calls your own touchesMoved method to handle the movement of the player's paddle.

```
-(void)touchesBegan:(NSSet *)touches withEvent:(UIEvent *)event {
    if (status == IN_PLAY) {
        [self touchesMoved:touches withEvent:event];
    }
}
```

Continuing down the chain of touch events, the touchesMoved:withEvent: method updates the position of the player's paddle by repositioning the paddle to the new position of the player's finger. The other thing you decided to do in this method was change the paddle image depending on its position. If it is to the left or right of the centerline, then you flip the left-right orientation of the paddle to simulate forehand or backhand. If it is near the edges, as defined as 101 pixels to the left or right of the centerline, which is the approximate edge of the table, then you change to the slightly tilted paddle image.

```
-(void)touchesMoved:(NSSet *)touches withEvent:(UIEvent *)event {
     UITouch *touch = [[event allTouches] anyObject];
     CGPoint location = [touch locationInView:touch.view];
     CGPoint xLocation = CGPointMake(location.x,playerPaddle.center.y);
     playerPaddle.center = xLocation;
     if (playerPaddle.center.x > (self.view.bounds.size.width /2))
             if (playerPaddle.center.x > (self.view.bounds.size.width /2)+101)
                     playerPaddle.image = playerPaddleRightUp;
             else
                     playerPaddle.image = playerPaddleRight;
       else
             if (playerPaddle.center.x < (self.view.bounds.size.width /2)-101)
                     playerPaddle.image = playerPaddleLeftUp;
             else
                     playerPaddle.image = playerPaddleLeft;
}
```

Note that this has the unnatural effect of instantly moving the paddle to any position (left-right) that the player places his finger. This is something that certainly should be corrected in a final version. But since later you will be using a potentiometer in your game controller to position the paddle, this won't really matter. The potentiometer is a linear device unlike your finger. For example, to get to position 128 from position 1, the potentiometer has to go through positions 2, 3, 4,..., all the way until it gets to 128. This is different than your finger that you can simply lift off of position 1 and bring it down on any position you want.

The last method to discuss is actually the first method to execute. You set up the viewDidLoad method to initialize your game when the player starts it by tapping the icon from the iPhone springboard. It loads up the four images you need for the paddle so they can be quickly changed, displays the name of the game in the playing area, sets up the sounds, initializes the scores to 0-0, sets the initial status to NOT_STARTED, positions the ball for the first serve, and finally sets up the NSTimer to run the game.

```
- (void)viewDidLoad {

        playerPaddleLeft      = [UIImage imageNamed:@"playerPaddleLeft.png"];
        playerPaddleLeftUp    = [UIImage imageNamed:@"playerPaddleLeftUp.png"];
        playerPaddleRight     = [UIImage imageNamed:@"playerPaddleRight.png"];
        playerPaddleRightUp = [UIImage  imageNamed:@"playerPaddleRightUp.png"];


        winOrLoseView.text = @"PONG!";


     // SET UP SOUNDS
     CFBundleRef mainBundle;
     mainBundle = CFBundleGetMainBundle ();

     // Get the URL to the sound file to play
     paddleSoundFileURLRef =      CFBundleCopyResourceURL (
                 mainBundle,
                 CFSTR ("paddleSound"),
```

```
            CFSTR ("aif"),
                 NULL);
    AudioServicesCreateSystemSoundID (
                 paddleSoundFileURLRef,
                  &paddleSoundObject);

        playerScore = 0;
        compScore          = 0;

        status = NOT_STARTED;
         [self setServePosition];
         [NSTimer scheduledTimerWithTimeInterval:0.05 target:self
selector:@selector(gameLoop) userInfo:nil repeats: YES];
     [super viewDidLoad];
}
```

NOTE: While sound is integral to any good game design, I chose to leave out a detailed discussion of sound because, for what you are doing, it is only incidental. Simply put, in your game you basically load an aif sound file and convert it to system sound with an ID that you call when you need to make the hit sound.

Summary

You've quickly built a practical Pong game to which you can add your game controller. In doing so, you learned that there are three steps to the life cycle of any iPhone application: (1) the program starts when its icon is tapped, (2) it does its thing, and (3) it ends when the user presses the home button.

Like any C program, an iPhone program written in Objective-C has a main() function that is generated by Xcode. However, your main does very little and most of the work is done by the UIApplicationMain() function that is called from within. Most of the time, you never need to modify the main() function. One time that you might change main() would be if you needed to override a method specific to the UIApplication object.

Your starter version of Pong (without the game controller) has an application delegate and a view controller with the view controller doing all the work. You went through the construction of your program focusing on getting something up and running quickly, so you could get on to the process of adding the game controller. Nearly all of this should have been familiar to the reader.

In the next chapter, you will get into the heart of this book and show how you can add a hardware accessory to an iPhone application.

KEY POINTS

- There are three stages to the life cycle of an iPhone App: (1) start, (2) run, (3) terminate.

- The main() function generated by Xcode generally is never modified.

- Subclass UIApplication if you need to control a method that is not handled by the UIApplicationDelegate protocol.

Chapter 7

Adding the Game Controller

Once again, it's time to break new ground. Previously, I've talked about the new frameworks for connecting iPhone OS accessories and you've even developed a test program for your game controller. In the last chapter, you created a simple Pong game that you're now about to modify to use external hardware.

The Game Controller Test Program

Let's talk a little bit about the test program you created when you were developing your game controller. The program consisted of four major sections: the application delegate, the root view controller, the primary view controller, and the actual controller object.

The application delegate performed the simplest of functions in the world of delegates. It merely launched the navigation controller with a table view controller as its root view. The table view only serves to display the list of connected accessories to which you can connect. Although it is table view, you will only find a single cell filled out representing the single accessory that Apple's EA Framework currently supports.

When you select the accessory by tapping on its cell and then tapping on the protocol from the action sheet, you are taken to the EADAccessoryDetailsView controller where you stay as long as you are working with the accessory. The fourth element, the EADAccessoryController provides the data connection between the actual external hardware and the EADAccessoryDetailsView controller.

What you need to do is to extract the relevant parts of the test program and add them to your Pong game. Since your Pong game currently consists of just the application delegate and the view controller, you'll need to place the hooks to use the data from the controller into the pongViewController object.

The accessory sends two different data values to the iPhone OS; in addition to signaling the iPhone when the pushbutton is pressed, it also sends a value from 0 to 255 to let you know the position of the knob. You're going to use the knob position to tell you where to put the paddle and you'll use the button press to activate the serve.

Since you use the notification system to send the data, you first need to set up the viewDidLoad method to register for notifications. Let's add the following four lines of code to the implementation file.

```
[[NSNotificationCenter defaultCenter]
addObserver:self
        selector:@selector(accessoryConnected:)
name:EAAccessoryDidConnectNotification
        object:nil];

[[NSNotificationCenter defaultCenter]
        addObserver:self
        selector:@selector(accessoryDisconnected:)
        name:EAAccessoryDidDisconnectNotification
object:nil];

[[NSNotificationCenter defaultCenter
        addObserver:self
selector:@selector(pbPressed:)
        name:@"PBPRESSED" object:nil];

[[NSNotificationCenter defaultCenter]
        addObserver:self
selector:@selector(potTurned:)
name:@"POTTURNED" object:nil];
```

The first two lines add support for your object to receive information from the system when an accessory is either connected or disconnected. The second two lines you added for the two events that are generated by the player interacting with the game controller. The player causes these notifications to "fire" when he either presses the button to serve the ball or turns the knob to position his paddle.

You might ask how you're getting the messages when you haven't specified the EAAccessoryDelegate protocol in your header. The reason is that these are coming as notifications from the NSNotificationCenter. The fancy name "Notification Center" shouldn't drive you away; it's just Apple's name for the service in their Framework that implements message passing.

As I mentioned earlier, message passing provides one of the central constructs in embedded processing. But it's more critically employed in real-time operating systems. Review any RTOS product literature and one of the first things you'll see is information about message passing. But don't assume that the iPhone OS is a real-time operating system.

A real-time operating system has several key characteristics; a task scheduler, inter-process communications such as message passing and semaphores, a predictable interrupt scheme, etc. The central theme of a RTOS is predictability. You set up your various tasks and processes so that you know exactly (within certain well-defined limits) when they start, how long they last, and when (and how) they stop. Any variability or uncertainty in the whole process can have disastrous results. Think about a flight control computer on a plane or even the Space Shuttle. You wouldn't want it to have a lot of flexibility as to when it moves an aileron or fires a thruster.

But don't think that an RTOS is only applicable for critical life-threatening situations. The irony is, most phones (by some accounts 85%) actually run an RTOS. While iPhone OS, Android, and Symbian OS (all non-real-time OSes) seem to be in most cell phones, Mentor Graphics' Nucleus, ENEA's OSE, followed by WindRiver's VxWorks, all populate hundreds of millions of phones.

The tradeoff comes with flexibility and the capability to add functionality. As iPhone developers, we can add any of 140,000 different applications (at the time of writing) to our iPhone. The iPhone or Droid is more of a computing platform than a phone.

Now that I've pointed out the fact the iPhone OS isn't an RTOS, you must tread lightly when using such tools as the scheduler or NSNotificationCenter. Primarily, because you have no assurances that messages will be delivered in a predictable manner, you cannot rely on them for real-time operation.

Look at Figure 7–1 to see the flow of data for either a pushbutton press or a rotation of the paddle knob.

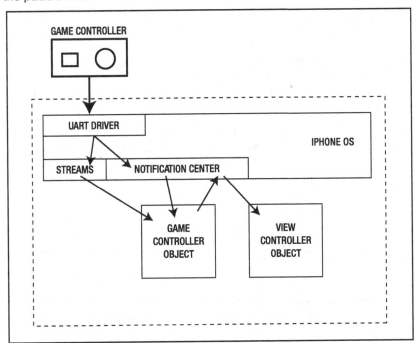

Figure 7–1. *Game controller data flow*

When the player performs an action on the game controller and sends data to the iPhone, the UART driver equivalent in the iPhone OS lower level first receives the information. Universal Asynchronous Receiver-Transmitter (UART) refers to serial data transmission, and most often the chip or portion of a chip. An alternative in this case would be to use USB. At the level of the EAAccessoryFramework, it doesn't matter which method you use. In fact, Bluetooth wireless is a third alternative. All that would change on Figure 7–1 would be a different name for the driver.

The UART driver within iPhone OS tells the notification center to "announce" the connectivity of your accessory which in turn is relayed to any object that has registered for accessory connect or disconnect notifications.

After that, most of the data passes from the accessory (game controller) through the UART driver to the iPhone OS Streams software. As you have seen previously and will see again shortly, your game controller (software) object gets and puts data to external devices using NSStreams. This simplifies things immensely for you but at a cost of abstracting things.

Think of a stream as a pipe from which you pull out data with another similar pipe where you stuff in data. The only thing is that you can't define when you take data from the pipe or put data into the other pipe. The iPhone OS lets you know when data is available on your input pipe and when there is space available to put data on your output pipe.

This is the first point at which you've lost any semblance of a real-time performing system. Your game controller (software) object is completely at the mercy of the streams mechanism within the iPhone OS. In other words, there is no predictability as to when you will receive or when you can send data.

To make things worse, as you continue along the route your data traverses, you decide to use the NSNotification mechanism to send data from your game controller (software) object to other parts of your system, i.e., the view controller where you will position a paddle or start the serve.

You construct a message along with passing your data using a dictionary object attached as userInfo in the notification and send it to the notification center. The center then looks up every object that is registered for this type of notification and sends out the message. You receive it through the notification registration you perform in the view controller and finally extract the data.

As you can see, you have two major sources of latency (delay) in your processing. First, you rely on the NSStreams mechanism to deliver data in what may or may not be a timely fashion. If that weren't enough, you purposefully added more potential latency using the notification system to transfer data.

> **NOTE:** I use latency here to mean the delay in a system, more specifically the time between two events. Though related to, latency is different than bandwidth or speed of a system.

You have no control over the first mechanism. That's just how Apple designed the EAAccessory Framework to operate; it uses streams. What you have to decide is whether to go the easier route and use message passing via the notification center, or take a different route to speed up your data transfer. In any case, you will always be a slave to how fast or how slow data is transferred via streams.

For now, you will continue to develop your data transfer scheme as you first outlined it; you will send the data from your game controller (software) object via the notification system and attach the actual information as a dictionary object using the userInfo notification parameter. Later, I'll show an alternative mechanism for getting the data to your view controller, and an even more important reason for not using the notification mechanism.

Continuing on with your process, add the following #import to the interface file.

```
#import <ExternalAccessory/ExternalAccessory.h>
```

Because you're using EAAccessory notifications, you have to include the ExternalAccessory reference. But that won't get your project to build correctly because you need to add the External Accessory framework to your project. In the "old days" this would be what you called adding a link library to your project. Say you were writing a scientific program and needed to use math functions such as $sin()$ and $cos()$, in addition to including the proper header (.h) files, you would need to include the math library (libm.a) when you linked the project.

You should know how to add a framework to your project by now, but as a refresher, place your cursor over the frameworks folder icon on the left side of your Xcode window. Right-Click and select Add ➤ existing frameworks, then click ExternalAccessory. If you try building your project now, it should complete successfully.

A question you might be asking right now is, why did I put all four notifications in the view controller? It's really a designer decision as to where things go, to a certain extent. With a simple system such as the Pong game you're building, everything is run from the single view controller. Remember, you didn't even add a setup page so there's just one screenful of content that you're managing.

Throughout the development of your examples, you're going to find many opportunities to do things better. I hope that you will act on these and improve upon the basic groundwork that I'm laying out.

The Game Controller Object

Although you will be making changes to the view controller object to handle the new I/O, first let's add your new game controller object. So, create a new NSObject class in Xcode, both the interface (.h) and the implementation (.m) and name it GameController.

The Game Controller Interface

Starting with the GameController.h file, you need to include the ExternalAccessory interface file. I will generally also add a reference to the project's application delegate so that, if you need to, you can access any common variables at that level.

```
#import "pongAppDelegate.h"
#import <ExternalAccessory/ExternalAccessory.h>
```

Next, let's design the interface section. You'll need access to a particular accessory instance, the EA session that you're opening and closing, a protocol string for the accessory, and a place to put data that you want to write to the accessory.

```
@interface GameController : NSObject <EAAccessoryDelegate> {
    EAAccessory *_accessory;
    EASession *_session;
    NSString *_protocolString;

    NSMutableData *_writeData;

        pongAppDelegate *appDelegate;
}
```

Note that I've also added a way to access the application delegate. You'll be using that a little later. Because the GameController object will act as a delegate for the _accessory object, you must also add the EAAccessoryDelegate protocol statement.

> **NOTE:** In the Game Controller object, the leading underscore (as in _accessory) is a common practice used to identify instance variables.

Since the game controller object stands alone, much like the singleton application object, you create a non-instance method of accessing it. Note the "+" instead of the usual "-" before the void.

```
+ (GameController *)sharedController;
```

Add the other method definitions that you need. I generally add more than is actually required here as I tend to call methods using [self <methodname>] to be a little more explicit.

```
- (void)setupControllerForAccessory:(EAAccessory *)accessory
                withProtocolString:(NSString *)protocolString;
- (BOOL)openSession;
- (void)closeSession;

- (void)writeData:(NSData *)data;
- (void)_writeData
- (void)accessoryDidDisconnect:(EAAccessory *)accessory;

Finally, add the property definition statements.
@property (nonatomic, readonly) EAAccessory *accessory;
@property (nonatomic, readonly) NSString *protocolString;
```

Next, you move on to the game controller implementation.

The Game Controller Implementation

In the game controller implementation we've grouped our methods into five categories using the #pragma directive. The #pragma statement is a great tool for organizing your objects and for quickly locating the sections you're interested in within Xcode.

The Instance Method section includes the primary methods that we reference from outside our game controller object. These include _writeData, _readData and sharedController. Note that there is no underscore on the sharedController method because it is not an instance method.

To send data from the view controller (our game) to the accessory—to turn on or off the LEDs—the calling object uses the writeData method. From the view controller this appears as:

```
[GameController sharedController]
        writeData:[NSData dataWithBytes:buf length:2]];
```

This is one of the lines of code where you send the command to the accessory controller to illuminate one of the LEDs. Note that you call the public version of writeData. Inside your game controller object, the writeData method is defined as:

```
- (void)writeData:(NSData *)data
{
    if (_writeData == nil) {
        _writeData = [[NSMutableData alloc] init];
    }

    [_writeData appendData:data];
    [self _writeData];
}
```

This very simple function does three basic things; first it checks to see if the _writeData mutable string (not the method) exists. If it does not—as would be the case where this method is called for the first time—it allocates and initializes the string.

Next, since the method call includes the parameter *data where the caller places the data it wants to write, you append that data to the _writeData string. Finally, the instance method _writeData is called to do the actual heavy lifting—send the data to the accessory.

Now, looking at the instance method _writeData you begin to see where the data is actually moved to the accessory. Note again that this is where the possibility of a real-time construct begins to break down. In the very first line of code, the while statement references the notification "hasSpaceAvailable" from the NSStreams object. This means that until there is room, the data is going nowhere. Also notice that the method returns if there is no more data to write.

```
- (void)_writeData {
    while ((([[_session outputStream]
                hasSpaceAvailable]) && ([_writeData length] > 0))
    {
        NSInteger bytesWritten =
                        [[_session outputStream]
                        write:[_writeData bytes]
                        maxLength:[_writeData length]];
        if (bytesWritten == -1)
        {
            NSLog(@"write error");
            break;
        }
```

```
        else if (bytesWritten > 0)
        {
            [_writeData
                    replaceBytesInRange:NSMakeRange(0, bytesWritten)
                        withBytes:NULL length:0];
        }
    }
}
```

If both conditions are favorable—there is space and you have data to be written—you get the appropriate data stream [_session outputStream] and call the stream's write method. This function returns the number of bytes written because you are not guaranteed that all the bytes will be written on the first attempt.

If the function returns a –1, then there was a problem sending the data to the accessory and it must be handled appropriately. But, if the bytesWritten is positive, then you need to remove the bytes that were sent from the _writeData string object so that only the bytes that weren't sent will be transmitted next. This is done of course by the replaceBytesInRange string method.

If you look carefully at what I just talked about, you might be asking how _writeData gets called. The calling object (our view controller) calls the method writeData (without the underscore) and passes the data it has to send. All that is done by the method in our game controller object is that the data is copied to the _writeData string object.

> **NOTE:** I've purposefully included the three different types of references of the term "writeData" to follow the way examples within Apple's documentation are presented.

The way that _writeData gets called is by the streams notification system. In the following, you see code that handles any stream event. The two key events that take place are the NSStreamEventHasBytesAvailable and the NSStreamEventHasSpaceAvailable that we use to call _readData and _writeData respectively. The user should handle the other stream event as appropriate to his system.

```
 (void)stream:(NSStream *)aStream
handleEvent:(NSStreamEvent)eventCode
{
    switch (eventCode) {
        case NSStreamEventNone:
            break;
        case NSStreamEventOpenCompleted:
            break;
        case NSStreamEventHasBytesAvailable:
            [self _readData];
            break;
        case NSStreamEventHasSpaceAvailable:
            [self _writeData];
            break;
        case NSStreamEventErrorOccurred:
            break;
        case NSStreamEventEndEncountered:
```

```
        break;
    default:
        break;
    }
}
```

Figure 7–2 summarizes the four basic steps of the process to write data from your view controller to the accessory hardware.

The view controller calls writeData with data to send.

The writeData method copies the data to the _writeData string object.

When space is available, a streams event causes the _writeData method call.

The _writeData method sends as much data as there is room for until the next stream event.

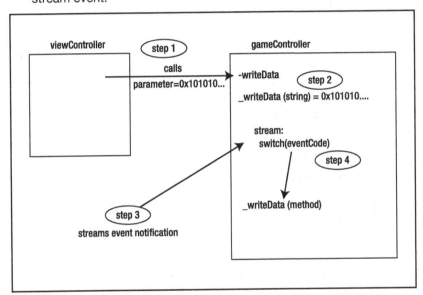

Figure 7–2. *Writing data to accessory hardware*

The _readData method, shown in the following code, waits until the output stream has data from the accessory that is to be sent to your view controller. In essence, this works like the reverse of the writeData process.

The _readData method is called when a streams event is received that indicates the data is available and needs to be removed from the inputStream. You allocate a buffer of sufficient size and check that the inputStream does indeed have bytes available. Although the streams event has "said" that there is data available, you make sure that the stream itself has a positive number of data bytes available to be read.

```
- (void)_readData {

    uint8_t buf[EAD_INPUT_BUFFER_SIZE];
```

```objc
while ([[_session inputStream] hasBytesAvailable])
{
    NSInteger bytesRead = [[_session inputStream]
                    read:buf maxLength:EAD_INPUT_BUFFER_SIZE];
    NSLog(@"read %d bytes (%d) from input stream",
                    bytesRead,buf[0]);

    // for now, we only expect two different command bytes from the accessor
    // 0x10 - means that the pushbutton was pressed and no additional data
    // 0x20 - means that the knob (potentiometer) has changed position and an
    //          additional  byte follows which represents the knob's position

            if (buf[0] == 0x10) {
                    [[NSNotificationCenter  defaultCenter]
                    postNotificationName:@"PBPRESSED" object:self];

            }
            if (buf[0] == 0x20) {

                    //NSLog(@"Data = %@",data);
                    unsigned char i = buf[1];
                    NSNumber *posInt = [[NSNumber alloc]
                    initWithUnsignedChar:i];
                    NSLog(@"_readData position = %d",[posInt intValue]);

                    NSMutableDictionary *dict =
                            [[ NSMutableDictionary alloc]
                                                            init];
                    [ dict  setObject:posInt
                    forKey:@"parameter"];
                    [[NSNotificationCenter  defaultCenter]
                    postNotificationName:@"POTTURNED" object:self
                                    userInfo:dict];
                    [dict release];
                    [posInt release];
            }
    }
}
```

After reading the data bytes sent from the controller, the method executes one of two conditions depending upon the first byte in the buffer. The first byte indicates the type of data we are getting from the accessory and is either a 0x10 to indicate that the serve button has been pressed or a 0x20 indicating the new position of the knob.

> **NOTE:** In a production system you should check that you have received enough data bytes to execute whatever functions you have planned. In the implementation you receive at most two bytes and can assume that you got that many. In the real world, you would want to check the value of bytesRead to make sure you can continue. If you did not get all the data you were expecting or needing, you would need to temporarily store what you received and wait for at least the next call to _readData.

In essence, all you do in _readData is to get the data from the inputStream and then make a decision as to what to do based on the contents.

If the data indicates that the pushbutton was pressed, you send a notification with the PBPRESSED notification name and you're done.

On the other hand, if you were sent data indicating the new position of the player's paddle (the knob position), you need to do a little bit more. First, you create a dictionary object to which you insert the second byte received (the position) with the key of "parameter". You can use any key name you want here as long as it's the same in both the accessory controller (your game controller) and the object where it is used (your view controller). The dictionary is then sent with the notification and you're once again done with processing the input data.

What you've just shown has a very subtle issue; you sent the data (your position) off and hopefully you get it at your view controller. But what happens in between? In most cases, this is not too big of a concern. But suppose the data that you sent was sensitive in nature, say, a person's social security number, or, in the case of a credit card reader attachment, all the information from their Visa card?

Because you released the dictionary object at the end of the _readData method, and it was taken over (retained) by the notification process, you can't erase it. So somewhere floating around is your customer's credit card information—something he would probably not like you to keep.

The simple way to handle this is not to transmit any sensitive data via means that you do not totally control. You can still use the notification center as your message passing mechanism; you just won't send any data that way. Look at the modified version of _readData in the following:

```
- (void)_readData {

        //
        // get appDelegate (pongAppDelegate)
        //
        appDelegate = (pongAppDelegate *)[[UIApplication
        sharedApplication] delegate];

    uint8_t buf[EAD_INPUT_BUFFER_SIZE];

    while ([[_session inputStream] hasBytesAvailable])
    {
        NSInteger bytesRead = [[_session inputStream]
                    read:buf
                    maxLength:EAD_INPUT_BUFFER_SIZE];

            if (buf[0] == 0x10) {
                    [[NSNotificationCenter  defaultCenter]
                    postNotificationName:@"PBPRESSED"
                    object:self];

            }
            if (buf[0] == 0x20) {

                    //NSLog(@"Data = %@",data);
                    unsigned char i = buf[1];
    //
```

```
//  Convert character received to a real number
//
                        NSNumber *posInt = [[NSNumber alloc]
                                initWithUnsignedChar:i];
//
//      put the number somewhere that we control
//
                        appDelegate.paddlePosition = posInt;

                        [[NSNotificationCenter defaultCenter]
                        postNotificationName:@"POTTURNED" object:self];
                        [posInt         release];
            }
        }
}
```

What you've done is to use the appDelegate reference to get access to a global variable paddlePosition that you can set from the game controller object. You still use the notification system to alert the view controller that data is available, but you don't pass any data as userInfo dictionary parameter.

> **NOTE:** You don't have to use global variables if you're of the mindset that they are "evil." Just as easily, you could put the information directly into parameters that the view controller has made public.

While the notification is used to alert the view controller that a new position is available, you don't even have to do it this way. Remember that your game operates as a gameLoop that is called periodically by an NSTimer that you set up. All you really need to do is to update the position of the paddle using the variable that you set. The gameLoop, or its enclosing object the view controller, doesn't care that new data is available. It always uses the paddlePosition variable on each iteration through the gameLoop.

This way you now completely control where your data from the accessory is used as well as reduced the latency of your system by eliminating the notification center for the more real-time aspect of your system—the paddle updates.

To access the game controller object, you need to create the sharedController method that returns the reference to the game controller singleton.

```
+ (GameController *)sharedController
{
    static GameController *accessoryController = nil;
    if (accessoryController == nil) {
        accessoryController = [[GameController alloc] init];
    }

    return accessoryController;
}
```

Each time you call sharedController, you remove the reference to any preexisting game controller by setting it to nil. Then you alloc-init a new instance and return it to the caller.

By making your game controller instance a static variable, even if you do call sharedController multiple times, you're always referencing the single instance.

In your Pong game design, you chose to put the delegate methods for when an accessory is connected or disconnected in the view controller. I'll discuss changes to the view controller to accommodate the game controller accessory a bit later in this chapter, but for now I need to mention that when the controller is connected you need to set up your session. In the view controller's accessoryConnected method, you call the following game controller method:

```
- (void)setupControllerForAccessory:(EAAccessory *)accessory
        withProtocolString:(NSString *)protocolString
{
    [_accessory release];
    _accessory = [accessory retain];
    [_protocolString release];
    _protocolString = [protocolString copy];
}
```

What happens in setupControllerForAccessory is that you make sure to release any accessory instances that have been hanging around and retain the accessory that the caller has passed by incrementing its retain count by one. Similarly, you release any previous protocol strings that might be present setting your instance variable to the new string that the view controller has passed in.

The final key elements of the game controller object are the methods to open and close the communications streams that is done via the open and close session methods.

In the following openSession code, the first thing to happen is that you assign this object (self) as the delegate for the accessory instance _accessory that was just covered in the setup routine.

Next, you open a session through the usual method of alloc-init, passing in the accessory instance and the protocol string.

```
- (BOOL)openSession
{
    [_accessory setDelegate:self];

    _session = [[EASession alloc]
                initWithAccessory:_accessory
                forProtocol:_protocolString];
    //_session = [[EASession alloc]
                initWithAccessory:_accessory
                forProtocol:@"COM.MACMEDX.P1"];

    if (_session)
    {
        [[_session inputStream] setDelegate:self];
        [[_session inputStream]
                    scheduleInRunLoop:[NSRunLoop currentRunLoop]
                    forMode:NSDefaultRunLoopMode];
        [[_session inputStream] open];

        [[_session outputStream] setDelegate:self];
```

```
        [[_session outputStream]
                    scheduleInRunLoop:[NSRunLoop currentRunLoop]
                    forMode:NSDefaultRunLoopMode];
        [[_session outputStream] open];
    }
    else
    {
        NSLog(@"creating session failed");
    }

    return (_session != nil);
}
```

You can see in the previous code that you've commented out one of the lines of code to illustrate a couple ways to pass the protocol string. Remember that a protocol string is a uniquely defined string written in reverse DNS notation. In the commented out line you can see that you've used the literal string "COM.MACMEDX" for the domain macmedx.com. You've also appended P1 to indicate that this is protocol number one. What follows the reverse DNS is totally up to the manufacturer of the accessory. You can use P1, P98, the name of your cat...whatever you want so long as it is unique. But you don't actually use this line in your program; you use the instance variable _protocolString and everything works fine.

The _protocolString is retrieved for you by the system. You enter it when in your project's property list file, as shown in Figure 7–3 using the Supported external accessory protocol key, new to iPhone OS 3.0. In general, this is where you always want to reference your protocols that your project uses and not directly in the code.

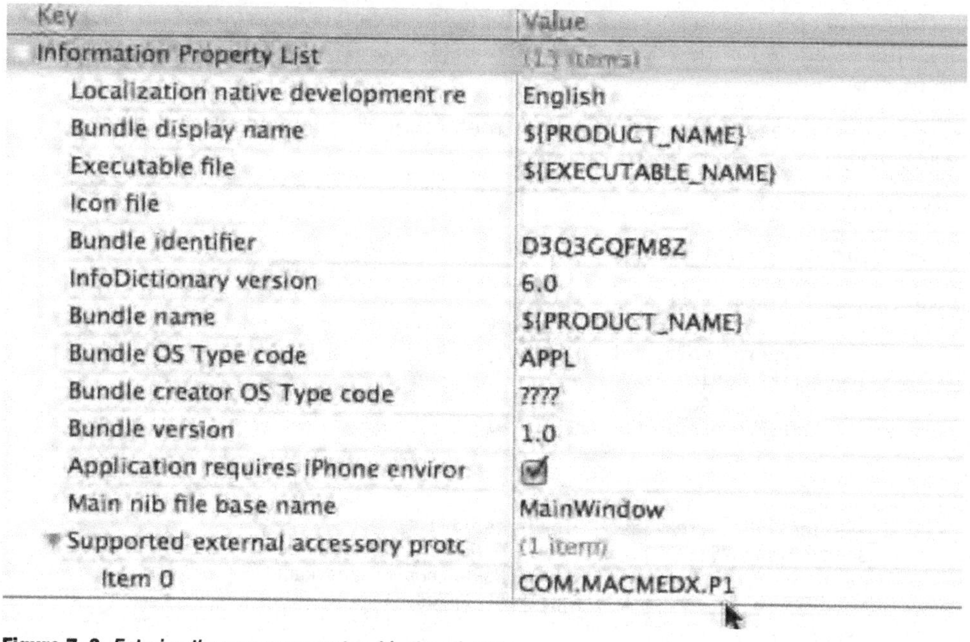

Key	Value
Information Property List	(13 items)
Localization native development re	English
Bundle display name	${PRODUCT_NAME}
Executable file	${EXECUTABLE_NAME}
Icon file	
Bundle identifier	D3Q3GQFM8Z
InfoDictionary version	6.0
Bundle name	${PRODUCT_NAME}
Bundle OS Type code	APPL
Bundle creator OS Type code	????
Bundle version	1.0
Application requires iPhone enviror	☑
Main nib file base name	MainWindow
Supported external accessory protc	(1 item)
Item 0	COM.MACMEDX.P1

Figure 7–3. *Entering the accessory protocol in the plist file*

Continuing with the _openSession method, if a valid (non-nil) session is returned, then for both the input and output streams (remember that streams are one-directional), you perform three functions.

1. Set the stream delegate (here you use self).

2. Schedule the stream events in the run loop.

3. Open the stream.

Once this is done you start receiving the stream notifications that I talked about earlier. When you're done and ready to close things up via the _closeSession method shown below, you just do the reverse, setting the _session instance to nil (clearing it) and releasing the space back to the pool.

```
- (void)closeSession
{
    [[_session inputStream] close];
    [[_session inputStream] removeFromRunLoop:[NSRunLoop
            currentRunLoop] forMode:NSDefaultRunLoopMode];
    [[_session inputStream] setDelegate:nil];

    [[_session outputStream] close];
    [[_session outputStream] removeFromRunLoop:[NSRunLoop
        currentRunLoop] forMode:NSDefaultRunLoopMode];
    [[_session outputStream] setDelegate:nil];

        _session = nil;
    [_session release];

}
```

Should the user need to handle things when the accessory is removed, the following method gets called. Here you simply log the message that the controller was removed. What should be done is to signal any objects that depend on input from the accessory that they will have to get the data another way. For your Pong game, this might be a flag that is set in the view controller object or even the appDelegate as a global variable. The gameLoop method inside the view controller object would then decide whether to use touches or the paddle position set by the game controller for where to move the player's paddle.

```
- (void)accessoryDidDisconnect:(EAAccessory *)accessory
{
        NSLog(@"Controller Removed");
}
```

Finally, when you're totally finished, you call the closeSession method that shuts down your I/O streams, calls the setupControllerForAccessory method with nil to clear everything, and then you clear and release the _writeData string you use to send data to the accessory.

```
- (void)dealloc
{
    [self closeSession];
```

```
        [self setupControllerForAccessory:nil
                 withProtocolString:nil];
         _writeData = nil;
        [_writeData release];


        [super dealloc];
}
```

View Controller Modifications

The game controller object that you just added to your system handles most, but not all of the things you need to do to work with the accessory game controller itself. You have to add the following lines within the interface section of the interface (.h) file.

```
        pongAppDelegate  *appDelegate;

        EAAccessory * _accessory;
    NSMutableArray * _accessoryList;

    EAAccessory * _selectedAccessory;
    GameController * _accessoryController;
```

Because you may be using a global variable, you add a way to access the application delegate by declaring a local instance of the pongAppDelegate object. You also need a way to reference the accessory (_accessory), the _accessoryList, the _selectedAccessory from the list, and the controller object (_accessoryController) that you built in the last two sections.

Earlier, I talked about how the Accessory Framework presents a list of available accessories and you have to handle it as an array. While this is the way the framework functions, currently Apple only allows one accessory per session. Of course, you couldn't connect two accessories to the dock connector, but remember that the Accessory Framework also works with Bluetooth wireless. So you could have a physically connected accessory, and one or more Bluetooth accessories once the restriction is lifted.

The final addition to the interface (.h) file are the definitions of the methods to turn on and off the green and red leds. By defining them this way, you can use the [self turnOnRedLED] format to call the methods.

```
//
//      LED Control Routines
//
- (void)turnOnRedLED;
- (void)turnOffRedLED;
- (void)turnOnGreenLED;
- (void)turnOffGreenLED;
```

The first thing you need to add to the implementation (.m) file is the setup code to receive notifications and to access the game controller. Add the following code at the top of the viewDidLoad method:

```
        [[UIApplication sharedApplication]
```

```
            setIdleTimerDisabled:YES];        // disable sleep dimming
    //
    // get appDelegate (pongAppDelegate)
    //
    appDelegate = (pongAppDelegate *)[[UIApplication
                  sharedApplication] delegate];


    [[NSNotificationCenter defaultCenter]
         addObserver:self
         selector:@selector(accessoryConnected:)
         name:EAAccessoryDidConnectNotification object:nil];

    [[NSNotificationCenter defaultCenter]
         addObserver:self
         selector:@selector(accessoryDisconnected:)
         name:EAAccessoryDidDisconnectNotification object:nil];

    [[NSNotificationCenter defaultCenter]
         addObserver:self
         selector:@selector(pbPressed:)
         name:@"PBPRESSED" object:nil];

    [[NSNotificationCenter defaultCenter]
         addObserver:self
         selector:@selector(potTurned:)
         name:@"POTTURNED" object:nil];

    [[EAAccessoryManager sharedAccessoryManager]
         registerForLocalNotifications];

    if ([[[EAAccessoryManager        sharedAccessoryManager]
             connectedAccessories] count] > 0) {
         NSLog(@"Connected accessories");
    } else {
         NSLog(@"NO Connected accessories");
    }


    _accessoryController = [GameController sharedController];
    _accessoryList = [[NSMutableArray alloc]
         initWithArray:[[EAAccessoryManager sharedAccessoryManager]
         connectedAccessories]];
```

In the very first line of code, you assign setIdleTimerDisabled the value YES. Because you're using an accessory and not touching the screen, the iPhone OS will see this as no events and put itself to sleep unless you disable the idle timer. As such, you need to add the following line to the viewDidUnload method to restore the idle timer and prevent undue drain on the battery.

```
[[UIApplication sharedApplication] setIdleTimerDisabled:NO];
```

Next, you get the reference to the application delegate. Although you won't be using it right away, you will need it shortly when you start to make modifications to the structure of your program.

In the next four lines you register yourself with the notification center. The first two set you up to receive notifications when the accessory (game controller) is connected or disconnected where you call the methods accessoryConnected: and accessoryDisconnected: , respectively. The next two notifications are for the ones that you created in the game controller object indicating a pushbutton press or a new knob position. These notifications call either pbPressed: or potTurned: when they come in.

Take a step back; for the four conditions that are governed by the game controller accessory (connecting, disconnecting, pressing the button, or turning the knob) you've set up a method to handle each of them.

When the game controller is connected, the first thing you do is pull the name of the accessory from the notification's userInfo field and add it to your accessory list. Because it is the only accessory list, when you retrieve it you know it is at index 0. After that, it's just a matter of calling setupControllerForAccessory and opening the session.

```
- (void)accessoryConnected:(NSNotification *)notification {

        NSLog(@"Game Controller Connected");

    EAAccessory *connectedAccessory =
                [[notification userInfo] objectForKey:EAAccessoryKey];
    [_accessoryList addObject:connectedAccessory];
      _selectedAccessory = [[_accessoryList objectAtIndex:0] retain];


        [_accessoryController
        setupControllerForAccessory:_selectedAccessory
        withProtocolString:[[_selectedAccessory protocolStrings]
        objectAtIndex:0]];
         [_accessoryController openSession];

}
```

In the accessoryDisconnected: method, you get the accessory from the notification and check to make sure it is in your accessory list using the enum design pattern:

```
for(EAAccessory *accessory in _accessoryList)
```

All that really happens here is to remove the accessory from your _accessoryList if you found it in the list and to notify you otherwise.

```
- (void)accessoryDisconnected:(NSNotification *)notification {

        NSLog(@"Game Controller Disconnected");

    EAAccessory *disconnectedAccessory =
                [[notification userInfo]
                objectForKey:EAAccessoryKey];

    int disconnectedAccessoryIndex = 0;
    for(EAAccessory *accessory in _accessoryList) {
        if ([disconnectedAccessory connectionID] ==
                                        [accessory connectionID]) {
            break;
        }
```

```
            disconnectedAccessoryIndex++;
    }

    if (disconnectedAccessoryIndex < [_accessoryList count]) {
        [_accessoryList removeObjectAtIndex:disconnectedAccessoryIndex];
    } else {
        NSLog(@"could not find disconnected accessory in accessory list");
    }
}
```

If you get a notification that the button has been pressed, then recall that what you want to do is to serve the ball. This is handled in the following function.

```
-(void) pbPressed:(NSNotification *)notification {
        [self    serveAction];
}
```

All it does is to call the serveAction method. Note that serveAction is called either by pressing the screen button and initiating the action that you linked in Interface Builder or by pushing the game controller button. As you will see next, you've engineered the player's paddle movement to work the same way; the player can use the knob or touch the screen to move his paddle.

What you did in the potTurned: method is to copy the code that you used in the gameLoop for when the player moves the paddle with his finger. Before that you added code to retrieve the position as an NSNumber from the userInfo part of the notification message. Then you convert it to an integer value and scale it. What happens is that, when the knob is all the way counter-clockwise, the value sent is 255. Conversely, when it is all the way clockwise it sends 0. Therefore, you basically flip the values so that 0 is all the way CCW and 255 is full CW.

NOTE: The value of 255 is not arbitrary. The value you are able to get is 8 bits, which allows you 2 to the 8 possible values. Beginning with all zeroes, your upper limit would be all ones, or 11111111b, which equates to 255.

Just before you move the paddle, you scale the value from 256 to 320 (the width of the screen and convert it to floating point. Then you use 'j' to do the movement of the paddle.

```
(void) potTurned:(NSNotification *)notification {
        NSNumber             *position = [[notification userInfo]
        objectForKey:@"parameter"];

        int i = [position intValue];
        //int i = appDelegate.paddlePosition;
        i = (-i + 256);

        float j = (float)i * (320.0/256.0);

// SAME CODE BELOW AS IN gameLoop
```

```
            CGPoint xLocation = CGPointMake(j,playerPaddle.center.y);
            playerPaddle.center = xLocation;
            if (playerPaddle.center.x > (self.view.bounds.size.width /2))
                    if (playerPaddle.center.x > (self.view.bounds.size.width /2)+101)
                            playerPaddle.image = playerPaddleRightUp;
                else
                            playerPaddle.image = playerPaddleRight;
                else
                            if (playerPaddle.center.x <
                                    (self.view.bounds.size.width /2)-101)
                                    playerPaddle.image = playerPaddleLeftUp;
                    else

                                    playerPaddle.image = playerPaddleLeft;

    }
```

Continuing on, in the implementation file let's also add a couple of local Boolean variables that you set, reset, and check as to whether an LED is on or off.

```
//
//      INSTANCE VARIABLES
//
BOOL    redLEDOn        = NO;
BOOL    greenLEDOn      = NO;
```

Sticking with the LED functionality, you add the four LED control functions. You can see that they function exactly as I talked about earlier. A command value 0x98 is sent to the accessory using the writeData method of the GameController object. The 0x98 value is defined by the interface definition of the accessory, as are the commands for any particular LED control information. Here, you use 0x01 to turn on the red, 0x02 to turn the red one off and so on.

```
- (void)turnOnRedLED
{
    const uint8_t buf[2] = {0x98, 0x01};
    [[GameController sharedController]
        writeData:[NSData dataWithBytes:buf length:2]];
        redLEDOn = YES;
}


- (void)turnOffRedLED
{
    const uint8_t buf[2] = {0x98, 0x02};
    [[GameController sharedController]
        writeData:[NSData dataWithBytes:buf length:2]];
}
- (void)turnOnGreenLED
{
    const uint8_t buf[2] = {0x98, 0x03};
    [[GameController sharedController]
        writeData:[NSData dataWithBytes:buf length:2]];
        greenLEDOn = YES;
}


- (void)turnOffGreenLED
{
    const uint8_t buf[2] = {0x98, 0x04};
```

```
[[GameController sharedController] writeData:[NSData
        dataWithBytes:buf length:2]];
}
```

Now you have to decide where and when to signal using the LEDs. The game controller layout is such that the green LED is at the top and the red LED at the bottom. This makes the green LED appear further away from the player and thus a good candidate for indicating when the computer's paddle hits the ball. You can see in the following code that I've added a line to turn on the green LED just when the ball is changing directions after contacting the computer's paddle. The same approach is used for the player's paddle and the red LED.

In addition, at the very start of gameLoop, you check to see if either of the LEDs are on and turn them off. This prevents you from sending any commands to the accessory. You only send a command to turn on an LED with a paddle and ball contact and to turn that LED off on the next iteration through the game loop code.

```
-(void)gameLoop {

    if(status == IN_PLAY) {
        ball.center = CGPointMake(ball.center.x + ballSpeed.x,
                        ball.center.y + ballSpeed.y); // move the ball

        //
        //     If we turned on an LED in the last loop, then turn it off now
        //
        if (redLEDOn) {
            [self turnOffRedLED];
            redLEDOn      = NO;
        }
        if (greenLEDOn) {
            [self turnOffGreenLED];
            greenLEDOn      = NO;
        }

        // Has the ball hit the edge of the room ?
        if (ball.center.x > (self.view.bounds.size.width - WALL_MARGIN) ||
                        ball.center.x < (0 + WALL_MARGIN)) {
            ballSpeed.x  = - ballSpeed.x;
        }

        if (ball.center.y > self.view.bounds.size.height || ball.center.y < 0) {
            ballSpeed.y = - ballSpeed.y;
        }

        // player scored against computer
        if (ball.center.y < 0) {
            // set status to hold
            status = POINT_OVER;
            playerScore++;
            playerScoreView.text = [NSString
                    stringWithFormat:@"%d",playerScore];
            if (playerScore == GAME_WON)
                {
                    winOrLoseView.text = @"YOU WIN";
                    playerScore = 0;
```

```
                compScore    = 0;
                status                    = GAME_OVER;
         }
           [self setServePosition];

    } else
    // if player didn't score, did the computer score?

         if (ball.center.y > self.view.bounds.size.height) {
                 // set status to hold
                 status = POINT_OVER;
                 compScore++;
                 compScoreView.text = [NSString
                         stringWithFormat:@"%d",compScore];
                 if (compScore == GAME_WON)
                 {
                         winOrLoseView.text = @"YOU LOSE";
                         playerScore = 0;
                         compScore   = 0;
                         status            = GAME_OVER;
                 }
                 [self   setServePosition];
         }


    // Did the player's paddle make contact with the ball
    if(CGRectIntersectsRect(ball.frame, playerPaddle.frame)) {


         AudioServicesPlaySystemSound (self.paddleSoundObject);

         // Reverse front-to-back direction
         if(ball.center.y < playerPaddle.center.y) {
                 ballSpeed.y = -ballSpeed.y;
         }

         // Reverse the X direction if we're off to one side of the table
         if  ( (ball.center.x > (self.view.bounds.size.width /2)+100) ||
              (ball.center.x < (self.view.bounds.size.width /2)-100) )
          {

                 ballSpeed.x = -ballSpeed.x +
          (ball.center.x - playerPaddle.center.x)/5;
         }
         [self   turnOnRedLED];
    }


    // Did the computer's paddle make contact withthe ball
    if(CGRectIntersectsRect(ball.frame,    compPaddle.frame)) {


         AudioServicesPlaySystemSound (self.paddleSoundObject);

         // Reverse front-to-back direction
         if(ball.center.y > compPaddle.center.y) {
```

```
                             ballSpeed.y = -ballSpeed.y;
                             // each time the computer hits the ball, speed it up
                             ballSpeed.y++;
                 }


                 if  ( (ball.center.x > (self.view.bounds.size.width /2)+100) ||
                        (ball.center.x < (self.view.bounds.size.width /2)-100) )
                            ballSpeed.x = -ballSpeed.x;
                   [self   turnOnGreenLED];
             }
             [self compPlay];
         } // end if
}
```

Those should be all the changes you need to make to get the Pong game to work with the game controller. Don't be alarmed if the game play seems a little jittery. Remember that this is not a real-time operating system so you are subject to how iPhone OS handles things. In the next chapter, I'll cover a few modifications to make the game operate a little more smoothly.

Summary

In this chapter, you've taken the game you created in Chapter 6 and combined it with what you learned about Apple's External Accessory Framework to make one of the most advanced pieces of consumer electronics act as if it were from more than two decades prior. Pretty cool, huh?

If you had any trouble following the piecemeal way that I discussed modifications and additions, I've included the complete source for the game controller object and the modified view controller. Just make sure to add the protocol for the game controller in your projects plist file in Xcode.

Chapter 8

Improving the Design

Now that you have a working game that uses your accessory controller, it's time to make some changes. While the game itself could use a lot of work, I will focus on the interface to the game controller and improving performance and security of the system.

Performance Concerns

Let's look at Figure 8–1 to review what goes on when you turn the knob and send a new position to the game.

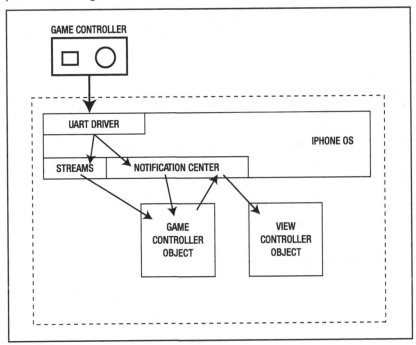

Figure 8–1. *Data movement through the game*

The game controller generates a byte of data representing the position of the knob that you want to translate into the position of the paddle. From the processor residing on the game controller, you command the onboard USART to send the two bytes—the command and the position—to the iPhone.

> **NOTE:** When working with the types of small processors used by your game controller, you will typically see the terms USART and UART thrown about. These terms refer to both the hardware inside the processor that performs serial I/O as well as the code that controls that hardware. Some processors such as the PIC series microcontrollers from Microchip have adopted the convention of calling their on-board serial hardware USART for Universal Serial Asynchronous Receive-Transmit. Programmers using the PIC series tend to name their code UART dropping the "Serial."

When data is sent out at the USART hardware level, it is just "shoved" out the port or wire that connects to some other piece of hardware, likely with its own USART. At this point in the process, there is no knowledge that what's on the other end of the line is an iPhone, another computer, or a terminal. The "what's on the other side of the fence" is what your UART code takes care of. You have to develop it.

When the two bytes are transferred over this wire to the iPhone, there are several steps to go through before it gets to a point where you can use it. Luckily, the things that are out of your control happen quickly. I'm talking about the USART hardware on the iPhone. The circuit reads and reconstructs the data (the bit order may have to be reversed, parity checked, and data retransmitted, etc.) quickly before passing it to the iPhone OS.

Once the phone's operating system takes over is where things get a little messy. Data gets passed through both the streams and notification system. Your code is notified that there is data on the stream. You pull the raw data out (your game controller object) and then pass it to the view controller via the notification system.

One of the big problems with message passing using the notification system is that it's easy. A programmer starts off with a fairly simple, well-structured design. Then, maybe one more view controller is needed to make things better. However, because you've added another view, you need to get data to it. Maybe it's a composite view and you need data from several of the other views. You start to write the code, but the data is local to those views and you didn't set up a means to get it out.

It's easy to say what you should do here, but the truth is that most programmers, including myself, will take shortcuts telling ourselves that once we do this "proof of concept" we'll go back and make things right. And what is that quick and dirty approach that we usually adopt in such cases? Most of the time, it is message passing using the notification system. We create a quick set of key-value pairs, put them in a dictionary, and send them to the new view. Before long, we've lost control in this rabbit's warren of interconnecting message paths weaving though our system.

Good programming habits are beyond the subject of this book. What I want to stress is that no matter what the complexity of your system, it's easy to get on the wrong track. Stepping back for a moment, what I'm really talking about in this book is just sending information from point A to point B and back again. That's what all this External Accessory stuff is about at its core level. What it really comes down to is using the right tool for the job.

In general, you have two options. You can do things simply by letting the system (the iPhone OS) take care of things for you. This is what you did in the last chapter. Your other choice is to take more control of the process and do most of the work yourself.

At first glance, this second choice might seem pretty stupid. I mean, isn't that why we invented high-level programming languages or advanced operating systems…to do the grunt work for us? Unfortunately, these conveniences come with a price.

There are reasons that you might want to not use these convenience methods and do things "the hard way." The first reason is performance. Let's face it; no matter how fast the latest and greatest iPhone executes apps, you're always going to want more. The thing is, the real problem isn't processor speed at all. The problem you're concerned about is latency or the delay in getting things done.

What you're really looking for is a way to accurately predict when something will happen. As I talked about earlier, this goes to the heart of real-time processing. You need to know that if an event of interest takes place that it will be handled within predictable time constraints.

For your game program this means that, if the player turns the knob to get to a fast moving ball, your program can respond and move it predictably. Note that I didn't say it would get to the ball in time as that wouldn't be fair. Part of the game is for one player to get the other player out of position enough so that, if he can place the ball far enough away, his opponent won't get to it.

What you do need is for the game to respond to events the same way each and every time your events occur. What you do not want to see is the player turn the knob and the paddle not move for an instant while the game's run loop is delayed for something else. In your Pong game, from time to time you will turn the knob and the paddle will seem to stick for a short while. This is because the iPhone OS has other things to do such as periodically checking e-mail or push notifications, responding to changes in signal strength from WiFi or the phone network, and so on.

Simply put, you're not likely to get absolute real-time performance. When you connect a hardware accessory to an iPhone or iPod touch, even though you have a fast physical interface, the underlying OS has to do its job, at the same time creating overhead that slows things down. This impacts performance. I mentioned that there were other reasons for not using the conveniences of modern operating systems and programming languages; so what are they?

Security Concerns

What might possibly be the most important reason of all is data security. Before going on, I'll point out that security is boring, especially for the new accessory developer. In most cases, especially early on, it's not really a concern unless you're developing for business applications. So, if you're strictly into gaming or an area where you feel security isn't an issue, you can skip this section and come back later if needed.

Consider again Figure 8–1 and your code from the last chapter. When your game controller object (software) is notified that a new position is available for the paddle you packed that data into a dictionary object and sent out another notification.

On the other end—inside your view controller—you read the notification, pulled out the data (position byte), and moved the paddle. But what happened between the time you sent the notification and when you received it? The fact is that you don't know. Look again at the potTurned method from your viewController.

```
-(void) potTurned:(NSNotification *)notification {
        NSLog(@"Pot Turned");
        NSNumber        *position = [[notification userInfo]
            objectForKey:@"parameter"];

        int i = [position intValue];
        NSLog(@"Position Received = %d",i);

        i = (-i + 256);

        float j = (float)i * (320.0/246.0);

        CGPoint xLocation = CGPointMake(j,playerPaddle.center.y);
        playerPaddle.center = xLocation;
        if (playerPaddle.center.x > (self.view.bounds.size.width /2))
                if (playerPaddle.center.x > (self.view.bounds.size.width /2)+101)
                        playerPaddle.image = playerPaddleRightUp;
            else
                        playerPaddle.image = playerPaddleRight;
            else
                if (playerPaddle.center.x <
                        (self.view.bounds.size.width /2)-101)
                        playerPaddle.image = playerPaddleLeftUp;
                else

                        playerPaddle.image = playerPaddleLeft;

}
```

Can you count all the places you used the position information? First, there's the userInfo dictionary object. From there, you extract the position and put it into an NSNumber using the key "parameter". From the NSNumber, you need an integer value so you convert it using the intValue method. But the position of the paddle is a floating-point number so there's another conversion. Then, you have to create a point using GCPointMake so you can use the x position to set where you want the paddle to be relocated.

In all fairness, this is being overly conservative in order to illustrate each step of the process to make things clear. But let's say you eliminated all the steps between when you received the position from the notification and were able to stuff it right into the position of the paddle. Imagine you could write the following:

```
playerPaddle.center.x = [[notification userInfo]
                                  objectForKey:@"parameter"];
```

That fixes all this nonsense about security, doesn't it? I mean you've eliminated all the middle management of the data so aren't you a lot more secure? Thinking back to the question I asked a few paragraphs earlier: What happened between the time you sent the notification and when you received it? The fact is that you don't know. You trusted the operating system's notification system to handle the transfer for you, but after all is said and done can you be sure that the actual information isn't still hanging around?

What's the big deal? Why do you care if a number is still hanging around in the system? The storage area has probably been released and you can reuse the space so you're probably not going to have memory leaks.

Imagine that the data was your social security number, or your bank account, or possibly your credit card number. Would you want that hanging around for any amount of time after it was no longer needed?

The Payment Card Industry

As of the time of writing, there were over twenty apps in the App Store that could be used to process credit cards. With prices ranging from $49.95 all the way down to free, small businesses have a lot of options for increasing their sales.

Why talk about the payment card industry in a book on accessories? There are two major reasons. First, small business applications are one of the most lucrative areas for third party iPhone development. While games get all the notice, investors (both individuals and venture capital firms) are looking for the next big small business app.

Second, small business represents a mostly untapped market because change is coming. Throughout 2010 the Payment Card Industry will require changes to the way small business operate to insure security and reduce fraud. Rather than play "catch up" once these changes go into effect, an accessory developer (or app developer for that matter) that has something ready ahead of time will have the market edge. So as boring as security may be for some, stick with it and you may come up with that invention that makes it big.

Take, for example, a merchant who makes weekend trips to crafts fairs where he does most of his business. Up until recently, he has maintained a cash business or graciously taken checks. If he did choose to take credit cards then he was probably forced to use something like the "knuckle-buster" manual swipe shown in Figure 8–2.

Figure 8–2. *Manual credit card processor, also known as the "knuckle-buster"*

The merchant has no way of knowing if there are sufficient funds or credit for the customers' purchases. Further, because of the manual processing, the per transaction cost of doing business this way cuts deeply into his profit.

The answer lies in mobile, wireless processing. But, even with the subsidies offered by merchant processors, a wireless terminal starts at nearly $800, well beyond the reach of the small businessman.

With the iPhone and its sophisticated operating system, innovative developers quickly provided a solution; credit card processing apps for the iPhone (Figure 8–3). The iPhone requires no power other than an occasional good charge and can use either the phone line or WiFi as a medium for connectivity.

A customer brings his purchases to the vendor who types in the card number, expiration date, and the amount of the purchase. Many apps also provide the capability of Address Verification System (AVS) whereby vendors can enter additional data such as the CVV code of the card and the street address/zip code of the customer. The vendor sets up the AVS feature if he wants to accept cards with an increased sense of security that the transaction is not fraudulent.

Although it may seem complicated from the outside, the actual code to perform the transaction is no more than a POST operation to an http server. The connection is made securely using SSL/TLS (Secure Sockets Layer/Transport Layer Security) protocols that are already part of the iPhone OS. This means sending data to a web address prefixed by "https//" which takes care of network security concerns.

Figure 8–3. *A typical iPhone credit card processing app*

But what about security within the application? How do you know that the app itself isn't just storing up all the card numbers it reads and that nice little old lady selling tomatoes from her van isn't going to go home and clean out everyone? The fact is that you don't. And that's where PCI comes in.

The Payment Card Industry Security Standards Council is a group of credit card providers (American Express, Discover, JCB, MasterCard, and Visa) that have formed a regulatory board that enforces security standards on, among other things, vendors of transaction processors such as credit card apps for the iPhone.

When the Government decided that individuals would only be responsible for a maximum $50 of fraudulent charges on stolen credit cards, that burden shifted to the credit card providers. The companies banded together to try and minimize their losses (estimated at over $4 billion annually).

> **NOTE:** PCI security standards encompass a lot more than just credit card processing applications. For more information, go to www.pcisecuritystandards.org.

For developers of applications that process credit cards, whether it be iPhone apps such as the one shown in Figure 8–3 or simple web apps that use the https:// post mechanism, come July 1, 2010 all applications must be certified by the PCI Security Council. What this means is that any applications that are not certified as being in compliance will not be usable.

To understand what this means you need to visualize what happens when a credit card is processed by an iPhone application such as that described.

The process illustrated in Figure 8–4 represents the typical flow in processing a credit card from an iPhone app. As you already know, the basic process of the app is to make a secure POST with the card number, expiration date, charge amount, and any other supporting data over the unsecured network using the secure SSL/TLS protocol. These transactions are processed by a merchant Gateway provider. The Gateway either approves or declines the transaction based on the cardholder information. The Gateway provider does not, however, move any money around.

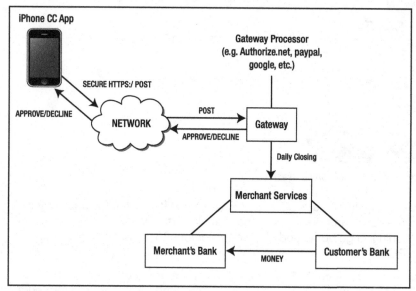

Figure 8–4. *Credit card processing flow for an iPhone app*

Another company called a merchant services provider does the actual movement of money from the customer's account to the merchant's account. This is typically a more secure firm such as a bank or "bank-like" corporation. At the end of the day at a time usually set by the merchant, the merchant services provider closes the daily transactions collecting all the Visa, Amex, etc., by card type transactions and puts the amounts into the merchant's account. The money typically takes from one to three days to show up in the merchant's account.

When a business sets up its credit card processing system, it will have both a gateway processor and a merchant services processor. With the typical brick and mortar business, all this is set up by the card services rep. The business owner gets a credit card system set up and he swipes cards throughout the day and sees his money show up in a day or two.

Though not any different, setting up one of these credit card apps requires more work on the part of the business owner. In addition to acquiring and setting up the app on his phone, he must also set up a gateway account as well as a merchant services account.

With the gateway account, the merchant will get a minimum of three pieces of information: a gateway address (`https://`) to post the transaction, a user id for the account typically called an API_KEY, and a password which is sometimes referred to as the API_KEY.

In addition, the business will apply for and receive, after a credit approval, a merchant services account that will handle the transfer of funds. As part of the merchant services application, the business owner will be required to define what application or device he uses for processing credit cards.

Come July 1, 2010, the name of the application or device that the business intends to use will be required to be on the PCI certification list. This means that the app or device has undergone validation by an authorized testing facility. If the application is not on the list, the merchant services company will not process the transfer of funds. This means that all those twenty-plus apps need to either become PCI compliant or they will cease to function.

> **NOTE:** There are several types of PCI compliance ranging from business compliance to compliance of physical CC processors to compliance of applications. As you are concerned with apps, the relevant certification comes from the PA-DSS Payment Application Data Security Standard. Starting July 1, 2010 any iPhone (or other) app that processes credit cards will need to be PA-DSS compliant.

So what does PA-DSS or PCI compliance mean for us? If you go to the PCI security web site you will find a detailed list of requirements that an app must meet to achieve certification. These requirements include passwords, data protection, and internal company processes for software development.

The essence of all the requirements boils down to one thing: *protecting data*. When a merchant enters a customer's credit card number, after he gets notified that the transaction was either approved or declined, the data is usually no longer needed and should not be anywhere on the device's memory.

> **NOTE:** There are some exceptions to this of course, primarily for merchants that do a lot of repeat customer business. A customer can allow the card information to be retained by the merchant so he doesn't have to reenter it every time. However, PCI requires that this data be kept secure and that such methods as encryption are used to make the data secure. For the type of small business being discussed here, storing customer-sensitive data is discouraged.

It's been a long, roundabout discussion, but I'm hoping you can start to see why using convenience methods such as message passing via the notification system to transmit data is a bad idea. Imagine that you used the notification to send the customer's card number from the accessory controller to the view controller. You, of course, can nil out all your variables that stored the number, but how do you know what the OS does?

Suppose you lose your iPhone and someone uses data forensic tools to scan memory. Would they find valuable information?

> **NOTE:** As part of PCI Compliance PA-DSS testing, certification houses use these very tools to check and see if any sensitive data is retained, either knowingly or not, within the memory of the iPhone executing the CC processing app.

Now you don't really care about the position of your game controller or if the CIA or KGB finds your iPhone and learns the secrets to your beating the computer player. On the other hand, after you finish with this Pong game you're probably going to want to write something a little more substantial and likely to make a profit. New requirements such as PCI offer you the opportunity to level the playing field somewhat. There are no longer twenty-plus developers ahead of you, as everyone has to start over.

Code Changes

You can make changes to enhance security. Whether you need to do it is up to you and the type of application or accessory you choose to develop. If you're a game developer or just tinkering, it's probably not that important. If, however, you're developing for the small business where security is a concern, then you'll want to know what you can do.

The changes you need to make are simple. You even laid the groundwork early on when you were designing the game controller addition to your system. Although this is not always the best approach, you're going to add a global property (variable) made public from the application delegate that you'll use to pass the new position of the knob. You will need to do the following:

1. Add a publicly accessible parameter in the application delegate.

2. Add access to the application delegate in the game controller object.

3. Add access to the application delegate in the view controller object.

4. From the game controller object set the position into the global variable.

5. In the view controller, when you receive notification that the knob has changed, move the paddle to the new position identified by the global variable.

In addition to the preceding generalized steps, you also need to modify the notification that you use to alert the view controller by removing the userInfo parameter.

Step 1

First, open the interface code for the application delegate and add an integer to represent the paddle's position.

```
@interface pongAppDelegate : NSObject <UIApplicationDelegate> {
    UIWindow *window;
    pongViewController *viewController;

        int    paddlePosition;
}
```

You'll also want to add the following property statement before the @end of the interface file and the @synthesize statement in the implementation (.m) file in order to set up the getter and setter functions.

```
@property   int   paddlePosition; // goes in the interface file
@synthesize paddlePosition;   // goes in the implementation file
```

Step 2

This code should already be in your file, but just to reiterate—add the following two lines to the game controller interface file in the appropriate positions.

```
#import "pongAppDelegate.h"
```

```
pongAppDelegate *appDelegate;
```

In the implementation file, at the top of the _readData method, add the following line to be able to access the application delegate:

```
        appDelegate = (pongAppDelegate *)[[UIApplication
sharedApplication] delegate];
```

Step 3

Here, you just want to repeat Step 2 for the view controller interface and implementation files.

Step 4

In the _readData method section that deals with the new knob position, set the value in the appDelegate.paddlePosition variable. Also, be sure to modify the notification scheme to no longer create a user dictionary to pass the userInfo field.

```
while ([[_session inputStream] hasBytesAvailable])
    {
        NSInteger bytesRead = [[_session inputStream]
                    read:buf maxLength:EAD_INPUT_BUFFER_SIZE];
        NSLog(@"read %d bytes (%d) from input stream", bytesRead,buf[0]);
```

```
                    if (buf[0] == 0x10) {
                            [[NSNotificationCenter defaultCenter]
                                    postNotificationName:@"PBPRESSED" object:self];

                    }
                    if (buf[0] == 0x20) {
                            unsigned char i = buf[1];
                            [[NSNotificationCenter defaultCenter]
                                    postNotificationName:@"POTTURNED" object:self ];

                    }
            }
    }
```

Step 5

Change the potTurned method to move the paddle in the view controller when the
notification is received, by using the appDelegate.paddlePosition variable.

```
-(void) potTurned:(NSNotification *)notification {
        NSLog(@"Pot Turned");
        int i = appDelegate.paddlePosition;
        NSLog(@"Position Received = %d",i);

        i = (-i + 256);

        float j = (float)i * (320.0/246.0);

        CGPoint xLocation = CGPointMake(j,playerPaddle.center.y);
        playerPaddle.center = xLocation;
        if (playerPaddle.center.x > (self.view.bounds.size.width /2))
                if (playerPaddle.center.x > (self.view.bounds.size.width /2)+101)
                        playerPaddle.image = playerPaddleRightUp;
                else
                        playerPaddle.image = playerPaddleRight;
                else
                        if (playerPaddle.center.x <
                                (self.view.bounds.size.width /2)-101)
                                playerPaddle.image = playerPaddleLeftUp;
                        else
                                playerPaddle.image = playerPaddleLeft;

}
```

The complete listing can be found in the Appendix. Make these changes and you should
find that the game performs pretty much the same as it did before. You will still be able
to move the paddle using either the knob or your finger.

These changes have eliminated using the notification system for passing operational
data. While this is not important in this example system, it provides a path for the secure
handling of potentially sensitive data in future projects.

If the data were sensitive, then, after it had been used and no longer needed, the
variables can be cleared and then returned to the pool. By overwriting variables that

hold sensitive data after their use, you eliminate the possibility of such data persisting past its need.

Summary

This short chapter focused on eliminating unnecessary and potentially unsecure methods within the systems we develop. Certain applications such as those in the financial industry dealing with sensitive personal information such as credit cards or social security numbers must be handled with care.

Identity theft and credit fraud are serious concerns for the iPhone/iPod touch application and accessory developer. Standards and compliance organizations are already in place and setting the bar ever higher for financial applications. Beginning July 1, 2010, all mobile apps including iPhone and iPod touch will be required to comply with the Payment Card Industry's (PCI) Payment Application-Data Security Standard (PA-DSS).

While this can be seen as an additional burden the mobile app developer must bear, it also allows some of us a chance to catch up. This is basically a restart of the financial app sector. It makes the game a little harder by raising the initial ante and forcing us all to comply to the same standards. But the main thing is, it gets us into the game.

Chapter 9

Apple Developer Programs

Throughout this book, I've referenced the Made For iPod/Works With iPhone (MFi/WWi) program from Apple. However, the company actually offers several programs designed to help the developer and budding entrepreneur.

In essence, there are three major programs you should consider joining. The Mac Development Center focuses on trends in Mac OS X and Cocoa development methodologies and techniques. Like other developer programs, the MDC offers various levels of membership.

Mac Developer

You can generally join any Mac developer program for free at the entry level. As with anything offered for free, what you get is generally limited to newsletters and access to information that will help you in your development progress. Think of it more like a portal to which you can go to research and find information.

One step up from free is the student membership, allowing you, for the annual price of $99, everything offered in the free membership plus one purchase through the Apple Developer Hardware Purchase Program. It may seem like a small benefit, but you can save far more than the hundred-dollar cost of membership. As a person who generally shops the refurbished area of the Apple Store looking for the best deals, I can personally attest to getting an even better deal here. It's a great program for students as the name implies, but as a professional engineer who regularly takes refresher courses at the local university, you're eligible to take advantage of it as well.

Probably the mainstream choice of the bunch is the Select Membership which offers (in addition to everything at the lower levels) access to ADC on iTunes, access to developer forums, two uses per year of the compatibility labs, and two technical support incidents. If you've ever run into a snag in your software that you thought you would never get out of, these TSRs (technical support requests) are absolutely essential.

Just about every program offers some kind of access to technical support once you get to the level where you're shelling out a few dollars. Speaking from experience, when your head is against the wall and you're ready to give up, handing over your problem to the Apple guys to figure out can get you out from a real jam.

Of course, everyone else out there with the same level of membership can use these two so your response time will not be measured in minutes. From my experience, and I've used the system for at least half a dozen issues, I generally get an answer within the week. Your times may vary.

The last part of the Select Membership, and the most valuable, is the access to software seeds. This means that you get the latest release of tools and operating system advances well ahead of the rest of the crowd.

What's even more important than getting to test drive these seeds, is the chance to make changes and have input on future releases. Apple, like any good company, listens to their customers. It's not unique to Apple; it's just good business.

This can also give you an edge over your competition. When the latest iPhone SDK came out, the version that ran only under Snow Leopard was far and away better than anything in the previous version. I was able to test and use the latest and greatest features of the SDK long before my competitors…at least those competitors who weren't part of the program.

The final level of the Mac Development program gives you more of the things you get in the next lower level, but also a pass to the World Wide Developer's Conference (WWDC) held each year in San Francisco.

The WWDC to some may seem like just a chance to go to the Bay Area and "hang out" for a week, but it's far more than that. In fact, if you own or are a significant part of a company that does Mac or iPhone development, missing the WWDC is like handing your business over to the competition.

For the past three years, the latest iPhone has been announced at the WWDC along with other operating system, technology, and product improvements. Not only announcements which are generally available to the public, but you also get the inside scoop on how to use these new features through presentations, tutorials, hands-on labs, sample code, and interaction with the people that made them in the first place.

Proceedings from the WWDC seem to become available for purchase about two months or so after the conference. That gives you a two-month head start on any of your competition that did not attend.

iPhone Developer

My guess would be that every person, or at least 99.9%, who bought this book has joined the iPhone developer program. You can download the SDK, sample programs, the iPhone simulator, and in a matter of minutes make magic happen right on your computer screen.

As with the Mac Developer program, there are several levels within the iPhone program, though they are organized a little differently. As you already know, you can join the program at no cost, download the SDK, and start building apps. You are limited, however, to only being able to run those apps on the simulator, i.e., you can't run them on your own iPhone.

To go farther, either you as an individual or a company can join the next level of the program for $99 per year and get access to the iPhone program portal. The portal allows you to go to the next step and create the tools and identities needed to take the program you built and download it to your phone. To even begin to think about creating accessories for the iPhone, the use of the program portal and running apps on your iPhone hardware should be second nature.

I've got to warn you though, if you haven't been through it, you **will** get frustrated, as there are several steps you need to go through and they are anything but intuitive.

The basic process centers on making sure that an application that is created for the iPhone is traceable to a credible source. As an iPhone developer, you have to go and get credentials that say Apple has entrusted to you the ability to create sound apps for the iPhone. You do this through the iPhone program portal.

After you download that identity to the Mac you will be developing on, you install it using Keychain. Take a look at the Keychain Access program in your utilities folder. This is where the authentication and certification processes are centered. I can't go into too much detail as I'm not sure where and how the NDA (Non-Disclosure Agreement) with Apple kicks in regarding how much can be revealed by developers to not-yet developers. If you want to find out more, use Google to search for "iPhone development certificate," or "provisioning profiles." You'll find a lot of frustrated developers.

While you will find a lot of frustration out there for the iPhone development system, it really does work if you follow the procedures. It took me a few restarts my first time through, and every now and then I come up with a problem. What I found that works well is to research the process carefully well before trying it. Don't just do the research at the Apple site; check out some of the other developer sites and read what others are doing. Again, Google is your friend.

There's more to it than identity certification as well. You need to define the devices you'll be using, create app ids, create things called provisioning profiles, deal with expired profiles, and so on. There are different configurations to choose from: Debug, ad hoc distribution, App Store distribution, etc.

The main problem I find is that certain pieces of information that are needed to do something—say ready an App for sale in the App Store—have to be placed in different locations, especially if you move back and forth between debug and production systems. You can put things in your project's property list file, in the project settings, in the target settings, and which one of these will depend on which configuration you're using.

I wish there were a single place I could tell you to go that summarized everything perfectly, but there isn't. You can Google a problem or issue and you might find half a dozen different answers to the problem. Interestingly, all of them are valid depending on several other factors surrounding the problem. The process simply is not worked out yet.

Probably your best source of information would be to look at some of the WWDC videos that discuss the development process. If you're just setting up your system processes, then these videos will help you immensely. It's quite possible that, if you're just setting up your first system, and you follow the video closely, you could, in less than an hour, work through the process successfully and have your apps running on your hardware. Of course, the problem then is the cost and availability of the videos.

You can set up your $99 account for yourself as an individual or a company. Whatever name you choose will be associated with the name used to sell or distribute your app through the App Store. It won't necessarily be the same as you can specify the name to be used as the seller when you begin to setup things in the App Store to make your product available. When you get ready to sell or freely distribute your product, you actually use a different part of the system called iTunes Connect.

Much like the program portal within the iPhone developer system, iTunes Connect helps you to setup and manage all your apps in the App Store. You upload your executable, program icons, sales information, screen shots, setup your bank accounts for all that money you're going to make, you set your price, determine where you want your product to sell, and many other things.

While this book is about iPhone accessories, you'll need to be able to use the iPhone developer site and program portal as well as iTunes Connect to offer a complete solution.

> **NOTE:** There is actually a third developer center for Safari and Safari technology that I will not be covering. For more information go to http://developer.apple.com/safari

Apple Developer Connection

Although not a specific developer area in and of itself, Apple Developer Connection (ADC) provides the container for your developer resources much like QuickTime is a container for media. Figure 9–1 depicts the relationship between the various programs. You use ADC to access the resources you've purchased through any of the other specific developer programs. For example, you might have a hardware purchase option though both your iPhone developer membership as well as your Mac developer membership. In ADC, under the assets options you can keep track of all these. You'll want to do this periodically as these assets are use 'em or lose 'em. They don't rollover like cell phone minutes to the next year.

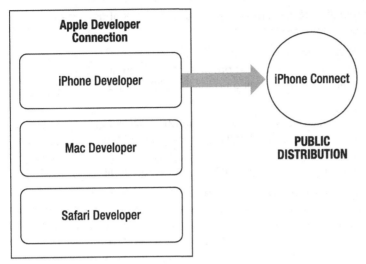

Figure 9–1. *Apple developer program relationships*

Made For iPod/Works With iPhone

The MFi/WWi program provides developers the tools and information they need to create accessories that connect to the iPod and iPhone. Approved membership makes you a licensed developer and grants you access to the technical information, materials, and logos for your product. Full information can be found at developer.apple.com/ipod.

Have you ever wondered which pin does what on the dock connector or why you can't take a standard headphone plug and wire them to your own set of iPod speakers? You can search and search on the Internet, but the best you'll come up with is anecdotal evidence and a few brave souls who have dissected the various pieces and come up with the way they think things work.

When I first started considering iPhone accessory development, I did the online research and it quickly became clear that I was never going to get anywhere trying to work the problem as an outsider. The MFi/WWi program grants you access to everything you need, including technical support to make your accessory a reality.

While the internals of the program are covered by an NDA that every developer agrees to, there is a good, generic way to look at the program that I'll be talking about. I hope to get across the concept that joining the MFi/WWi program is very much like acquiring a managing partner in your development.

Running a Business

Joining the MFi/WWi program means that you will need to conduct your business with order and professionalism. You will develop plans and schedules and there will be order to your operations. Working in the program moves you from the level of garage or bedroom hobbyist to a true small business owner.

Joining is simple. You simply go to the website and click the Apply Now button. You will be asked to respond to a series of questions and provide information about your business. It's not that much different than signing up for the $99 iPhone developer program.

However, unlike an individual developer, when you join the MFi/WWi program you will need to be an actual business. Part of the verification will be to submit documentation that proves you are a real operation. You may need to provide articles of incorporation, business licenses, FEIN numbers, or other information to verify your legitimacy.

If you don't have an actual business but are considering becoming an accessory developer, look into organizing your own business structure. Limited Liability Companies (LLCs) provide a low-cost, straightforward way to begin setting up your organization. The law varies from state to state or country to country on these, so check your local regulations.

The time it takes to become active from when you initially apply will vary depending on a variety of circumstances ranging from things you will need to do such as setting up your company to things well beyond your control. All in all, my advice would be to expect it to take at least a month or more from when you click that Apply Now button until the time you start digging into the internal of Apple products.

Although I can't provide details on the secrets of the program, if you take a formalistic stance in your day-to-day operations, you will be right in sync with the essence of operating under the program.

Look at it this way. Joining the program will affect you in two distinct ways. First, as I talked about, you will be granted access to all the tools you need to develop your accessory. This is the technical side of things. The second way that it will affect your business is that you will become accountable.

I'm not going out on a limb to say that you will be receiving Apple confidential information. You'll need it to do your job. How else can you figure out what goes where on that 30-pin connector. The thing is you've become responsible for its protection just as if you were working at Apple in Cupertino. It's part of your NDA agreement. You must protect any and all information that you're given.

At first, it doesn't seem like too big a deal. Just lock up the papers and don't let other people see them. Like any set of technical information, things change from time to time. After being in the program close to a year, I've seen changes on the order of once a month. Everything doesn't change, but a load value here, a command byte there…you get the idea. It's just like being in any technically progressive company. (Hey, your design is going to change way more than the Apple docs.)

The key thing here is to protect them. You'll have access to information in both electronic and paper form. It goes without saying to limit access to your electronic information (and Apple's). No technically savvy developer leaves his or her design work lying around where anyone can click and see it. The same thing applies to any paper manuals that you print out.

I work far better with paper documents than those on my computer. I can write on them, cut and paste, move things around...I just work easier with paper. As I mentioned, the documents will be updated from time to time and you will likely print out new paper and want to dispose of the rest. My advice is to get a shredder. While I probably can't disclose the means of doing it, your documents are traceable back to you. If someone posts sensitive Apple information and they trace it back to you, well, I'm sure you can understand that being kicked out of the program will likely be the least of your worries. Any major business, not just Apple, takes its information seriously. After all, all the value in the company is in the information.

The same thing should apply to your business as well. If you do establish a commercial presence, don't leave your information out for anyone to see. On the other hand, having a good-looking prototype of your product will get people talking. They don't need to know your secrets to making it work, only what it will do for them.

In my daily schedule, I operate my design business (the part that makes accessories) from my small shop that does Apple computer and iPhone screen repair. As more than 95% of my business is iPhone repair, customers are very interested in what's new and exciting for the iPhone. They're tired of apps; they want to see hardware. When I bring out my little accessory, no matter what it is, their eyes light up and they show a lot of interest. I've even had a few become investors. It's great to use someone else's money to work on this kind of stuff.

The point of the conversation is to be mindful of what you show and what you keep sight unseen. Spur their interest but never at the expense of revealing your secrets or Apple's.

Another part of running a business is schedules and inventory. Again, not getting into revealing details, you will need to develop schedules for what you're developing as well as keeping track of things.

Let's talk about schedules. Imagine you're starting a restaurant. You're a great chef, can make meals in quantity for low prices, and you've got some start up money. That initial money will only last a certain while. You know that you'll have to buy or lease equipment, furniture, and space. There's staff you'll need to consider. You have to develop your supplier relations and so on. Your initial money will last you only so long.

Suppose you're getting that money from a bank or some other form of a loan. In all but the most charitable cases, you will need to provide a lot of information to get the cash. You'll especially need cash flow predictions and sales predictions. You'll have to estimate how much you will sell and when. You'll create sales projections.

I have never in my life seen a scientific end-all way to make realistic sales projections. I mean, maybe, for a restaurant you could look at restaurants in the area, their traffic pattern, the demographics, and so on. In the end, you're guessing. We all guess.

Think of the benefits you get from the MFi/WWi program as a loan to you by Apple. That's really what it is. Apple is saying that, from the information you've shown them, that they think (hope) that you will be successful in your accessory endeavor. They trust you enough from what you've told them to grant you access to their secrets. Think of it as money from the bank.

Therefore, you want to think about what your accessory will do in the open market. Obviously (or maybe not) you don't want to make something that there is already a couple dozen of in the open market. The exception would be if yours was far and away the better product, or yours was significantly cheaper. Don't be an "also ran".

On the other hand, making something too unique will limit your market potential because there just won't be a big enough market for it.

As an example, the credit card reader I depicted in Chapter 1 was my first accessory product. It addresses the small business owner's need or desire to accept credit cards at a cost far below merchant services offerings. Something like over 90% of the businesses in the country are small businesses so the market potential is there.

However, if you look at the number of apps in the App Store, there were over twenty available ranging from free up to $50. Why develop a piece of hardware for something that a small business owner with an iPhone or iPod touch could already get?

For me, there were two answers; security and cost. I don't know about you but I never want to speak my card number aloud over the phone—even if I made the call to make a purchase. It just unsettles me. All the current products require the merchant to manually type in the customer's card number and expiration date. By having a swipe mechanism, I never have to see the customer's information. I don't even have to handle their card. I can position the reader so that they can swipe it themselves so that their card never leaves their hand.

That's pretty cool, but is it enough to warrant developing the product? You're going to face this and similar questions that you'll have to answer. Don't forget about competition. Just because it isn't out there yet, don't think that someone else isn't already working on it. To make an honest assessment, assume your competition is ahead of you, or at least at the same place. After that, make your decision.

I've talked about security in the sense of keeping your and Apple's information safe. I also discussed the need for a good business plan that includes sales forecasts. How many of your widgets can you sell? What is your price? What's your profit? These are things you will want to have thought about and documented.

Another closely related area that you will need to address is your schedule. You cannot go into this thinking that you're going to get all the Apple information goodies and something will "come to you." It doesn't happen that way and Apple knows it. Like any business, to get off the ground, you need to know what your business is about.

A restaurateur doesn't start a restaurant and then on opening day decide that he's going to go Italian. Similarly, you can't go into this thinking you're going to make iPhone accessories and after you get set up, then decide what accessory you're going to make. Apple won't let you in the door.

Let's face it. There will be things that Apple probably doesn't want you to make. Frankly, when I found out that Apple began using an iPod touch based device in their stores as a point-of-sale terminal, my heart kind of sank. After months of development and conceptualizing, I thought they'd never want to allow a competitive product like mine. Turns out it wasn't as much in the same market space as I thought.

On the other hand, I had an idea that I thought Apple would absolutely love. I figured it would bring lots of people over to Apple products not just the ones that already had an iPhone or iPod. Turns out that's the one they didn't allow. The main point is that you will need a specific idea or product that you will want to implement.

There's another benefit to being specific and that is it will give you some knowledge about how you will go about implementing it. Suppose your accessory was something that required minimal user input, maybe none at all. That may be a lot easier to develop than a User Interface—perhaps a game controller—with lots and lots of knobs and sliders and buttons. On the other hand, maybe not; maybe the game controller is just simple commands to the iPhone. Your idea could be a complex super cipher key to user hardware encryption of your iPhone data so that, unless someone had the physical key, your data was unreadable. While it might just be a few ICs to implement, the US Government export controls would cost you a huge amount of time.

Again, it's all about schedule. You need to know your schedule. Your investors need to know your schedule and remember that I said, by allowing you access to their sensitive information, Apple is an investor. Follow the dots.

How are you going to deliver your product to your customers? Go into any electronics store—a Best Buy, a Fry's, even an Apple Store—and take a look around. It's not like a flea market with widgets thrown about the place is it? There's an order to things. Some products are hanging up on hooks and some may be on shelves. The cheaper gizmos might be on a table in the middle of the aisle with a "Sale" sign while others costing a few hundred dollars may be under lock and key or even have alarm tags on them.

The thing they all have in common is packaging. How you present your product to your customer says a lot about what is inside. Something stuffed into a cheap cardboard box with computer printed stickers on it says a lot about what's inside. To most customers it says the business didn't care that much about the packaging so you have to wonder how much they cared about the product development.

Look at some of the phrases on the site at apple.developer.com/iPod, the MFi/WWi program page:

- *Participate in the Made For iPod licensing program*

- *Licensed developers gain access*

- *iPod and iPhone compatibility icons*

- *Made For iPod and Works With iPhone logos*

- *Certified by the developer to meet Apple performance standards*

Just these few phrases should make you understand that if you make it through the hurdles of the program, your product's packaging will stand out from the rest of the stuff on the shelves. Go to any of these stores that have an Apple products section and pick up each and every one and study it. Imagine where your product might fit in. Think about its size and shape. Imagine what the key colors of your package will be. Do you want it to stand out or fit in?

What I did when I was considering packaging was to buy several things where the packaging might be appropriate for my product. I redesigned at least half a dozen packages this way to see how my product will look. Chances are you might want more than one. It's never too early to start thinking about how you want to present your image to the world. Is this required by the program? You'll have to join to find out for sure, but ask yourself this: Do you think Apple would want to give any product developer the unconstrained ability to use their "logos" or "compatibility icons" any way they wanted without some input?

Getting back to the actual development process for a moment, ask yourself something else: would Apple ever let you release a product that they haven't seen or tried out? If you create an app that you want to put into the App Store, there is a review process in place to verify that the software meets certain requirements. Sure, there's a lot of talk about App Store approval being arbitrary, but I don't think it is. I've never gotten an app in without fixing it and each and every time I got feedback, it was clearly a technical issue or I in some way violated the Human Interface Guidelines.

Do you think, given that Apple rigidly tests every single app that they're going to put into the App Store, that they wouldn't test your product that connects to and (in the case of iPhone OS accessories) talks to their products? In keeping with the NDA, I cannot and will not talk about what goes on "behind closed doors." Hey, I haven't seen behind them doors myself. But in this case, use common sense.

By common sense, I mean that you need to make your product robust. It should work each and every time. It should never cause your app to crash. Think about it this way; imagine yourself showing your product to the guy who is going to give you all the money you need to start production. For whatever reason, it is an absolute certainty that everything that could possibly go wrong will. Assume the worst.

In my mind, the absolute worst thing that could happen is if I started my program, connected my accessory, it worked, and then the person watching said "what happens if you connect it first, then start the program?" There are three possible outcomes. One, you've planned ahead and show him—no problem—works perfect every time. Two, you connect it and it crashes. Three, and the absolute worst of the lot, you don't know. You can gamble and say "no problem," then if you try it and it crashes you are totally screwed. You could say "I don't know" which is honest, but if it were me as the investor, I'd see someone that doesn't plan.

The only "right" answer is to do your best and try to account for every contingency. Start with boundary conditions: starting, stopping, initializing setting, installing the app, deleting the app, and so on. That's a good start. A simple example is that I once added a "done" button in the table view of an app. I needed the "done" button because I was using a numeric pad and there's no enter button—no way to signal that I was finished and thus, no way to get rid of the keyboard. So I added a "done" button to the table view's header that is perfectly legitimate.

An even better idea is to give people your app to try out. Usually, and my wife has done this many times, they'll find things you didn't even think of or see coming. Be sure the people you use for testing are "iPhone-savvy". Even those who have had an iPhone for a year or more may not know how to set preferences on the phone that may seem simple to you. One of my first testers complained that my app kept shutting down. The real thing was they had left the iPhone auto-lock at 1 minute and blamed it on the app.

I tested it for every field that I entered even if it didn't have a numeric keyboard. The thing I forgot to test was what happens if someone presses it before they've entered something in a field. Bam! I had used a method to save the field identity in an ivar and when "done" was pressed, to use that ivar to release the first responder and get rid of the keyboard. Know what happens if you release a first responder on something that is nil? Yes, that was the first thing they found.

The moral of the story is, when testing, to really hit those boundary conditions. I thought I had done so, only the "done" button concept turned out to be a fix to a fix that slipped through the cracks. The thing was, I had tested my product with several different people. We found dozens of issues that we were able to correct. But something as simple as this wasn't found by any of us.

Therefore, testing has to be a focus of your development process. There are three things that need to work perfectly: your app by itself, your accessory by itself, and the two of them together. I don't mean to say that your accessory has to work and function normally without software, it just better not crash the system. The same thing goes for the app. Your app should provide some indication to your user about the status of the accessory. As mentioned earlier, if you connect your accessory and a suitable app is not present, the iPhone OS does ask the user if he wants to get the app from the App Store.

In terms of testing, you'll also need to consider the quantity of units you develop throughout your process. Without getting into any insider details, do you imagine that someone from Apple is going to come to your little shop to check out your product? When you submit an app to Apple, you send it to them to be checked out. A reasonable person might infer from that a similar process for hardware accessories. Not saying anything for sure you understand, but infer what you will.

If there were such a need to follow a similar path for your hardware accessory as is clearly stated for apps, then, if it were me, I'd probably not want to send my only unit anywhere. It could get lost. This fictional place I *might* be sending it to could take a while leaving me without something to continue my work with or to show around. Consider making several prototype units. Three is good, five is better. One will almost always break. Even more important is to keep baselines units as you change the design.

During this process of building an accessory, you will create a logic board that will be fabricated and have the parts soldered to it. More than likely, you'll want or need to change something at some point. Even if everything works fine, maybe you want to change the ground planes or add bypass capacitors. Whatever it is, don't get rid of your old working units. Even if, when you get them back, assemble them and do an initial test that works—keep the old working boards around. You'll make a simple firmware change that cannot possibly have any effect on things, but it does. You'll pound your head against the wall for hours (said the man with dents in his head) and then think about trying the same change on the old board. If you have the board, you can make the change and try the fix and immediately isolate the area of the problem—hardware as in the new board, or firmware. You will need more than one unit for each stage of your design so plan ahead.

Summary

Apple offers many programs to hardware and software developers who want to leverage their ideas using products such as iPhones, iPods, Macintosh computers, Mac OS X, and Safari. The Mac Developer, iPhone Developer, and Safari Developer programs focus on the software aspects of their respective underlying platforms. Each program provides several levels of membership that offer varying degrees of benefits. Obviously, the higher the benefit, the more the cost of membership.

All three programs can be viewed as subclasses of the Apple Developer Connection membership. The ADC provides a resource "umbrella" from which you can manage your assets of any and all program memberships.

The Made For iPod/Works With iPhone program, like all other Apple developer programs, comes with strict non-disclosure agreements which participants must agree to and sign. Violation of the NDA from any program can have serious consequences including termination of your membership in any and all programs.

Because of NDA agreements, I am unable to provide details in order to help you choose whether or not you should participate in the MFi/WWi program. However, Apple is a business, like any other technology corporation, and is in this for profit. As such, by adopting and following sound business practices that any successful technology firm adheres to, a prospective participant should be able to understand what is in store for them should they choose to participate.

Part III

Designing an Accessory

Chapter 10

Hardware Design

You've decided to make the plunge and signed up for the MFi/WWi program. The widget you plan to create for your accessory has undergone rigorous scrutiny by your friends, peers, potential customers…basically, anyone you can trust to give you reasonable feedback but not reveal or steal your idea. It goes without saying that you need to be careful to whom you give information. Right now, your idea is all you have.

Your goal has become to make that idea a reality. Where do you start? At first, this question will seem daunting. Daunting is actually too weak a word. The tasks that lie ahead of you will probably seem insurmountable. You have no money, you're not skilled at hardware design, and your software skills are shaky at best. This translates to: you can't hire someone to do it and you can't do it yourself so why bother?

If you can't answer that question (why bother?) then you probably shouldn't proceed. Things will only get tougher from here on, so, if you stumble now and there's even the possibility of quitting (not failure as the possibility of failure is ever present) in your future, you better make that decision now before you put your heart (and life savings) into it.

Getting Started

Designing the hardware with all its transistors, milliamps, and multilayer boards may seem like the hardest part, but it's really gotten pretty simple over the past few decades. You don't code in assembly language much less enter ones and zeros with switches to create your program. You use a higher-level language such as objective-C, C, or C++.

Hardware design continues its advance in much the same way. In fact, you could create the electronics you need to build using a programming language such as C. However, that type of design methodology is generally reserved for very specialized devices that you won't be using it here. In essence, the way you'll develop your hardware will be even easier.

The parts that make up electronic devices today can contain a wide range of functionality. In the not too distant past, a Dual Inline Package (DIP) such as that shown in Figure 10–1 might contain a few basic Boolean functions such as a few Nand or Nor gates.

> **NOTE:** Because the reader is expected to have a general level of programming knowledge, I will assume a basic understanding of Boolean logic for these discussions.

Figure 10–1. *Basic DIP IC*

Creating usable functionality from such devices was done by hand using pencil and paper as well as lots of trial and error. Once a suitable design was solid enough to try out, the circuit was prototyped either by wirewrapping or soldering depending on the complexity of the circuit. Needless to say, even the simplest design required hours of checking and rework to achieve the desired results.

So much for history. Today things are far simpler. Just about anything the hobbyist needs for his design is either available already or can be programmed into a generic processor circuit. The type of design the hobbyist performs and that you will adopt is through the use of building blocks. You pick the parts that you need and connect the appropriate lines (wires) between them.

While it really is that simple, a sound knowledge of basic electronics principles goes a long way to helping create a circuit that works as opposed to a mess of wires, time, and money that has no hope of succeeding.

The good news is that vendors of the parts that you'll use want you to succeed. They provide very detailed specifications that can be several hundreds of pages for a single part. Their web sites contain application notes on how to use the parts in typical circuits, FAQs covering every aspect of the part, forums to provide user interaction with each other and company representatives, and many provide webinars available any time day or night to view.

While the glut of information can be a problem in itself, forcing the designer to look through potentially thousands of pages for information about a single part, most parts in a family tend to work well together. Sticking with a single manufacturer and its recommended product lines gives the novice a good way to get started.

The best thing that can help the beginning designer is to purchase evaluation or prototyping kits such as that shown in Figure 10–2 for the PIC microcontroller line from Microchip.

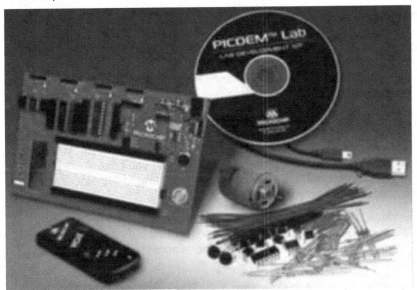

Figure 10–2. *PIC microcontroller evaluation kit*

For the designer of iPhone accessories who doesn't have an extensive hardware engineering background, but wants to begin developing hardware, evaluation kits cannot be beat. For any processor family that a designer would consider to use in an accessory design, there are several evaluation kit options. These kits offer the hardware you need to get started. They include the processor with its associated circuitry, software development tools (generally a limited set), and tutorial projects to get you going. Each project builds upon the last and the whole "course" can generally be completed in a day or two.

None of these kits will turn you into an electrical engineer, but they will give you enough knowledge to get you moving in the right direction. The kits range in price from less than a hundred to several hundred dollars.

As discussed, the central part of your hardware accessory will be some type of processor, i.e., a small computer. Most everything else in your accessory will be supporting data acquisition. In general, most accessories are either going to take data into the iPhone or send data out.

So really, your accessory will be (1) a processor of some type, (2) a connector to get to the iPhone (provided by Apple), (3) some other I/O devices such as buttons, knobs, LEDs, etc., to move data back and forth, and (4) other support circuitry such as power or security.

Now that you know the basic design of your accessory, you want to look at the process involved to get from your idea to a product that you can test with your iPhone.

Design Process

The goal in the design process is to take your idea and turn it into hardware. For now, you're going to forget about any iPhone software or even processor firmware that you need to create and focus entirely on the actual hardware accessory. You'll even delay talking about any case design for your circuit board.

There are probably an infinite number of ways to talk about the design process and no single way is totally right or wrong. I use a six-step process flow where someone else might use seven or twelve or any other number. Every process has some entry conditions that you will assume. For my process, I assume that you have an idea of what you intend to develop and maybe a basic diagram. Before getting to the process, let's draw out what the accessory roughly looks like.

Remember, all diagrams are going to be about the same because most accessory designs perform the same basic functionality; they connect to the iPhone to put data in or send data out. In that regard, take a look at the generic accessory diagram shown in Figure 10–3.

One of the most important facets of this diagram is that the processor is central and everything else revolves around it. Each of the four blocks surrounding the processor represents one of the major areas of your accessory.

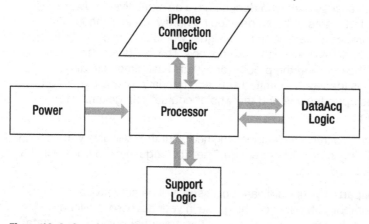

Figure 10–3. *Generic accessory block diagram*

The accessory will, of course, need power and require a method to connect to the iPhone since that's your purpose for building it in the first place. In many cases, you may be able to get your power from the iPhone or iPod touch depending upon your needs. Though you cannot go into specifics because of Apple's NDA, it's safe to assume that the lower your power requirements, the more likely that Apple might give you a little power. For now, let's assume they are separate.

As stated, the major purpose of just about any iPhone accessory is data acquisition. Here, you use data acquisition to mean acquiring data *for* the iPhone or *from* the iPhone, meaning you're sending data to the iPhone or from the iPhone to somewhere else. Finally, there is a fourth area that you'll call support logic. Support logic could range from something as simple as bypass capacitors that you put on your ICs to specialized logic for secure communications.

Again, hiding behind Apple's NDA, I make the claim that the iPhone connection logic shown in Figure 10–3 will be more or less "taken care of" for you. What I mean by that is that Apple obviously wants anything that connects to their products to be done properly. So it is safe to assume that they will provide you with enough guidance to do so without causing problems.

Let's look at the obvious; you know you'll attach via the dock connector that has 30 pins. Those pins represent signal, power, or ground. There really isn't anything else they can be so at the most there are 30 lines that you have to interconnect to the rest of your device. Let's set that aside for now with the belief that it's the easy part.

In essence, what all this soft pedaling around the details boils down to is that you have to connect your processor chip to a bunch of other stuff that you're going to place on your board. The processor forms the central part or core of your accessory. What part are you going to use?

That question, "What processor will you use?" is likely the most difficult part of the process and forms that initial step in the six step process shown in Figure 10–4.

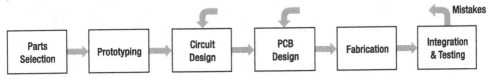

Figure 10–4. *Six-step accessory design process*

You come into this process with a good understanding of what needs to be done and, assuming you have joined the MFi/WWi program, the knowledge of how to connect your accessory to the iPhone. Given that knowledge, the first thing you'll need to do is select which parts you plan to use. Primarily, this means selecting a processor to use.

Parts (Processor) Selection

If you take a really good look at the processor options available for your accessory, it can seem daunting. One of the first options that stood out for me was using a customizable Field Programmable Gate Array (FPGA) from a company such as Altera or Xilinx. Your mileage may vary.

FPGAs give the designer a programmable module of logic that he can turn into pretty much anything he needs. While each FPGA architecture is unique even within the same manufacturer, in essence, an FPGA part contains a large number of flexible logic cells and a programmable interconnection matrix. Through design tools, you create a program or diagram of what you want to happen. You can use Hardware Design Languages (HDLs) such as Verilog or VHDL and, in some cases, a language like C can be used to program the chip. Let me say that one more time; you can use the C programming language to configure hardware.

While this at first glance seems pretty cool and exactly what the software engineer migrating to hardware design might need, it is not the way to go. To begin with, the parts and tools are fairly expensive. While FPGA providers do provide low-cost entry systems for evaluation, to create parts that you can use in a product for sale requires licensing. The larger functions you create using FPGAs are made up of smaller blocks of IP, or Intellectual Property. Like a song or movie, someone created this IP logic block and expects to be paid each time it is used. So, if you need a serial module for your FPGA, there's certainly IP to do that so you don't have to create it from scratch, but it will cost you. FPGAs are not the way for a first time accessory designer to go in all, but the most specialized designs.

If the cost doesn't scare you away, the power requirements may or probably should. While there are FPGAs that have low power requirements, these will also have the lowest functionality. If you're trying to use all those cool, high-level functions, you're going to pay for it in power consumption.

Another option for processor selection, a step down from sophisticated FPGA devices are microprocessors such as the Intel 8051 family of devices. Invented by Intel in 1980, making it 30 years old, the 8051 has been replaced by a family of devices based on the original design and is now known as MCS-51. Designed as an embedded processor from the start, the 8051 architecture contains a CPU, RAM, ROM, Interrupt Logic, Timers, I/O, etc., all in a single package as shown in Figure 10–5.

The MCS-51 architecture is even available as IP for high-density FPGA devices. Over the years, however, use of 8051 designs has waned in favor of more specialized microcontrollers. In fact, Intel dropped its MCS-51 product line in 2007.

These days most designers of projects such as an iPhone accessory will typically use a microcontroller based on one of four architectures: (1) the ARM 32-bit RISC, (2) the Texas Instruments (TI) MSP430, (3) TI's C2000, or (4) Microchip's PIC. Like everything else there are dozens of variations within each family. What's more, family lines are made by different, even competing companies. For example, in addition to their own MSP and C2000 lines, TI also makes an ARM product.

Intel 8051 Microarchitecture

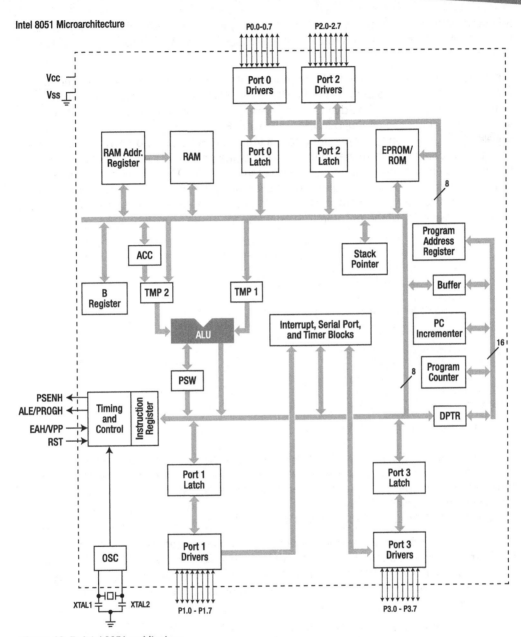

Figure 10–5. *Intel 8051 architecture*

While each product line is likely to have its own set of fanboys, I've found that pretty much any one of these can be used for what you're trying to accomplish. Taking a maturity approach, I wound up selecting Microchip's PIC16 line of products for my own development. The PIC16 is an 8-bit microprocessor line that has plenty of I/O including analog-to-digital and digital-to-analog conversion, built in oscillators, built-in serial functions, internal and external interrupts, and very low power requirements. Microchip has several parts in their nanoWatt line that use less than a microamp of power in low-power mode.

What I found was a significant PIC community with lots of available design examples and help. Microchip also provides the MPLAB development environment and HiTech C optimizing compiler. For the adventurous, there are even several realtime operating systems available such as Salvo from Pumkin Inc. Every designer will likely have or develop his "go-to" part. For me, that part is the PIC16F690, as shown in Figure 10–6. Able to fit probably ten of these on top of a dime, the part sports an internal oscillator that meets all my timing needs with enough memory and I/O to tackle most jobs at very low power consumption. While the Apple NDA again prohibits getting into specifics, let's just say that this was the central part in my first Apple approved accessory. With all that, I still have over 45% of the program memory free for future growth.

Figure 10–6. *PIC16F690 microcontroller*

Choosing to use a Microchip part is in no way an endorsement of this part over any other. Practically speaking, a designer should, if time and money permit, have a large toolset that encompasses various processors. Personally, while I am currently using the PIC16 line in my projects today, I also have an effort underway to migrate several designs to the ARM architecture. But let's get back to power.

All in all, power is going to be your number one adversary when developing the hardware design for your accessory. Power is expressed in watts and is defined in one formula as $P = IE$, where P is power in watts and I is current in amps, and E represents voltage. Power for the types of parts you are considering generally center on the milliwatt region.

While watts are the defined units for power, as a new board designer you'll almost never use them. More often than not, you will be measuring your power consumption by looking at the amount of current a device draws measured in milliamps. More specifically, in the general section of the product's specification sheet, you're going to see something that refers to normal operating current at a specific voltage and maybe a frequency.

A couple of the design parameters you will have to decide upon when developing your processor-driven accessory will be what speed to operate the processor chip and what voltage level to provide. Modern processors can operate on a range of voltages typically from something as low as 2.0 volts up to 5.0 volts. Most often, you will choose something around the 3.0-volt level that is normal for these types of designs. There are other considerations as well. Have you ever looked up the voltage of an iPhone battery? 'Nuf said.

Another consideration is at what clock speed you will run your processor chip. The off-the-tongue answer is "as fast as possible." That answer lasts for about a minute until you realize that the faster the speed the more power consumed. Processor speed selection isn't an arbitrary decision. You have to consider other clock speeds within your system.

For example, take an RS232 serial connection to some device. Unlike a desktop computer, where you can pretty much set any speed on your modem, a microcontroller is different. You are generally limited to a small set of connection speeds. What's more, some of the speeds will be more accurate than others. For example, you might run 19.2 kbps with a 2.5% error but have an error of 5.5% if you run the connection at 9600 bps. The serial connection speed is derived from multiples (or subdivisions) of the processor's clock speed.

This means that you may have to work backwards from your specific rate requirements (e.g., serial speed) to get to your clock speed. If you need a 19.2 kbps clock at less than 2.0%, you look up in the processor's specification which processor clock speed can provide that accuracy. So it's not an arbitrary decision.

Also, be sure to check all processor I/O that requires deterministic clock speeds. For example, you could have two serial connections, maybe an RS232 and a SPI interface. Once you find a set of rates and accuracies that work, you'll have your processor's clock.

To get the processor's clock, you had to derive it from the requirements for any other clock derived interfaces. Your purpose in deriving the clock speed was to determine power requirements. Now that you have selected a voltage source (level) and a clock speed, you can determine the amount of current your accessory will draw.

NOTE: Clock speed of the processor can really drive your design, even going as far as forcing you to switch to a different model or even a different family of chips. Some processors have an internal oscillator that provides a clock you can use without adding parts such as external RC networks or crystals that drive up power and cost. On the other hand, internal oscillators tend to be less accurate. That loss of accuracy can trickle down to parts of your system where a specific speed must be met. Like anything, it's a trade-off.

Now that power and clock speed have been dealt with, the next thing to consider is I/O. Processors generally provide increasing amounts of digital I/O along their family lines. As I/O pins increase, so does the number of pins on the device that causes it to get larger. The PIC16F690 I use comes in a 20-pin package, and you saw how small it was by looking at Figure 10–6. Basically, every pin except power and ground is (or can be used as) an I/O pin, so the PIC16F690 has 18 pins available for I/O. These must be shared across any other function that you need to use.

For example, if you want to use the built-in serial I/O function of the part, you lose two I/O pins to transmit and receive. Decide to add an oscillator to create a super-stable clock, another two pins. Use a part-to-part link such as SPI or I2C and there go another three or four pins. Therefore, pincount is a critical part of your design parameters as well.

> **NOTE:** Many chips provide both on-chip and off-chip capability. First time designers should consider using as much as possible provided by the chip, such is the on-chip oscillator. Oscillator design is one of those areas that looks simple at first glance but can really eat up your time trying to tweak things to get them correct.

Never go into the process targeting 100% utilization, that is, have every I/O pin accounted for in the critical elements of your design. Give yourself some wiggle room. I always use two I/O pins on all of my designs to drive diagnostic LEDs. While there are debuggers and single-step tools available, once your part is soldered onto your board, you need a quick-and-dirty way to tell what's going on. LEDs are the embedded engineer's equivalent of printf() statements.

Another very critical parameter you need to consider is memory. Microcontrollers such as the PIC16F690 have three main types of memory. Program memory is generally how a part is identified. The PIC16F690 is a 4K-part meaning that it contains 4K (4096) program words. It also contains 256 bytes of static RAM (SRAM) and 256 bytes of EEPROM. Look again at those numbers; that's 4K of program space and 256 bytes of space for any variables you need, loop counters, program variables, etc. The Mac I'm writing this book with has 4 GB of memory.

Program memory is where the machine code generated by your compiler is kept. It's actually executed from there as well so there's no swapping to RAM. Of the 256 SRAM bytes, some of those are used for other things so you lose a little bit there as well. EEPROM memory can be used to store data elements that may change from assembly to assembly; serial numbers are a good thing to store in EEPROM.

To a seasoned programmer that 4K number has got to be pretty frightening. But remember what I said earlier, in my first Apple approved design, a credit card reader, I had 45% free program memory. Looking at it another way, my software used 55% of the available program memory to do all functions including identifying itself to the iPhone, handling communications with the iPhone, data transfer, and processing stripe data from a credit card. For the game controller accessory the numbers were closer to 50% utilization as well as 50% free space.

How do you know how much memory to select? The short answer is to look at what I did. I am no expert in programming intricate, tight loops in PIC assembly code. In fact, I used C and made the structure of my code as reusable and understandable as I could.

In other words, seasoned embedded programmers would call me sloppy. I leaned heavily on the optimization features of my compiler to get me where I am.

That brings me to another point; the compiler you choose can have serious make-or-break consequences for your design. I actually tried a couple of compilers when I was programming my accessory firmware. I'll get more into firmware in the next chapter, but another reason I chose the PIC16 line of processors was that there were several compiler options. I could start out with a free version that came with my evaluation kit, but because of licensing agreements couldn't distribute the code. From there, I progressed to a low-cost version that I could use for code distribution and verify that my design was workable.

Later, after becoming familiar with the PIC16F690 after several projects, I felt secure enough in my decision to go all out and invest in professional optimizing compiler. Most companies will let you try out even their high-end versions for a limited time. You'll need about a week to convert from one compiler to another, but after that you can see how much an optimizing compiler might buy you. For my credit card reader, I went from a 99% utilization of program memory (meaning I had very little space left) to my 55% number. The increase in free memory made the significant investment in an optimizing compiler worthwhile. Why? Because now I can use this part with which I have become very familiar, in even more complicated designs. I don't have to learn a whole new part; I can continue to use the PIC16F690 for new designs.

In reality, any of the four microcontroller lines that were mentioned earlier should be suitable for anything you're looking to build. Your goal should be to pick a line that you feel comfortable with because you'll probably wind up sticking with it for a while. Derive the requirements for what your accessory needs to accomplish. Look at the product line you've selected and make sure that the part that works to fulfill your needs isn't at the high end of the list of parts. Give yourself some room to grow.

Although I called this section "Parts Selection," I've focused only on the processor as that is the key component of your accessory. Although there are other parts to the system, LEDs, resistors, chip capacitors, switches, potentiometers, etc., you'll tend to purchase these based on distributor and availability rather than manufacturer. Like the processor you will need to specify all these other components. For example, to add diagnostic LEDs to a system you need to consider forward voltage (the voltage at which the LED illuminates) and current draw. You can't put an LED with a forward voltage of 5 volts in a 3-volt system.

Prototyping

I talked earlier about the value of prototyping. Simply put, if you don't already have experience with embedded hardware design, then you must prototype as much of your design as possible. This will save you time and money.

Each manufacturer of embedded processors typically offers several evaluation kits with breadboard (or prototyping) areas, as shown in Figure 10–2. Each kit will include lesson materials to bring you quickly up to speed using the device. Some kits may offer multiple processors on the same board. If you can, choose a kit with a processor that meets your project's requirements. That way, most of the prototyping you do will be reusable in your final project. For example, I selected the PICDEM eval board from Microchip that contained the PIC16F690 processor (as well as two others). Since this part met the needs for my accessory, I was able to reuse much of the code that I created while learning the part. Specifically, I created and worked out the details of my UART serial routines and SPI routines even before my first card reader design iteration.

Using a prototyping or evaluation kit also provides a chance to use sophisticated debugging tools such as an In-Circuit Emulator or Debugger (ICE/ICD). These devices let you stop at any point in your program, look at registers and memory, evaluate conditions, and single-step through your program. Once you've fabricated your boards you lose that kind of intimate access to what's going on in your device.

One of the most important, practical things this ability offers you is the debugging of your firmware's communications protocols with the iPhone OS. Again, a lot of the details of the protocols are locked up inside the MFi/WWi program and covered by Apple's NDA. But, you can assume that the communications mechanism is nontrivial. There will be a major piece of software that you need to create (from scratch) to talk to the iPhone. The ability to single-step and look at registers and memory values, for me, proved invaluable in getting this part of my project accomplished successfully.

From your breadboarding area, you can create a cable interface to connect to the iPhone (see Figure 10–7). Early on in your project create a PC board to which you will mount your 30-pin dock connector. You'll learn how to obtain these parts once you're accepted in the MFi/WWi program. This is really good practice as you will most likely have to create a PCB footprint (more about this later) for the connector. Add the appropriate connections from the connector to solder points on the board. From those points, you can attach a cable to connect back to your prototyping board. Now you can connect the 30-pin connector to the iPhone (or iPod touch) and create your code using your evaluation system.

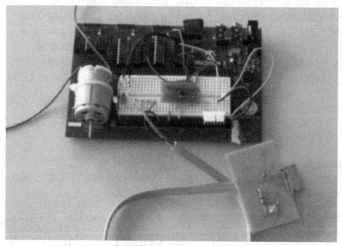

Figure 10–7. *Prototyping kit with iPhone interface cable*

By doing it this way, you're able to handle most of your testing without yet doing any major electrical design work. There are several quick turnaround PCB fabrication businesses on the Web with simple tools you can use to get a taste of PCB design. This also provides a gauge to measure your ability to perform the design and handle dealing with the fabrication vendors. If designing a board such as this is a "no brainer" for you and it works the first time, then you can be pretty confident in your skills. On the other hand, if this seems way beyond your capability, then hire someone. Most fab houses can generally refer you to several designers they've worked with to handle what you need to offload.

Unless you are already far overburdened with too many other things to do, give this process a try. Even if you wind up outsourcing most of your design work, you'll want to be able to talk to your designer in a knowledgeable manner. The iPhone interface board in the lower right of Figure 10–7 cost less than a hundred dollars including shipping. Believe me, unless you're very, very skilled (and if you were you probably don't need to read this book) or very, very lucky, you're going to make mistakes of the couple hundred-dollar variety throughout this process. Taking this step early on will go a ways to reducing the number and cost of those mistakes.

> **NOTE:** I haven't really talked about what all this (creating an accessory) is going to cost you. As with anything, there is a lot of variation depending on what you're trying to do, what you can borrow or get as a loan, etc. It's very common to negotiate with vendors to get lower rates; I've personally done that on just about everything. As a practical matter, you can expect to spend a minimum of a couple thousand dollars to get to the point where you have a working accessory. By "working accessory," I'm talking a board that you can plug into an iPhone that contains all your electronics, i.e., no mechanical housing. Let's face it, if it were easy or cheap, everyone would be doing it.

Circuit Design

I'm sure you'll agree that one section of one chapter is not enough space to teach you electronic circuit design. There are many good introductory texts on the subject, as well as tutorials available free on the Internet.

The main thing here is not to get bogged down in the details. Introductory courses will almost always start with Ohm's law and how it works. The gist of it is a way to define the primary three DC (direct current) parameters in circuits: voltage, current, and resistance. I discussed these earlier and, for the most part, that little bit is all you need to know.

Think of designing a circuit, like so many other things in life, as using a set of smaller elementary items to make something more complex; the building block approach. In the "old days" we designed using very basic parts such as resistors, capacitors, transistors, such as the simple lamp circuit in Figure 10–8. We still design using these elements, but through the growth of technology, we've also been given a set of very complex blocks to build even more complex things. Consider that, way back when, someone took a bunch of parts and made a car. Now, society takes cars, buildings, roads, and people to build communities or cities.

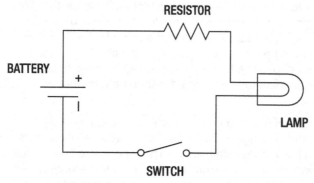

Figure 10–8. *Simple circuit*

It should be clear that your iPhone accessory circuits will be much more complicated than the lamp circuit in Figure 10–8. After all, they do so much more than turn a light on or off. On the other hand, if you view them as complex blocks arranged correctly, as in Figure 10–9, then your job doesn't look so daunting. Figure 10–9 is the top-level diagram of your Pong game controller.

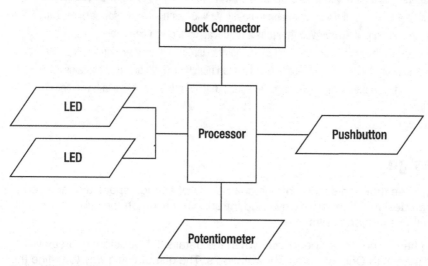

Figure 10–9. *Your Pong controller accessory*

NOTE: Certain elements of the Pong Controller have been hidden due to stipulations in the Apple Non-Disclosure Agreement.

At first, you might say, "Yeah, but there's a whole lot more in Figure 10–9 than you're showing!" My response would be, "Not really." Take another look. There's a processor in the middle that you'll program to handle the I/O with all the other parts. Then, there's the user side of things: the button, the potentiometer (knob), and the LEDs. Finally, there's a connector to attach the iPhone or iPod. What's missing is the complexity of the lines that interconnect things.

> **NOTE:** Experienced electronics designers will note that I am excluding certain elements such as oscillators, RC timing circuits, and even bypass capacitors here in favor of simplifying the discussion.

Figure 10–9 can be created using any simple drawing software or even on the back of a napkin. After that, you have to turn each single line into the correct number of connections needed to make the circuit work. For example, to light up an LED, you need to send a signal to the LED to give it power and there has to be a return path for the current to flow. So there are at least two wires that connect to the LED. As the complexity of the block increases, so does the number of connections.

At the high end, there will be many lines that go from the processor to the connector and back. Think of the connector as actually being the iPhone since that's what it attaches to. The connector itself can be thought of as just a pass-through mechanism. Since the iPhone is a computer and so is your processor, then you can anticipate a complex set of wires that travel between the two.

So where are you now? Essentially, I've broken down the job of creating the electronic representation of your accessory into putting together a set of building blocks (the easy part) and connecting them together (the hard part). How do you complete the job?

It all comes down to the fact that there are two ways to finish the job and make the connections; you can do it yourself or hire someone to do it for you. Unless you have the knowledge, confidence, money, time, and resilience to suffer several setbacks, I suggest you hire someone.

Don't think of it as giving up if you hire someone at this point. You're hiring them to finish your circuit design, not to do it for you. After all, you came up with the idea and created the block diagram like the one in Figure 10–9. You thought of and designed the system. You're hiring someone to put the finishing touches on your work.

I know that sounds like a cop-out at this point, to "punt" when things get tough, and it is your decision. You can always "keep it in-house," meaning that you or someone on your team does the actual circuit design. Again, it comes down to resources.

If you do want to give it a go and try it yourself, start by getting all the part specifications together and studying them to see which connections you'll be using. Remember, the processor will have many more functions and I/O than you'll likely be using for your first design because you'll want some margin to grow.

Though you don't have to do it now, you'll want to decide which package you'll be using when you create your PC board. There's a variety of packaging types available for parts such as the dual inline package (DIP), plastic leaded chip carrier (PLCC), ball grid array (BGA), and the quad flat no lead (QFN), as shown in Figure 10–10.

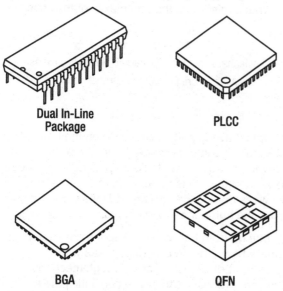

Dual In-Line
Package   PLCC

BGA   QFN

Figure 10–10. *Some IC package types*

I could go on and on about when you should use one type over another, but as an accessory developer you'll more than likely end up using the DIP and QFN types. When you start to route your connections, if you choose to do it yourself, focus on the DIP and QFN pin diagrams in your spec.

Why DIP and QFN you ask? A DIP part is easy to handle and design for. The pins are exposed and available, so it can be easy to mod (modify or change) a circuit even after the board has been created. Use DIPs to test your design concepts in the early stages, if you can afford it. It's not that DIPs are higher cost, in fact, just the opposite. But, by fabricating (making) test circuits and boards, you'll be doing at least twice the work.

Why do twice the work? By doing twice the work, you're not doing four, five, or ten times the work. By creating a test circuit that you can have access to the circuit traces and IC pins, you can make changes and get it right so that the next board you send in to be made is correct. On the other hand, if you use parts and create boards that cannot be easily modified, changing your design means fabricating the board again. Every change might require an extra fabrication cycle, and every fabrication cycle is time and money.

The reason for using QFN parts in your project is because that's how most parts for this level (complexity) of design are made. Since you'll be using parts that have fewer than about fifty pins, QFN will be the package of choice. The QFN package is designed as a good balance between spacing saving characteristics (note that there are no pins that visibly extend from the package) and cost.

The final piece of the circuit design step will be creating an electronic representation of your accessory in some sort of tool. The de facto standard EDA (electronic design automation) tool is the Cadence/OrCad suite. Not a single product, but a set of individual tools loosely coupled together, the Cadence suite is the most widely used product for circuit and PCB design. Should you wind up hiring someone to convert your design, there's a high probability he'll be using the Cadence suite.

If you want to try and do it yourself, start with one of the low-cost, quick-turn (quick turnaround time) houses such as ExpressPCB. I found ExpressPCB after researching various electronics and robotics hobbyist sites. Companies like ExpressPCB usually offer a free tool that you can download and use to create your schematic design. The process of going from an idea or hand drawn circuit is known as schematic capture. You're "capturing" your design from paper (or thought) into an electronic format.

You perform schematic capture graphically by picking your parts and then connecting the lines, as shown in Figure 10–11. Depending on the capability of the tool you use, you may have to create parts to put in your design library. This means that you'll use the part specification to create a block and all the necessary pin connections to represent your part. Common parts, such as the PIC series of microcontrollers, may already be in the library for you to click and drag your part to the drawing area. As with anything, the more it costs, the more it will probably do for you.

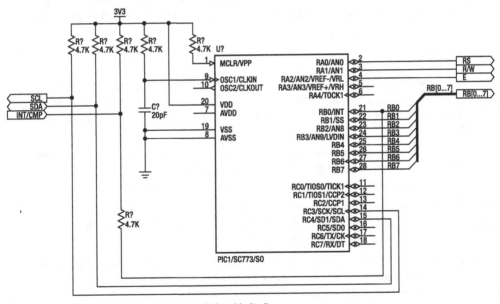

Figure 10–11. *Schematic capture (courtesy Altium Limited)*

In between the all-encompassing Cadence suite and freebies on the web, are a series of tools that offer a good balance for the occasional user. They provide everything necessary from schematic capture, PCB layout, simulation, and production support.

After looking at what was offered and what capabilities I needed, I wound up selecting Altium Designer. The tool suite did everything that I as a mid-level designer needed to do at a reasonable cost. You must do the research yourself, based on your needs and ability and especially budget. The deciding factor in my own case was the extensive set of help available in the form of both PDF and video tutorials.

Let's face it. Most tools are more or less equivalent and at the level of accessory design that you're doing, all will do the job admirably. You have to find something that you can work with comfortably. You'll also need to be able to afford it. Before selecting a tool, weigh the costs involved. Some products come with a stand-alone license that you buy and use on your PC. Others might have an electronic license that requires a connection to the Internet. Electronic licenses are lower cost, usually by a thousand dollars or more because the company can control how many copies you are using without resulting to the use of a hardware key (dongle) that they may have to provide.

> **NOTE:** While there are some EDA tools that work on the Mac, most are for the PC/Windows platform or Linux. So, yes, you need a PC to design for the iPhone!

In the end, you're going to want to use one of the free tools on the web first, such as that from ExpressPCB, to get your feet wet. You won't put out too much money and you'll learn a great deal even if you decide to hire someone to do your design work.

PCB Design

Once you have a schematic design that you're comfortable with, you'll make it real by converting the logical schematic representation to a physical one in the form of a logic board. Notice that, in each step of your process, you move your idea one step closer to reality.

If, in the last step, you chose to hire someone to capture your design into schematic form, then don't even think about doing this part yourself. PCB design is much more than getting your design to function as a combination of building blocks.

While the details of PCB design can be daunting, the basic concept is that you have a flat piece of something that is painted with copper; it's printed all the connections of your circuit onto it, and then you remove everything else.

More specifically, a sheet of insulator material is coated on the outside of both surfaces with copper. If you remove the unused copper on both sides so that only your circuit remains, then you have a two-layer circuit board. For complex designs many more layers maybe required. The sheets (called laminates) are stacked together with another material separating the laminates. You can therefore have two, four, six, etc., layer PC boards.

Because the unused material is removed before the laminate boards are layered together, as the number of layers grows, the precision needed increases. Because the circuits that run on the inner layers have to connect to a part or another layer (otherwise an inner circuit would do nothing because it could never connect to a part) inter-layer connections are needed. Called vias, these layer-to-layer connections must line up otherwise the board wouldn't work.

The good news is that most EDA tools provide mechanisms not only to convert the logical schematic into a mechanical representation, but also help with routing. In essence, you configure the shape and number of layers you want to use then convert your design to PCB representation. The tool can either place the parts for you based on some set of rules or you can do it manually as well as routing the connections for you or letting you do it. As always, the higher end tools provide more functionality at a higher price.

The essence of PCB design is the routing of traces on your board. While tools do provide autorouting, in all but the simplest cases, some traces (the copper paths that connect one part to another) will have to be done manually. When you first convert your schematic to the PCB layout, you'll usually be presented with the "ratsnest," as shown in Figure 10–12. This is a logic-physical hybrid representation of your circuit. The footprints (physical layout) of each part are shown with logical connections (lines) represented as straight lines.

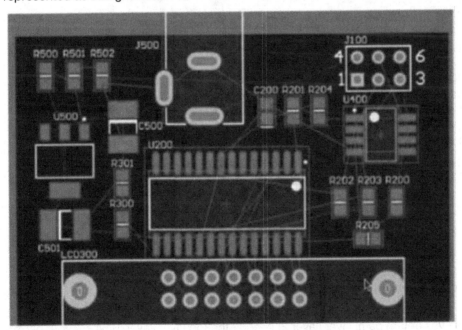

Figure 10–12. *Typical ratsnest*

This allows you to place your parts on the board where they need to be without worrying yet about the traces and how they'll be laid out. Once your parts are positioned as needed, you can proceed with routing. Generally, you'll attempt to use the autorouting feature of your tool and then finish up manually. Even if autorouting results in 100% completion, you may need to adjust things manually.

Once you've finished routing, your design will look something like Figure 10–13.

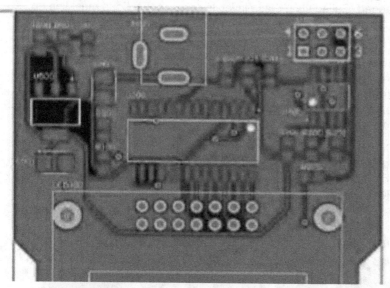

Figure 10–13. *Routed PCB*

While PCB design and layout can seem daunting, I advocate giving it a try with the free tools available from PCB manufacturing companies. You can do all the work without it costing anything except time. When you're ready to see if your design works, it'll cost you anywhere from one to a few hundred dollars. You'll have to judge whether or not you are confident enough in your abilities to fab a board.

Before moving on, I want to leave you with three suggestions to consider when implementing your own PCBs. First, consider a four-layer board with the two inner layers being power and ground, typically represented as Vdd and Vss.

NOTE: The Vdd and Vss terminology derive from the use of MOSFET transistors where d refers to the drain pin and s the source pin. You may see the terms Vcc and ground used which references the use of bipolar junction transistors (BJT). The main thing is not to confuse them as that can short out (and damage) your power source.

Place the Vss (return path) layer (layer 2) nearest the top layer (layer 1) where your parts will be soldered. In most boards of this type, you will wind up using surface mounted parts where there are no holes through the board. Even discrete components such as resistors and capacitors will be soldered to one side.

Place the Vdd (voltage source) on the other middle layer (layer 3) nearest the bottom of the board (layer 4). Putting power and ground in the middle does two things: first, it provides some shielding between layers helping to eliminate some crosstalk. Second,

Figure 8–2. *Manual credit card processor, also known as the "knuckle-buster"*

The merchant has no way of knowing if there are sufficient funds or credit for the customers' purchases. Further, because of the manual processing, the per transaction cost of doing business this way cuts deeply into his profit.

The answer lies in mobile, wireless processing. But, even with the subsidies offered by merchant processors, a wireless terminal starts at nearly $800, well beyond the reach of the small businessman.

With the iPhone and its sophisticated operating system, innovative developers quickly provided a solution; credit card processing apps for the iPhone (Figure 8–3). The iPhone requires no power other than an occasional good charge and can use either the phone line or WiFi as a medium for connectivity.

A customer brings his purchases to the vendor who types in the card number, expiration date, and the amount of the purchase. Many apps also provide the capability of Address Verification System (AVS) whereby vendors can enter additional data such as the CVV code of the card and the street address/zip code of the customer. The vendor sets up the AVS feature if he wants to accept cards with an increased sense of security that the transaction is not fraudulent.

Although it may seem complicated from the outside, the actual code to perform the transaction is no more than a POST operation to an http server. The connection is made securely using SSL/TLS (Secure Sockets Layer/Transport Layer Security) protocols that are already part of the iPhone OS. This means sending data to a web address prefixed by "https//" which takes care of network security concerns.

your boards. You can generally specify how many you want and how soon you want to get them back. Typically one week is the breaking point. The sooner you want the part, the more it will cost you. Much longer than a week and the price drop is not substantial.

If you've chosen to go more "high end" and use a professional tool, then you'll need to make sure that your design files are in the correct format for your PCB vendor. Once you've finished the PCB design part of the process you'll perform a design rules check (DRC) to make sure you haven't misconnected something or any other type of logical or wiring error. In addition, the PCB design will be checked for manufacturability.

The board layout will be tested for things like two traces being too close together, vias being too close, pads for soldering too small, and a host of other errors. Here's the kicker; you have to set those rules. Because you chose to use a generic toolset, it doesn't know what vendor you will be using, unlike a tool supplied by a specific PCB manufacturer. Before you can generate any files used to manufacture your board, you'll have to setup the rules of the system in accordance with the capabilities of your vendor.

Some vendors may only be able to do a certain width of board while others can go much thinner. Some can do very fine pitch (distance between pins) parts and others can't. Are those vendor specific, free tools starting to look more appealing yet?

The essence of the process is to create a set of computer aided manufacturing (CAM) files that you'll email to your vendor to create the board. You'll hear these referred to as Gerber files, which is the name used by a specific format of file.

There are several files created: one for each layer, one for each of the top and bottom layer's silkscreens, a drill hole file, and so on. Your PCB vendor will specify which files and in what specific format they need to manufacture your board. Some vendors have a file compatibility Web link to which you can upload your files to see if they'll work for that vendor.

While there are hundreds of PCB vendors out there, the correct choice is one that you're comfortable working with. Most vendors offer design testing before manufacturer and will contact you if anything looks like it might cause a problem. Many offer design support services such as helping with creating a footprint for a specific component.

I used this service for my initial board design. The PIC16F690 microcontroller is a QFN 20-pin package with a center pad to dissipate heat. In my haste to create the footprint, I made the center pad and pin pads too close which would create shorts when the part was placed on the board. My vendor helped me to find this issue and correct it preventing costly rework later on.

Another thing you'll want to consider is the assembly capability of your PCB vendor. Trust me, you'll want someone else assembling these tiny parts onto your board. Though you can find some QFN soldering techniques spread here and there throughout the Web, let the professionals handle it.

If it isn't obvious yet, you're going to want to order more than one board. The question of how many to order is a tough one. There used to be a commercial about a laxative and comparing it to the homeopathic effect of prunes. At that time—this was the 1960s—most families, especially in rural regions, used prunes as a laxative. The concept of chemical, over the counter laxatives was still new. The commercial started out asking a question as to how many prunes you needed to eat to relieve your constipation—was three enough—was six too many. Whenever I try to pick a number of boards to order, that commercial is always in my head.

Personally, I almost always order five boards because the cost of five is about the same as the cost of one. I always assume one will be bad. It never has been so far, but then I'm a pessimist. Also, even as good as I think my soldering skills are, I also assume I'm going to damage a board putting on parts. That I have done. That leaves three. One of those I get working and use as a "gold" reference. That is, after it works I never mess with it but set it aside to use for comparison. That leaves me two for testing.

The reason that five costs about the same as one is that most PCB vendors will panel your boards into arrays. There are certain standard panel sizes and if multiples of your board can fit, then it costs the same to make one as it does the number that fit on a panel. You can check with your vendor about what size panels they use then tweak the size of your board so that a nice multiple fits into that panel.

One thing to remember is to make sure you specify that you want your boards separated when you pick them up or they are delivered to you. It's very annoying to open your box of PCBs and find a panel of your boards rather than individual units. So remember to specify that your boards are to be de-paneled before shipping.

Try to find a PCB vendor close to where you are. You don't want to have to be shipping your boards and parts cross-country to save a few dollars, when that savings may get eaten up with shipping and rework charges. My PCB vendor is twenty minutes away and over the course of several design iterations that saved me a couple weeks of time I could use to stay ahead of my competition.

Integration and Testing

Although the title of this section sounds like a fancy term, I&T just means verifying that your board works when you get it back from your PCB vendor. Integration refers to combining your PCB with the rest of your system—the firmware, the App, and the iPhone test unit. As for testing, well, I'm assuming you know what testing means.

When you get your boards back from the PCB vendor, they should be separated (de-paneled) as discussed in the last section. Also, you should have had them install any surface mount parts, especially any leadless parts including all QFN packages.

More than likely, you'll need to add discrete components such as chip resistors and capacitors, as well as any through-hole connectors yourself. Of course, you'll need to attach the Apple dock connector. A good setup is to have a magnifying lamp with something to hold your board in place for you, as shown in Figure 10–15. Even then, you'll sometimes feel that you need an extra hand.

Figure 10–15. *Board solder assembly setup*

Be careful when soldering on the dock connector. While I cannot provide complete details on the specs of the connector, I can tell you that it is very easy to get it a little crooked. What I like to do, and this takes a little practice, is to slide the connector on and hold the board and connector with one hand then dab a little solder on one or two of the end pins. This dabbing, or tacking, will act to hold the connector in place so you can finish your soldering job. Figures 10–16 and 10–17 show the right and wrong way to hold the connector and board using this technique.

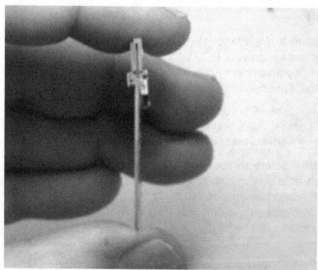

Figure 10–16. *"Right" way to hold the board and connector*

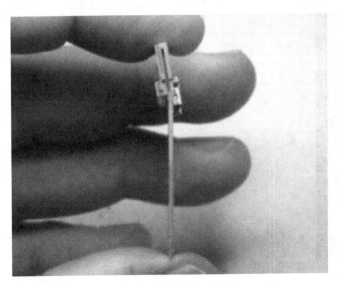

Figure 10–17. *"Wrong" way to hold the board and connector*

Once all the parts have been soldered in place, you'll want to download your firmware into your processor and test the board. If this is your first board, then it's good to do a couple of preliminary tests before trying to connect it to your iPhone. I'll talk about firmware in the next chapter, but the first test you'll want to do is to illuminate your LEDs. Simply include as the first line in your `main()` routine, the code to turn or off the LEDs. It's also good to put in some timing routines such as flashing an LED at one-second intervals. This also has the benefit of seeing if your chip setup parameters are correct relating to clock speed and timing.

In the I&T world—yes, there is an I&T world with books, specs, standards, conferences, etc.,—this would be known as "unit test." You're testing a single device (part, board, box) as a single, standalone unit. Once you've tested all you can at the unit level, it's time to move on to seeing if it works with other parts of the system. In this case, I mean the iPhone and App software.

A good idea before moving on would be to rest on your laurels a bit. Take a day away from things, relax and do something fun. Reward yourself for getting this far. The next steps may have you tearing your hair out and throwing things.

Assuming you have a set of firmware that you want to use in the end product, it's time to download it to your board and plug it into your iPhone and see if it works. I can almost guarantee you that you will get the message shown in Figure 10–18.

Figure 10–18. *The first time you connect your accessory*

If (or should I say when) you get this message, don't panic, we've all seen it. Part of your MFi/WWi membership includes the ability to purchase test equipment that will help you to solve this and other kinds of errors. When you talk with your Apple MFi/WWI manager, he'll tell you all about it. He will probably advise you to get the test equipment. Do it! In actuality, you can't complete the process without the test equipment. I can't go into details as to why—that whole NDA cop-out again.

Most of the firmware you will write for your accessory is to handle the communications between your processor chip and the iPhone OS. There are roughly a half-dozen steps that your code needs to perform to get to the point where you can start using your accessory as it was intended. At each step, your processor needs to talk to the iPhone OS and respond to it appropriately.

From this point on, it's going to be you against the Apple specifications. You will think that your code should work, but it doesn't. Your first inclination will be to ask Apple for technical assistance. Your MFi/WWi membership will give you that kind of support. However, it is not unlimited and it will be on Apple's terms as to when they get back to you and how much information they provide. My advice is when you are at the give up point and want to pass the problem off to Apple, take a break and come back in a day. I probably sent in four or five technical requests during my first development, and each and every time, I found the answer before Apple responded. In most cases, it will come to you. Also, understand that this has been done before. I did it so you can too. Go out and buy an MFi/WWi accessory and use it as a reference. Once you're in the MFi/WWi system, you'll get what I mean here.

That's about it for integration and testing. Like I said, most of your work is the battle between your firmware and the iPhone OS. You won't even need any App code (Xcode) at this point.

How long will this take? It's totally up to how you deal with these kinds of problems and how much time you have available. Generally, getting from a completed board with the initial firmware downloaded to the point where your board completes its startup and handshaking sequence with an iPhone will take a week or longer. Give yourself a month if you're doing it part-time. The good news is, once you're done with it, the code is reusable.

Summary

An accessory can be considered to be composed of: (1) a processor, (2) a connector to communicate with the iPhone device, and (3) other support logic. The processor in your accessory connects everything together and is the most critical piece of the puzzle. One of the first decisions you need to make is which processor you are going to use.

Although there may seem like a lot of processor options, it's really going to come down to some type of low-power embedded microcontroller such as the ARM 32-bit RISC, the TI MSP430 or C2000, or a Microchip PIC controller. There is no one best answer. It's a trade off of price, tool selection, power consumption, physical dimensions, capability, resources, and many others. For each type of processor, there will be evaluation boards with prototyping areas available at a reasonable cost. Select one or two that you think you'll feel comfortable with, try them out, and then make your selection.

I've described the accessory hardware design process as six basic steps: (1) parts selection, (2) prototyping, (3) circuit design, (4) PCB design, (5) board fabrication, and (6) integration and testing. If you break your process down into these measurable steps, the entire adventure won't seem as daunting as it might otherwise.

Chapter 11

Firmware

Just like the last chapter on hardware, a complete tutorial on firmware design would need a book (or several books) to itself. Even then, many would tell you that good firmware design takes more than recipes from a book; it's part art. What I'm going to do here is to give you practical tips based on my own experience.

As I discussed in chapter 4, firmware defines the program that you'll be writing and installing into your embedded processor. It's nothing magical or mysterious, just software like any other you write. Well, mostly. You'll need to take a step back from the protective world that Objective-C provides and handle most everything in your own code. In most cases there won't be any operating system support; if you need something, you'll most likely have to write it yourself.

Your first inclination might be to write your programs using the processor's native machine or assembly language. The part's spec sheets usually contain a lot of examples written this way leading the new developer to believe that's the way to go. In all but the most extreme cases, it's not.

Learning the nuances of a processor take weeks even for the most savvy and embedded designers. If you haven't had a lot (or any) experience working at this level, then you might be in for a couple months of study. Remember the bigger picture; this is about your accessory and not the details of one piece of the puzzle. Don't get bogged down in the details unless this is more about the learning experience.

I'm a PC

The first thing to understand about making accessories for the Apple iPhone and iPod touch is that you'll need to have a PC, specifically a Microsoft Windows based machine. That blows my mind every time I say it.

Most of the support tools that you'll use to create firmware for your parts, including the Integrated Development Environment (IDE), run only on Windows. A few support Linux and some compilers even run on Mac OS X, but you'll find that most of what you plan to use is Windows-based.

You could consider using Bootcamp to run Windows on your Mac, or use something like Parallels to run Windows and Mac OS X at the same time, but when a problem happens, you'll never be sure whether it's real or just something created because you're using an unusual configuration. You're going to have a lot of setbacks and frustrations as it is; my solemn advice is to minimize every problem that you can ahead of time.

Compilers

In most cases, you'll program your controller using some variant of C, typically either ANSI or not. What's the difference? You can find pages detailing the features and benefits on the Web, but, for embedded programming, one thing mainly stands out. An ANSI C compiler will adhere to strict naming conventions for functionality whereas a non-ANSI C compiler will be a little looser. Let me give an example to clarify the point.

As I've done before, I'm going to stick with the PIC16 series of microcontrollers from Microchip. One reason I chose PIC16 as a reference, especially in this section, is that there is an ANSI compiler and a non-ANSI compiler widely used for the part. The CCS C compiler for the PIC series from Customer Computer Services, Inc. is a widely used, cost-effective compiler with built-in functions that support PIC hardware. Another widely used PIC series compiler is the HI-TECH C compiler that was bought by Microchip, the manufacturer of the PIC parts.

CCS supports many built-in functions for the PIC chips such as byte conversion routines (make8(), make16()), I/O control (output_bit(),input()), and communications functions (spi_xfer(),spi_write()). Because these functions are "built-in" to the language, the compiler is not considered ANSI compliant. On the other hand, using the ANSI compliant HI-TECH C compiler, you would have to create your own function for something like make16 (convert two bytes to a 16-bit word) as follows:

```
int make16(char upper, char lower)
{
        return( ( upper << 8) + lower);
}
```

Why would you ever use the HI-TECH compiler if you have to make your own functions where the CCS version does it for you? One of the main reasons is portability. If you use the CCS compiler and its built-in functions, then the code you write is not portable to other systems that CCS doesn't support. You're locked in. You don't have to be of course. You could just code in an ANSI "style", not using any built-in functions, creating your own, so they're easy to port. But then, you're losing the advantages the CCS compiler offers. It becomes a tradeoff between ease of use versus compatibility across platforms.

If you never plan to switch platforms, then wouldn't sticking with the easier to use compiler be the right choice? However, ease of use is only one of the things you'll need to consider. In many cases, cost will be the most important factor. Fortunately, most compiler vendors offer a free version of their product for you to use; not just to try out, but to use. HI-TECH C does this with its HI-TECH C "LITE" product. It's not a trial version, but a free product. The idea is, of course, to set you up using their product and then if you ever want or need to upgrade, you're likely to stick with their product line. There's much less to learn by going with an upgrade rather than a whole new product.

Whatever route you take, carefully read the licensing agreements for the compiler. Although a company may offer you a free compiler, the license may still prevent you from commercially using the generated code in your product.

After ease of use and cost, another very important factor to consider in compiler selection is the amount of optimization offered. Because you're dealing with parts having very small memories, a good optimizing compiler can reduce memory use by as much as 50%. This means that while a non-optimized program might take up all of the memory in your part, a compiler with strong memory optimization might make a program that does the same thing and only takes up half the available memory. This is exactly what happened to me, so it's not just a theoretical possibility.

In addition to memory optimization, some compilers also provide speed optimization, meaning that the code will run faster. Sometimes speed optimization is important, but in most cases of accessory development, memory savings will be your main concern.

Programming

If you haven't programmed embedded chips before, then you're probably wondering how you get your code into one of these tiny parts. Learning how to program an embedded processor chip is another great reason to buy an evaluation kit when you're first getting started. The evaluation kit will usually contain a means to program your parts, generally in the form of an in-circuit system programmer (ICSP). Figure 11–1 shows the PICkit 2 programmer from Microchip that comes with most of its evaluation kits.

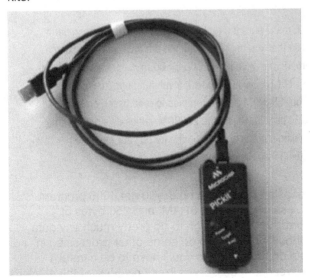

Figure 11–1. *PICkit 2 programmer for PIC16 microcontrollers*

Let's pause a moment and talk about the memory of your processor before going further into how you program that memory. As a programmer, you know that when an iPhone is advertised as having 8, 16, or 32 GB you don't get all that memory to use for your program. In fact, those numbers really refer to what is the equivalent of computer disk space but on your mobile device. Your 3GS iPhone comes with a whopping (sarcastic face) 256 MB of RAM, and if you have a 3G or Original iPhone, you're down to 128 MB. Oh, and the iPhone OS takes up part of that.

Your phone has two types of memories that you access: the solid-state drive that you use as bulk storage, and the RAM where the OS and your program execute.

Similarly, a microcontroller comes with several memory types, divided into program or data memory. Program and data represent what you put into the memory, not their design attributes. Sticking with your PIC microcontroller part, you'll be dealing with three distinct kinds of memory. The largest amount will usually be Flash and reserved for your program executable. The good news is that the program executes out of Flash and doesn't have to be loaded into RAM as with a typical desktop computer. Microcontrollers might have anywhere from 1 to 32K of program memory.

There are two types of data memory: static RAM (SRAM) and EEPROM, which I talked about earlier. SRAM stores short term values used in your program. These would be the data variables you declare such as loop counters, arrays, integer and string variables, and so on. These are elements that change or may change frequently.

You'll use EEPROM to store long-term data elements. These might be things like the serial number, hardware version, firmware version, or things like your EA Protocol. Remember the com.yourcompany.P1 values I discussed in the first part of the book? EEPROM is where you store them. It should be obvious to a seasoned programmer that you don't want to hard-code these kinds of values into your program source.

> **TIP:** When you store values in EEPROM, make sure the routines that access them are generic enough to support future modifications so that you only need change the data, not your source code. Let's say you have a protocol named: com.mynicelittlecompany.p1. Later you want to have a protocol called: com.mynicelittlecompany.p100, a value that is 2 characters longer than the first one. Don't set up your EEPROM access routines to read based on length as that can easily change. A good idea might be to always store EEPROM values as strings with a trailing 0x00 (null) then you could use a single string access routine for all your elements, assuming of course that you don't use 0x00 inside the string.

Taking the PIC16F690 microcontroller as a specific example, you get 4096 program words, 256 bytes (you read that right, I said "bytes") of SRAM, and 256 bytes of EEPROM. The program space (4KWords) is large enough to do pretty much any data capture and transfer to the iPhone. Should you want to do some other processing in your controller before passing the data on, that's where you'll have to be careful. I already mentioned that my credit card reader accessory utilizes only 55% of the 4KWord memory. So, if I can do it, you probably can too.

The place you'll want to watch yourself is the SRAM data memory. When you're moving data around, 256 bytes can be a little tight. This 256 has got to handle all your flags, counters, variables, etc. All you have to do is to declare a 100-byte string variable and you've eaten up nearly half your memory. Another little gotcha is that SRAM is not always purely contiguous. By that, I mean it may be broken up into "banks" of smaller amounts, typically 128 or 64 bytes. Again, watch out for string and array variables. Try to be frugal.

How do you program your part? Similar to the Xcode environment that Apple provides for developing Objective-C for the Mac and iPhone OS, Microchip provides the MPLAB IDE shown in Figure 11–2. MPLAB contains a desktop environment where you can edit files (program your code) or upload memory from your part to inspect your program and data areas. Everything is done as a project. You can configure a project using a wizard to specify which part you're using and which compiler. MPLAB allows other compilers to be used, not just HI TECH C.

MPLAB works with various programmers and debugging tools. Programming is just a pushbutton away. During setup, you specify which programmer and debugger you plan to use. Some programmers, such as the PICkit 2 that comes with most of the entry-level evaluation kits, offer some amount of debugging in the form of a single breakpoint where you can have your program stop.

Figure 11–2. *Microchip's MPLAB Integrated Development Environment*

Any decent IDE you use will offer a number of tutorials that will walk you through each step of the process. You'll create a project, add source files, compile, program your part, and debug your code. Most IDEs from parts manufacturers are free, but they'll only work on parts from them. More general IDEs are available that work across part types, but you'll have to pay a premium for them.

> **NOTE:** A very important thing to remember is that IDEs such as MPLAB are project based and each project should be kept in its own folder. Let me repeat that because it is that important. Keep your projects in separate folders. Never modify a project then just save it to a new name. Copy the whole folder and work on the copy. Lock anything you want to keep. The reason is that the IDE typically only saves the new project name. If you have several source files such as name1.c, name2.c, and so on, any changes to those files will be saved in the same source file—meaning that you've overwritten the good stuff.

Once you're familiar with using the IDE and compiling your code, you'll want to download that program to your controller to see if it works. The first thing you'll have to do is to connect the programmer to the evaluation board. You can see the PICkit 2 connected to a Microchip evaluation board in Figure 11–3. In many cases, the evaluation boards come with multiple parts to try out. The board in Figure 11–3 actually has three different PIC controllers. Each controller will have a port for you to connect the programmer. It may or may not be clear which port goes to which part. A common error when you cannot program your part from the IDE is that you've connected the programmer to the wrong port.

Many IDEs do not give messages telling you that programming has completed successfully. What you'll see is the lack of an error message. Check your IDE manual carefully to determine what indicators it gives you.

After a part is programmed, the program will immediately begin executing, usually from the start of your main() function. What I like to do is to flash an LED to indicate that the program has begun. Turn on an LED for a half a second or so, then turn it off. This lets you know your program is working and you can begin testing.

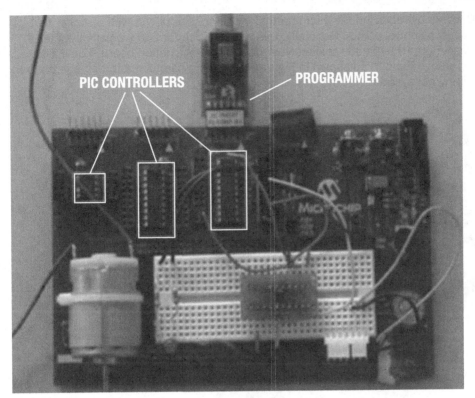

Figure 11-3. *Programmer connected to evaluation board*

Debugging

It probably would have been more politically correct to title this section "Testing" or some other more positive sounding word, but let's cut to the chase; your program will always have problems. You've misunderstood the specs for the part somewhere, or forgot to install the latest compiler update, yet it doesn't matter because something is bound to go wrong. And that's a good thing. It's from the mistakes you make and subsequently correct that you learn.

Your IDE will have a number of debugging tools you can use to figure out what's wrong with your program. In general, you should have a view utility to see the memory locations inside your part. There will be a way to single step through your program. You should have the capability to set at least one breakpoint; a place you can run your program up to and stop. This minimal capability should be a part of the basic evaluation kit.

For more advanced debugging, you might want to consider an In-Circuit Debugger (ICD), a more advanced hardware tool giving more control over your part. An ICD may also have the ability to program your part as well. The major benefit of an ICD over what you get in the standard evaluation kit is the ability to set multiple hardware breakpoints.

An ICD works by replacing the microcontroller chip in your circuit with a similar part that has more control points. Generally, this will be in the form of a small daughter board (see Figure 11–4) that replaces your part on the evaluation board. You'll first need to remove the part as shown in Figure 11–5, being careful not to damage the part or bend any of its leads.

Figure 11–4. *ICD daughter board*

Figure 11–5. *Extracting the microcontroller part*

When you insert the daughter board containing the interface for the ICD, be sure to observe the correct orientation of the part. Most evaluation boards use Dual Inline Package (DIP) parts and will have a small notch at the top of the part. This notch will also be shown on the part outline, usually in white ink, on the board (see Figure 11–6).

Figure 11–6. *Notch at the top of the microcontroller*

Once the DIP part has been removed, install the ICD daughter board, as shown in Figure 11–7. It's very easy to misalign or bend the pins as you're installing the board. A good technique to use would be to look down the side of the part as you're placing the pins atop the socket to make sure they line up properly

Figure 11–7. *Installing the ICD daughter board*

Once you've installed the ICD daughter board, connect the cable to your PC and configure the debugger in the IDE. In your source code window, double-click on a line of code to set the breakpoint. You'll see an indicator to the left of the line that may look like a "B" inside a circle or something similar depending on the manufacturer.

From this point forward, the debugging you do for your embedded code is similar to using GDB when testing your iPhone software from within Xcode. It's a good idea to get as much of your firmware debugged at this point as is possible. Remember, you're working on the evaluation kit, not the PCB you had or will have manufactured. Any connections you have designed onto your board, you'll want to try and incorporate them in the prototyping area of the eval kit. If there are parts of the system that you can't duplicate or would be too difficult to do on the eval board, comment them out, or jump around them temporarily.

To summarize, you're going to work with your code in two places. First, you want to test as much as you can with it executing on your evaluation kit so you can use the full capabilities of your ICD or whatever debugger you use. At a minimum, you'll have the ability to stop on a single breakpoint and examine the internal memory of the part. When you're ready to move to the PCB you've made, you're going to lose almost all of those tools. This is where those LEDs you installed will come in handy.

Unlike the evaluation kit, your board has the parts soldered directly to the board so there's no way to use an In-Circuit Debugger. You could, if you had the time and money, design your initial board to use socketed parts so that you could connect an ICD or other debugging system. It's going to depend on the complexity of your system.

Let's say you have a design like the game controller that uses only a few I/O lines to some switches, knobs, and LEDs. This is something that's easy to prototype on an evaluation board with the only unknown being how to connect to your iPhone or iPod touch device. As described in Chapter 10, a really good tool would be to have a connector mounted to a small PCB that you can wire to your prototyping area. I've shown this again in Figure 11-8.

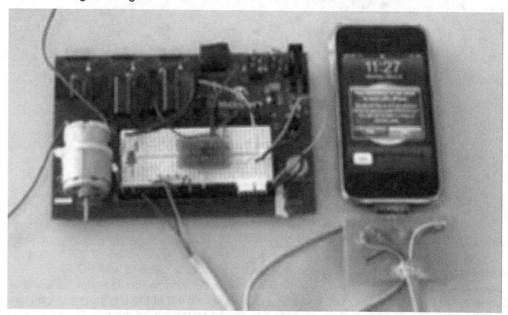

Figure 11–8. *Connecting the evaluation kit to an iPhone*

By connecting the evaluation kit to your test device (iPhone), you can use your IDE's debugging tools every step of the way. Conceivably, you could get your software running perfectly before even fabricating your first test board.

Just as when I described running Windows on your Mac to save the cost of buying a PC, you're apt to have some issues with this setup as well. One thing to consider is that you're now using a cable to go between your microcontroller part and the iPhone. This adds resistance to the circuit that could create timing problems. You're adding something to the system under test that won't be there in the final product. If problems show up when you're testing the real board, you'll need a way to determine whether a problem is real, or just there because of the way you set up the test system.

Overall, the benefits generally outweigh the negatives using a setup like the one shown in Figure 11–8. You save time and money by being able to debug all or nearly all of your firmware before dealing with the expense of fabricating a PC board. Plus you're not only debugging the firmware, but the overall design. You could, using this setup, discover for example that the LEDs draw too much current or maybe that the potentiometer needs a different base resistance. For the record, this was the way I debugged my first project.

Your PCB

If you didn't get enough of hardware in Chapter 10, I'm going to throw a little bit more your way now.

At some point, you're going to have to bite the bullet and fabricate your PC board. This is sort of like your "point of no return". If you're going to fab a board, you'll want to have your PCB vendor assemble, at a minimum, all the surface mount parts. You'll need to have purchased any parts needed, including those available through the Apple MFi/WWi program. This is all on top of any tools or design services you have already bought. Expect this phase—the board fabrication and preliminary assembly—to run about five hundred dollars. The actual cost will mainly depend on how soon you want to get your boards back. The quicker you want them, the more of a premium you'll need to pay.

For the brave of heart, there is a way to reduce the price a bit; you could consider putting the surface mount parts on yourself. There are two different ways to possibly go about doing this. The first would be to hand-solder the parts onto the board. It's hard but not impossible. You'll need to make the pads on your board extend out from the part a little more than normal. Generally, you'll want to increase the "toe length" by about 50% outside the boundary of the part. You can see this in Figure 11–9.

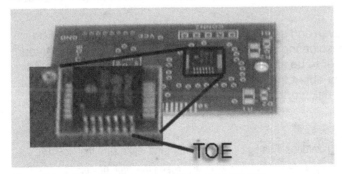

Figure 11–9. *Toe of the pad extended away from the part*

This allows you a place to touch the tip of your soldering iron. After you've cleaned the pads with soldering flux, align the part centrally to all its pads. This is where it gets tricky and requires a steady couple of hands. Apply a tiny bit of solder to the tip of your iron; you can't apply solder with one hand and hold the iron with the other as you'll likely bump the part out of position. Use your free hand to hold the part in place with a pick or tiny screwdriver or set of tweezers. Touch the iron tip to the pad as far away from the part as you can. The solder should "wick" or flow up to the part and make the connection. Once you've done this (it's also called tacking the part in place), you can then use both hands to apply solder, still staying as far from the part as you can. I did say it was hard. Chances are that you'll mess up a few times before getting it right.

The second way to assemble surface mount parts to your PCB uses the same technique as your PCB vendor. This procedure needs solder paste that comes in a tube or jar and costs a little more than standard wire-solder. You'll also have to buy a small toaster oven that can be found for less than fifty dollars in any discount store. You might even try a local thrift shop to get one cheaper.

There are a number of tutorials with descriptions and timelines on the web so I won't repeat the details here. However, the basic procedure is to clean the board as you did before with flux, then apply a small amount of solder paste across pins for all the parts you're going to mount. Here, you're going to be attaching all parts at once. Once the paste is applied, place the parts in their respective positions. Then, in essence, all you do is bake your board.

> **NOTE:** It's actually a little more than just "baking" the board with the parts on it. There's typically a very specific heating curve that needs to be followed depending on the type of solder you use. The oven has to heat to a certain temp, usually about 400 degrees F and then stay there until all the solder melts. This typically takes 60-90 seconds. All this is followed by a cool-down period.

The solder wicks or flows onto the pins of the part creating a nice, even connection. The great thing about this is that the part will naturally adjust to be centered onto the pads because of the way the solder flows. There are many examples of this with illustrations at various robotics and electronic hobbyist web sites. I've even had companies that sell soldering tools recommend this toaster oven technique for manufacturing quantities of a hundred or fewer parts.

Because you have to buy the oven and solder paste, your cost savings is going to be slightly less than with the hand soldering technique. Expect the cost of assembling your boards through your PCB vendor to be about one hundred and fifty dollars. You could get an oven and solder paste for about fifty bucks if you put some effort into it. The question you have to ask is the risk worth the hundred dollar savings. You'll need to make that choice.

> **CAUTION:** Solder fumes can be hazardous. Read all labels carefully and make sure that you use skin and eye protection and have adequate ventilation when performing this type of work.

When your board is ready to test, you'll program it using either the programmer that came with your evaluation kit or one you bought separately. Depending upon the type of part you selected for your accessory's controller, you'll have five or more pins that you'll need to connect to. These are power, ground, data in, data out, and a control pin used to tell the part that it is being programmed. These pins may or may not be shared with other functions; you or your designer will have addressed that much earlier.

A typical ICSP connector will be a five-pin header strip set at 0.1" spacing. You can see the ICSP header on your game controller accessory in Figure 11–10.

Figure 11–10. *ICSP header on game controller*

You install the firmware by connecting a programmer such as the PICkit 2 to the ICSP header, as shown in Figure 11–11, then initializing the download through the IDE.

Figure 11–11. *Connecting a programmer to the target board*

Structure

I've talked a lot about what it takes to test your firmware but have been skirting the issue of its design or more specifically, structure. Depending on the part you select and the amount of program memory it contains, you'll find three basic choices when it comes to designing your code. First, there's the bare-bones approach. Your code will run directly on the hardware with no other support like you get when running on iPhone OS or any other operating system.

At the other end of the spectrum, you can include a real-time (or near real-time) operating system (RTOS). Many companies provide an RTOS for various higher-end microcontrollers. The more functions and support you require, the more memory your part will need to have. In turn, this will drive your part cost, and more importantly, its power requirements. The trade-off is ease of use (through the services an RTOS provides) versus power consumption (by using a part with a low enough power requirement, you can use the iPhone as a power source and not have to add a battery circuit).

Between the extremes of a full RTOS and no OS support at all, you'll find a few alternatives. Generally these will be a set of support routines that may or may not include some kind of real-time kernel. In fact, a number of RTOS products are scalable so that you can configure the minimal support that you need. You generally start with the base kernel then add the features you need such as semaphores, locks, memory pools, mailboxes, etc.

What is a kernel? A kernel is the central part of the operating system; it's the layer of software that communicates directly with the hardware. The kernel deals with handling the processor's address spaces, manages any threads of execution, and may provide for interprocess execution. In a RTOS, the kernel will likely handle process scheduling and interrupt context switching.

Because a kernel is necessarily small and provides the sole interface between the hardware and your application, it can give you guaranteed context switch times for most of the things necessary in real-time embedded systems. There are many RTOS kernels available for common embedded systems. Symbian is the number-one OS found in mobile systems and runs on ARM processors. Pumpkin Inc. makes a very small RTOS called Salvo for embedded systems that runs on a number of different processors including 8051, ARM, TI's MSP430, and the PIC microcontroller series. Pumpkin offers a free "lite" version that you can try out.

When you look at a product such as Salvo, you can see the advantages of using a RTOS. Because Salvo runs on different processors, by designing your code to work with something like Salvo, it can be easily ported to different platforms.

While this might seem like a good thing, think about how many times you might need to port your accessory code to a different processor. More than likely, the answer is never. Even if you do have to, for some reason, port it to a new processor, it's far more likely that you'll just use another product in the same line. I can attest to this personally. While I've always had intentions of porting my code to an ARM processor, I've never had the need to do so. In one of my projects, I found that the PIC16F690 did not have enough memory so I selected another processor in the same line, the PICLF1936. Other than changing some I/O pins around, the code compiled and ran without a hitch.

Designing with an RTOS or even a kernel is outside the scope of what I plan to cover. I'd like to provide you with that information but the RTOS vendors will give you much better tutorials on their products than I can. Learning the nuances of using the features of an RTOS takes at least a week and that's in a class setting with customer support right there. More than fifteen years ago, I took the introductory VxWorks class from Wind River Systems, a major RTOS player. The class was a week long and at least half the class, all practicing software engineers, came away from the class still unable to grasp how to use the product. Yes, they could install it, create programs, and basic stuff, but they were still weeks away from meshing it with their own specific projects.

In some complex systems, you may benefit from or possibly even need an RTOS to get the job done. However, because this is your first accessory it should be far from complex. It's that whole walk before you can run thing you've got to get going here.

So if you're not using a real-time OS or any OS for that matter, then how do you structure your code? Most people will find the answer as horrible as saying you're going to write a flowchart; the answer is to use a superloop. A superloop is nothing more than a software loop that never exits. Generally, you create a superloop using while(1) { } and everything in the brackets just continually executes. The "1" in the parenthesis can be replaced with anything that always evaluates to true, but "1" is the usual value.

Therefore, a typical accessory program might look like the following code:

```
// begin source code
{ code to configure the processor }
#include …..
{ support routines and variables }
{initialization code }
{ establish communications with iPhone OS}
while (1)              // superloop
{
 handle everything
}

// end of source code
```

I admit it's a little simple, but this is pretty much the way it's been done for decades. You might ask, "Where's the interrupt code?" That's a good question. It's actually in two different places…well, sort of. Processors have various sources of interrupts, but there's typically one interrupt that fires. This means that you might have a single interrupt routine that gets called and it has to determine the source of the interrupt. This usually means examining certain interrupt flags and taking a certain action depending on which flag was set. It could be that multiple flags are set meaning that more than one interrupt happened at nearly the same time.

You might think that this interrupt code would be inside the superloop, but it's not. The interrupt code is really no more than a special type of subroutine that can get called. As such, it would be in the support routine section in the preceding pseudocode (another dirty word). The interrupt code will usually be defined by a special keyword much like a compiler directive. In fact, that's exactly what it is. Look at the following code:

```
interrupt
(void) isr_routine(void)
{
        if (RBIF) {
        flag1 = TRUE;
        RBIF = 0;
        }
        If (TMR1IF) timer_flag = TRUE;
} // end isr_routine
```

The "interrupt" is a compiler directive to make sure this routine is handled as an interrupt routine and not an ordinary subroutine. This usually means that fewer registers are pushed onto the stack which means you need to take care of such things. It also means that this routine will activate very quickly as there is much less overhead involved.

> **NOTE:** You cannot use `return` in an interrupt routine as `return` is for a typical subroutine and not an interrupt service routine (ISR). If you do use `return` in your ISR, your stack pointer will pop to a different point from where it was pushed and then everything will go downhill from there. You'll hear the term "lightweight" used to describe ISRs. This means that the work done to switch the program counter (PC) to point to the ISR is not bogged down (or made heavy) with unnecessary saves and restores of values.

Notice how small the interrupt service routine is. This routine checks for two different types of interrupts. The first part checks the RB flag and if it is set, makes the program variable flag1 TRUE and then clears the RBIF flag. Note that in the second check of the timer1 flag, you don't need to clear the flag. You'll need to check your processor specs to see which flags have to be manually cleared and which are automatically cleared when they are read. As with the first section, if the timer 1 flag is set, meaning the timer has rolled over, then you set the program variable timer_flag.

Resist the urge to do "stuff" in your ISR. It will be very tempting to just send out a byte or maybe read a program value from the potentiometer. That's what the superloop is for and the reason you set those program variables. In essence, your superloop could be a series of if statements that check to see if a certain program variable was set and then call the necessary routine. In the following code, your superloop checks flag1 and timer_flag calling the appropriate routine.

```
// superloop
while(1)
{
        if (flag1) get_external_data();
        if(timer_flag) reset_external_io();
} // end super loop
```

It's simple, crude, and ugly, but it works and it's quick. I'll point it out yet again; the competition is nipping at your heels and now is no time to try to be politically correct by adhering to the latest software fad.

Another aspect of structure I want you to consider early on is how you partition your code among the different files in your project. As you know, you'll have .h and .c files mirroring the .h and .m files in Xcode. The .h, or header files, contain the references to variables or function calls that exist somewhere in the program, but not in the associated source file. Let me describe an example to clarify.

One method that works well is to partition the major functions in your program into separate h and .m pairs. For my credit card reader, I use four such pairs. The largest section contains the code that makes the connection to the iPhone OS. As this pair will always be used in every accessory, I call the files BASE.H and BASE.C. Note that the file names are capitalized. This is the standard used by MPLAB, the IDE from Microchip.

The other sets of files I use are SERIAL.H and SERIAL.C for the code than handles the USART communications; SPI.H and SPI.C for the serial peripheral interface code, a master-slave chip-to-chip communications mechanism. You should learn to use the SPI interface, trust me. Finally, READER.H and READER.C contain the code specific to the card reader part.

Getting back to the references issue, take the SERIAL code for example. The SERIAL.C module contains all the functions that operate the processor's USART. The header file, SERIAL.H, contain the names of those functions with the keyword extern to indicate they are external references. This is because the BASE.C file will need to make USART calls to move data back and forth to the iPhone OS.

But SERIAL.H is also a place to store things like #defines that are specific to the serial code. This means that both SERIAL.C and other files such as BASE.C will include the SERIAL.H file. Again, the base code includes it to make sure that a call to something like write_serial() aren't flagged as errors but are instead treated as external references. The local serial code includes it because SERIAL.H contains all the specific stuff used by the serial algorithms.

Sounds okay, right? The problem comes because SERIAL.H has labeled the write_serial() routine as extern meaning that including it locally (in SERIAL.C) will cause an error. How do you fix it? The common way is to use the compiler directive #ifndef to exclude sections of the file if a certain compiler variable is not defined.

For example, the SERIAL.H file may look something like the following:

```
#define BAUD    19200
#define BITS    8
#ifndef _SERIAL_
extern  void    write_serial();
extern  void    put_c16()
#endif
```

Then, in the SERIAL.C file you might have:

```
#define _SERIAL_
#include "SERIAL.H"
```

What happens in the first bit of code is that the external functions are only defined at all if the compiler variable _SERIAL_ is not defined. You use _SERIAL_ to define the file it is in as the serial source file. Then you include the SERIAL.H file exactly the same way no matter where it is needed. Because the compiler variable is only defined in the SERIAL.C, or serial source file, that's the only place the functions are not declared externally. That's good because this is the source file where they are declared by definition locally. In all other files, including the SERIAL.H, files declare the functions externally so you can use them and the linker makes all the connections when you build the code.

Chip Configuration

The last point I want to make about your software is that you usually need to configure your chip as the very first part of your source code. Each processor out there has a variety of ways it can be configured. Some processors have the capability to protect the program memory so your competitors can't read it. Why would you ever want it not to be protected? If you can't read it then you can't debug it, so until you have an absolute final code build, leave the memory unprotected.

Most chips will also have a watchdog timer, or WDT. This timer runs in the background and when it rolls over (goes from all 1s to all 0s) it generates a WDT interrupt. The WDT interrupt may be very specific in that you don't create a WDT routine to use. So what happens? When the WDT interrupt is generated the program counter is set to zero to force a processor reset. This is great to keep your code from hanging up. Unfortunately, it adds complexity to your code in that you'll need to manually reset the WDT before if overflows.

Another common feature is master clear, MCLR. This is basically a reset line that you can use to reset your system. This may or may not be a good thing to have on an accessory. Think of it this way, if you provide a master reset, say, a little recessed button somewhere, then you've said to your customers, "Hey, this thing might hang up"; not a good start at establishing confidence.

But what if it does hang up? It's an accessory! Even the dumbest of users will disconnect then reconnect it to the iPhone to try and fix the problem (well, probably most of them). Since you've designed it that way—to reset when first connected to the iPhone dock connector—you don't really need a separate reset.

What else? The specific things you need to configure will, of course, depend on the particular part you're using. For example, when you use the PIC16 series, you can use a number of different oscillator options. An oscillator is basically a continuous series of 1s and 0s that drive the clock input of your processor. Without an oscillator or clock input, your processor doesn't run. So you have to have it.

A PIC16, like most embedded processor chips, has an option of an internal oscillator. It's not extremely accurate, but for most cases it works fine. One thing to keep in mind, every aspect of your processor's timing is derived from this clock. If you have a specific baud rate your RS232 port needs to use, check the spec to see (1) if the clock rate you select can be divided to create that rate, and (2) if the amount of error is acceptable.

What does it look like to configure the processor? Here's an example configuration statement from one of my projects:

```
__CONFIG( INTOSC & NOMCLR &NOWDT & UNPROTECT);
```

This statement is specific to a certain PIC processor and the HI TECH C compiler. Note that the CONFIG command starts with two underscores, not one. The command specifies that you'll use the internal oscillator. There is no master clear line, the watchdog timer is not enabled, and you are not using memory protection. Also, note the semicolon at the end of the statement. All compilers work a little differently so make sure to study how to set this up. Not getting the configuration set up correctly is one of the easiest mistakes you'll make.

Summary

I've tried to cover the most common issues that you'll need to address when creating the firmware for your accessory. First off, you'll more than likely want to have a Windows-based PC at your disposal for design work and firmware development. Though you could run your compiler and development environment on Windows running on a Mac, you'll find that running them on the machines they were intended for will eliminate uncertainty when problems arise.

Using any of the major embedded processors, you'll likely have a choice when it comes to compilers. Try out the free ones first, but don't skimp when it comes to choosing a final compiler. While the cost difference could be as much as several hundred dollars, one compiler could save you 50% in terms of memory utilization. The several hundred dollars you might save could be easily eaten up if you need to switch processors because your compiler wasn't efficient enough.

All embedded processors that you might use for accessory development come in evaluation versions that include the processor on a prototyping board, IDE and compiler tools, and lessons to get you started. This structured introduction could save you weeks of time in coming up to speed on a particular type of device. It's a "must have" for the beginning embedded systems developer.

The firmware you wind up developing to run on your embedded processor can be constructed as a superloop using interrupts to set local program variables. Then, inside the superloop, simple if-then statements can be used to test the variables to see what processing needs to be done. It's simple and crude, but works well for the types of simple, embedded systems used in accessory design.

Chapter 12

Everything Else

With the exception of the secrets that lie within Apple's MFi/WWi program that I've sworn a blood oath (and signed an NDA) to protect, I've given you most of the bits you need to begin working on your own accessory designs. You should now understand the basics of the EAAccessory frameworks and what you need to do to create an iPhone app that uses them. I told you why it's a good idea to look at joining the various Apple developer programs, including the MFi/WWi program. To reiterate, if you want to build an accessory, you must join the program. There's no other way to get the information.

Finally, in the last two chapters I tried to provide a lot of hints and tips in the areas of hardware and software design. There's simply too much material and not enough time to provide an exhaustive discussion of the design process itself. By now, you probably already have your "way" of doing things, especially in the software context. Rather than try to mold you into something else, I hope I've given you something that you can work with to possibly incorporate into your own process.

In this final chapter, I want to continue that help by giving you more stuff that you can hopefully use. This chapter covers all those things that don't fit nicely into a category such as hardware or software. I'll talk about tools and test equipment, mechanical design, packaging, and business processes.

Tools and Test Equipment

How much equipment you decide to purchase will depend on a number of factors. If you decide to do a lot of the board design work yourself, then you'll likely want to have most of everything I'm going to talk about. If, however, you decide to hire someone to do the hardware work, then you could significantly pare down the list. Just about everything can be found secondhand on Craigslist or eBay. Even high-end items like an oscilloscope can be purchased this way. Just the other day, I saw a Tektronx 465 dual trace oscilloscope on Craigslist for $150. It was one of those situations where the guy didn't know what he had (or at least that was the impression I got) and just wanted to get rid of it.

Tools

To begin, unless you plan to have someone else do all the hardware work for you, including assembly of all parts on the board, you're going to need a decent soldering iron. Generally, something like a variable temperature Weller, like the one shown in Figure 12–1, works really well. New, these units cost anywhere from $80 to $120. It's a fairly easy thing to find on eBay for under fifty bucks.

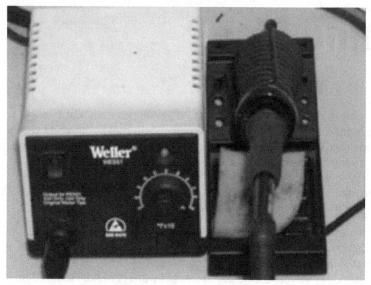

Figure 12–1. *Low-end soldering station with variable temperature*

Stay away from the cheap soldering irons you can buy for below twenty dollars. Generally they will have very large tips that don't offer you fine enough accuracy or a hot enough temperature. You'll want something that can get up to about 750 degrees Fahrenheit.

This type of system works well for soldering in basic surface mount parts such as chip resistors and capacitors as well as connectors and any through-hole parts you might decide to use. If you plan to do more of the work in house and possibly even see yourself trying your hand as soldering on chips, then you may want to consider a hot air station like the one shown in Figure 12–2.

Figure 12-2. *Hot air solder station*

A hot air station provides heated air through a handle that you can direct at the parts on your board. It offers a touchless solution reducing the risk of destroying sensitive parts. It's absolutely necessary if you ever need to remove a QFN or other surface mount package as it heats all the pins evenly. Make sure that you shop around before making this purchase, though. I found the unit in Figure 12-2 at a good price and it has served me well for rework and removing parts. However, I learned later on that the air stream was a little too strong to place surface mount chips on my boards. If you want to place (install) small parts, then look for a station with an airflow in the few cfm (cubic feet per minute) range. A flow of more than 10 cfm will blow your parts around too much to place accurately.

Speaking of placing parts, don't expect to be able to do it by hand. You'll need at least one good pair of tweezers. This is definitely something you can scrimp on. Because I do a lot of work with surface mount parts, I got the tweezer kit shown in Figure 12-3. It's definitely more than you'll need for just about any accessory project.

A single pair of cheap tweezers with a curved tip can be found at most hobby supply stores for about five dollars. You mainly want something that opens wide enough for the parts you'll be placing. So that you don't have to always apply pressure to hold a part, you can put a soft rubber band around the part of the tweezer you hold with your fingers. Then, the rubber band will keep the tweezers closed holding your part so that you can more easily maneuver it around the board.

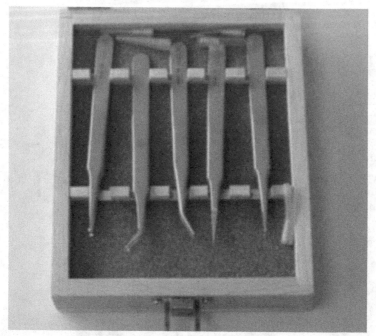

Figure 12–3. *Surface mount tweezer set*

To do any soldering you'll need—you guessed it—solder. Get a very thin, about 0.02 inch diameter, 63/37 solder. The numbers mean that the solder contains a mixture of 63% tin and 37% lead. This mixture is known as eutectic solder and has the lowest melting point to help minimize damage to sensitive components. If you want to do any major surface mount work such as soldering your own IC packages, then you'll want to get a solder paste.

You'll also want some solder flux and tip cleaner. You apply flux to the board pads before placing your component. Heat the flux so that it melts and cleans off all the connections. This will help to make the solder flow much better when placing your components. Tip cleaner comes in small tins and is used to make the business end of your soldering iron distribute heat more uniformly. A lot of people forgo tip cleaner because it seems such a little thing. Take a look at Figure 12–4 and the difference between a cleaned and an uncleaned tip. Trying to use the tip on the left side is like trying to cook on a pan that someone burned dinner in and never cleaned it.

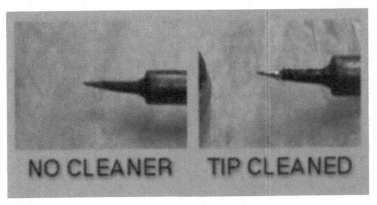

Figure 12–4. *Soldering iron tip before and after cleaning*

You may think that I've beaten soldering to death, but not even close. Remember, you're dealing with very small parts that can easily move on the board. You'll need some method to hold the board still while placing and soldering your parts. The simplest and least expensive way is to just secure your board at the corners with something like electrical tape. Then, you place the parts on the board and hold them with a pair of tweezers. It works well but you need to be careful of static discharge. Specifically, you don't want to do this on a plastic surface that could retain a charge that might destroy your parts.

While I'm on the subject of electrostatic discharge (ESD), you'll want to make every effort to reduce ESD in your work area. I could suggest antistatic mats and work surfaces as well as wrist straps to ground your body, but I know that's unlikely as I've never met another engineer that can wait to get started. If you can, at a minimum keep all your parts in their protective storage until they're needed and avoid touching ICs with your hands.

Your parts will come in antistatic bags or tubes from the supplier. Never take out a part into your hand then place it back into the container unless your body is properly grounded. Move parts from one protective container to another when pulling them out for assembly. Avoid touching parts by their leads even if you're using tweezers. The leads are the direct line to the sensitive internal components.

Here's the thing: a part can be damaged by ESD and you might not even know it. You might place the part and it works fine, then later on down the road when you're debugging software something weird keeps happening. You search and search for why your program isn't working. However, it's not the software at all but a part that's been damaged by ESD and the error shows up as an intermittent failure. It really does happen.

NOTE: I've been a little light on the subject, but ESD should be taken seriously. Ground yourself and your work area. Take precautions when handling any sensitive electronic parts. Don't add to the cost of your project by introducing problems that can be prevented.

Depending on how much PCB work you plan to do you might only need a simple board holder that uses alligator clips like the one shown in Figure 12–5. It should handle all the small, single board jobs you're likely to do starting off developing accessories. If you do plan to graduate to small quantity manufacturing, the Panavise shown in Figure 12–6 can hold a number of boards at the same time allowing you to scale up your production rate. Using the Panavise, you're able to assemble four accessory PCBs at a time.

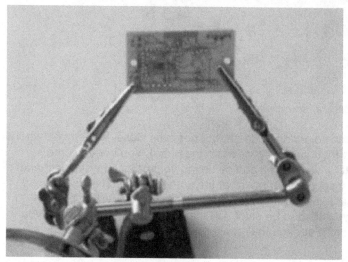

Figure 12–5. *Low-cost single PCB holder*

Figure 12–6. *Sturdy, multiple-board holder from Panavise*

Test Equipment

Once your accessory board is assembled, you'll need one or two pieces of test equipment to make sure things are working correctly. As part of the MFi/WWi program, you will have the option of purchasing an accessory test system. Because of the NDA, I obviously can't go into details or show you any pictures. The one thing I can say is to get it. Make no mistake; you cannot develop an accessory without it. It is an absolute must-have.

The next piece of equipment you'll want is a multi-meter that has a tone setting in the resistance (Ohm's) scale for tracing out paths in your PCB. In the early stages of testing your board with the firmware installed, you'll come across problems related to the path from one part to another. In the game controller, this might be from the processor to the pushbutton. For some reason, you might not be getting any response when you push the button. The first thing you'll want to do is to check for continuity between the associated parts.

With the pushbutton, this might mean from the voltage source to a pull-up resistor to one terminal of the button and then to the input pin of the microcontroller. Next, you'd check from the other pin of the pushbutton to ground. Because the board is so small and the pins on the parts are so close together, having an audible tone when the circuit is complete keeps you from having to take your eyes away from the board.

In fact, you may rarely, if ever, use the other parts of the multi-meter. On occasion, you might check a voltage level or the actual value of a chip resistor, but mostly you'll be looking for opens or shorts in your board. Remember how I talked about using a four-layer PCB design with the power and grown planes on the two internal layers? Because you're mostly going to be concerned with signal levels (not power or ground), you want to have access to the signal paths by putting them on the outer layers. Also, having accessible test points—places where you can touch the tip of your probe—means you don't have to try to place your probe on the edge of a part with fine pitch connectors.

Speaking of signal levels, you'll really want to invest in an oscilloscope. You're not so much concerned here with identifying the structure of each and every signal, but you do want to know if they are present and get a rough idea of how they look. A practical solution would be a dual trace scope with at least a 60 MHz bandwidth. A 200 MHz bandwidth would really let you see the nitty-gritty details of the signals and would be good if you plan to send higher speed signals such as audio or video through your accessory.

I found the scope shown in Figure 12–7 on eBay for a couple hundred dollars and it has served me well. In some situations, I would not have been able to continue if it weren't for the o-scope. In particular, if you are debugging something like a SPI or I2C serial connection between two parts on your board (trust me, you need to understand at least one of these), a scope can be invaluable. Certain levels have to follow certain patterns and without being able to see the signal levels, you're feeling around in the dark.

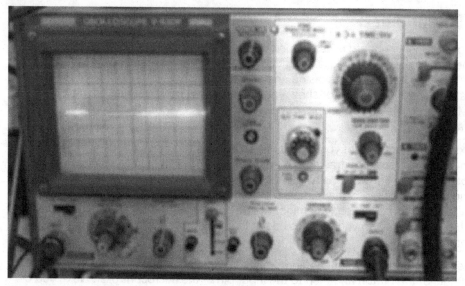

Figure 12–7. *A decent oscilloscope is essential to debugging certain signals*

If you're young and have great eyesight you can skip ahead, but the rest of us might want to consider some type of magnifying device to examine the boards. The pins on the parts you'll be using are so close together it's nearly impossible to single out a specific pin with confidence. Imagine trying to solder a jumper wire on the board from one pin to another without help.

Though a magnifying lamp is a good investment, if you really want to get up close consider a stereoscopic inspection microscope like the one shown in Figure 12–8. This is great for doing close-up work on very small boards and parts. A wide 5X set of optics works well; it gives you enough magnification with a wide enough field of view, so you don't have to continuously search for where you are working.

I found the unit in Figure 12–8 on eBay and picked up an LED lamp and 5X eyepieces for about $300. I actually bought it for my repair business but it came in very handy when working on accessory PCBs. It's not a "must-have" for doing accessory work, but if you're the type of person who plans to be really hands-on with the hardware side of things, you'll want to consider it. Also, the company I bought it from sells these new on eBay, so it's probably going to be available whenever you need it.

Figure 12–8. *Stereo inspection microscope*

I think I've beaten the tools and test equipment subject to death. But before moving on, I want to reiterate that you do not need everything I've talked about to perform accessory development. For what it would cost you to get all the stuff I've mentioned so far, you could probably hire a good, experienced engineer to develop your boards. What's more, by selecting a practicing engineer, you'll almost definitely have a higher success rate than if you tried it yourself.

Mechanical Design

When the point comes where your accessory PCB begins functioning correctly, you need to consider what the final product will look like. You can't ship your product as a circuit board; it will need some type of enclosure. Remember, you joined the MFi/WWi program so that you could get Apple's blessing on your product. It doesn't take secrets from inside the program to figure out that, if Apple is to "bless" your product, it can't look like a 12th-grade science project.

As with any other step in the process, you have a couple options. The higher cost approach is to hire a mechanical design engineer to work with you to create a model of the final product. You'll provide him with one of your PCBs—it doesn't need to be working—to use in making exact measurements. Depending on your engineer's other commitments, you can probably expect to see your design in a week or two.

Expect the cost to range from about $500 to $1500 just for the design. You'll also want to get prototypes made to check form, fit, and function. You can generally get prototypes for anywhere from $50 per item to a couple hundred dollars for machined parts that have been polished.

Lower-cost prototypes can be made by a process called Fused Deposition Modeling where the part is built up from scratch by applying successive layers of a glue-like substance. The part isn't very strong and is only used to check correct dimensioning. The good news is that the process is fast and relatively cheap. With a model, an FDM part can be created in a couple hours.

If you want something that looks more like the final product, then you should consider a part that is machined from a block of material such as ABS. The end result will be much stronger as it is made from the final material. Machining does leave marks on the part where the excess material has been cut away, but most shops can polish out the tool marks so the part has a nice shine to it. Expect this service to cost a couple hundred bucks per part.

> **NOTE:** Material selection is a whole science unto itself. Your manufacturing house or design engineer can help you with the selection. In most cases, you'll probably go for something like ABS (Acrylonitrile butadiene styrene), a common material for these types of projects.

You may have noticed that I've stressed the "per part" cost. This is because each part has its own processing that needs to be addressed. Consider a simple box to enclose your PCB like the one shown in Figure 12–9. The final "box" is in the middle of the figure with the two pieces to either side.

Figure 12–9. *Two-piece parts prototyped using FDM process*

These boxes were created as two pieces—a top and a bottom. As such, each part has to be prototyped meaning the cost doubles. In some situations, your mechanical designer could create a one-piece "clamshell" design where the bottom is more of a flap that is hinged to the top. I tried going this route, but it just didn't work for my accessory. I suspect there are very few cases where it would be successful.

For FDM prototypes, the necessity to create two pieces for a single part isn't too big a deal. Some fab houses will cut you a break on your parts, especially if they see more business from you in the future. After all, an FDM prototype is a kind of a "push the button and let it go" manufacturing process. Once the machine is set up and initiated, the operator can walk away and the machine runs until it is finished. For a machined part, the process is much more operator intensive. While the machining is still automated, an operator pays closer attention to the process to make sure things go smoothly.

As a real-world example, each set of parts (top and bottom) in Figure 12–9 cost me $77 to create using the FDM process and took a day to get done.

In the beginning of this section, I said that you had a couple options on mechanical design. I will get to the second option soon, but let me say a couple more things about your first option. So far, you've spent maybe a thousand dollars on a designer to create a model of your enclosure. You've also had some prototypes made using FDM costing you a couple hundred dollars so let's say you've spent about $1200 so far. Remember these are prototypes, not the final product. So how does the final product get made and how much does it cost?

The good news is that the final parts might cost you something like a buck apiece. It'll depend on quantity and complexity of the part of course, but it'll probably never be more than two or three dollars at most per part. You can probably live with that.

The parts are made by creating a mold based on the mechanical model. The mold is typically a hard or soft steel. The harder the mold, the more parts it can be used to make. A hard steel mold is typically guaranteed to make 500,000 to a million pieces. A soft-tooled mold might make a couple hundred thousand pieces.

Now, the bad news; a mold will cost from five to fifteen thousand dollars to make. The more complex the mold, well, you can guess which end of the price spectrum that'll approach. In fact, should you design to create an accessory requiring custom shaped, molded parts, expect the mechanical part costs to far outweigh any electrical design costs.

Think about that for a moment. You probably thought that all those tools and test equipment costs were going to put you out of the game; then I throw in something that costs $10K. You're probably thinking that because your box is two pieces, that means $20K not just ten. Not necessarily.

Molds are made up of cavities. A cavity is the area of a mold where the part is created. A mold can have several cavities. Two, four, and eight cavity molds are common. Of course, more cavities increase the cost. For the box design in Figure 12–9, my fab company created a two-cavity mold. The top part was in one cavity, the bottom in the other. While this didn't double the cost of the mold, it did increase the cost because the mold was now more complex.

In general, expect a two-cavity mold that contains the two halves of your enclosure part to add about 50% to the single cavity cost. These numbers are only examples of course. You'll need to discuss it with your design engineer and local fab houses to get your exact costs. Still, it's going to likely be the most significant cost of your entire project.

One thing you can do is to create your prototypes using machined parts to get that professional look, then go out and sell your accessory. I don't mean to actually take cash and hand over your prototypes; you'd never get a return on your investment doing that. What I'm talking about is pitching your product to potential distributors.

Get people to want your product early on so that you can test the waters and see if it's worth pursuing the making of a mold in order to mass produce your accessory. And remember, you'll also need to consider all the other pieces for mass production as well.

If nobody shows interest in your product, well, you sort of have your answer, don't you? Remember, you want to create a product that has mass appeal and that people will buy or there isn't any reason in doing it. On the other hand, if everybody wants one of your accessories, then you've at least got some indication of its potential. Now you have to get the money. Getting the money is the subject for another book entirely, but if you use the information I've provided in this book, it's a great start to developing your business plan for potential investors.

The Alternative to Custom Mechanical Design

You've waited and are totally disheartened and ready to quit. I can see why. A ten thousand dollar cost to make a case for your product that may never sell is a big bummer. However, there may still be a way.

If you haven't thought of it on your own already, you should have. Basically, all you really want is a box to enclose your electronics. Go to any Radio Shack and look in the hobbyist section (if your Radio Shack still has one) and you'll find all these little hobbyist project boxes. Typically, they're made of a plastic box with a metal plate that you drill out holes for your controls. You don't want these, but it should give you ideas.

Search on the Web for electronics hobbyist or project boxes and I'm sure you'll find something to suit your needs. For my first project, I found a company that makes these small plastic boxes that were originally intended as key fobs for cars. Take a look at Figure 12–10 to see how nicely they work for my PCB.

Figure 12–10. *Off-the-shelf electronics enclosure*

The part in Figure 12–10 is a two-piece enclosure very similar to the custom part shown in Figure 12–9. In fact, the off-the-shelf (OTS) part in Figure 12–10 is used in version one of my product. The custom version in Figure 12–9 was derived from this original version.

If you look carefully at Figure 12–10, you can see the cuts in the side of the box so the 30-pin dock connector can protrude. These were customizations made by the supplier. Many suppliers will have the capability to customize their parts for your needs. They generally won't be able to change the size or shape of the part, but making holes and cutouts can usually be done for a low fee.

In the end, the enclosures in Figure 12–10 wound up costing me about $2 each. I'm guessing you're starting to feel better now. Sorry I took you on that roller coaster, but I want you to understand that there are almost always workarounds for any problem you're likely to encounter. The difference between success and failure is often in figuring out workarounds.

You might ask why I chose to create a custom box like the one in Figure 12–9 when I can get parts for $2. I never said I actually created the mold for the custom boxes and the parts I've shown in Figure 12–9 are FDM prototypes. Ah ha, I can hear you say. The author DOES take his own advice. And, it's true; the first version of one of my products does use the OTS case. However, to add features to my design I did need more volume and plan to upgrade to the custom box as soon as I get enough interest.

I do hope this last section has scared you into thinking about your board's physical design early on. From what your accessory needs to do, you can get a rough idea of the physical dimensions, or more specifically limits, of your board. From that, search to find a suitable OTS enclosure that will work for you. Then, when either you or your PCB designer creates the board outline, make sure it conforms to the enclosure you've selected. By doing it first, you won't have to come back later and resize the board (spending another $500 or so) just to make it fit in the enclosure. This does require planning ahead and to be honest, I didn't do it and wish I had. I'm trying to help you not only with my successes but with my mistakes (failures is too strong a word) as well. Hold your applause.

Packaging

You've got to know you're getting to the end of the book when I start talking about things such as packaging. While packaging may seem like an easy thing to leave until last, it's still something you're going to have to consider.

By packaging, I'm of course talking about the outer part that a customer is going to see on the shelves of his local store. You could consider just shipping your product in a brown cardboard box to whoever buys one. However, there's that whole Apple-thing you have to deal with. I'll say it again, as consideration for them (Apple) granting you their holiest of holies (the specs from the MFi/WWi program) you're going to have your product held up to the highest standards—that includes packaging.

As always, I repeat my mantra—I can't divulge details because of the NDA with Apple— but it doesn't take a genius to figure things out. The simplest thing to do is to go to your local Apple reseller or maybe an Apple Store and look at the shelves. See what everyone else is doing and copy it. Well, of course you're not going to copy their logos or wording—I mean it wouldn't even apply to your product, unless you copied that. If you did, then I don't even want to know you.

Just take a look. You should quickly see a common theme among Apple iPhone and iPod touch compatible items. Examine the packages for commonality. Check out color schemes. See what materials are being used.

Originally, I wanted to go with a package for one of my products similar to the box that iPod Nanos came in. It was clear polycarbonate or acrylic material and two-piece with these nice smooth lines. Also, because it was similar to Apple's packaging, I thought it would make a great impression. Alas, these types of parts are molded. Remember that section on Mechanical Design? Remember the ten thousand dollar part? Now you're talking clear plastic parts so you must figure making a clear case is going to up the ante. It does. Say goodbye to the Nano box. Hello ULINE.

If you don't know about them yet, you should. ULINE is the company that small businesses turn to for shipping supplies. They have about every size, shape, and composition of shipping container you might consider. Of course, their products are standard sizes and you'll have to conform your materials to fit, but again, ten thousand dollars! So, yeah, it's something to do.

Check out the ULINE product in Figure 12–11. It's a simple 3"x3"x3" clear plastic cube, but they come in different sizes. You create an insert for all your labels; secure your accessory inside, and you've come away with a packaging solution for less than a buck with no start-up (mold creation) costs. Not bad!

Figure 12–11. *Low-cost packaging solution*

That's the basics of packaging. Like you've come across every step of the way, there are high- and low-cost alternatives, and which one you choose is up to you. Again, go take a look at what's out there. I think you'll find that most products come in plastic packages and use color and labeling to make them stand out. Color and ingenuity are a lot cheaper than a ten thousand dollar mold.

Of course, you can create the design for all your packaging yourself. When you're going to get to it because of all the other work you have to do, I don't know. So you might want to consider a professional for this part. Do you want to leave the first impression your customer sees to an overworked individual? (In case you didn't get it, I mean you.) There are a lot of graphics designers out there and all of them have portfolios for you to check out. Look for themes that you connect with and that match what you're trying to convey about your accessory.

This is one of those areas where you don't want to be cheap. Remember, first impression! This is what will cause the person walking the aisle at Best Buy to lean down and take a look at your product. All the great hardware and software design are nothing if no one sees it.

Business Processes

Okay, I've really got to be getting near the end with a section title like this. In truth, most of your processes can be handled by writing down everything in a decent composition book. However, there are a couple of things I want to mention that I've learned by going through the complete cycle of accessory development.

First, you're probably going to need a way to wire money from your bank account. I know you're thinking credit cards or even bank checks, but trust me on this. Some of the parts you're going to need will come from overseas distributors. They will generally only take payment by wire transfer. Some will, if you have established business credit, open an account for you. Then, you'll get a bill every month (that you make purchases) for the net due. If you don't have a business that's been around at least a year and with good credit (business credit), expect that you'll need to make wire transfers.

Like everything else, wire transfers cost money—a wiring fee. It could range from as low as twenty to as high as seventy dollars. If you only make one purchase, then a higher fee isn't too big of a deal. Expect to make at least two to four purchases so look for a good rate on wires.

Another thing to consider is the ease of which you can make a transfer happen. Most banks offer online banking, some with wire transfer capability. If you're comfortable using online financial services then this could be a good way to go. Otherwise, you'll have to make a trip to your bank each time you need to make a parts purchase.

Remember that composition book? You really need to keep up to the minute records of your expenses. Here's a scenario; you get a set of boards back from your manufacturer and they don't work. You drop everything and find the problem. You forgot to include a line from your processor chip to another part of the board. It's an easy fix, but it'll cost you. Very quickly, you spend another $350 or so. A couple of these can very quickly drain your resources. It's just something to keep close track of.

A good idea might be to keep this in a spreadsheet that's always open on your desktop. Make the total amount of capital that you have remaining stand out in a huge font. This way, every change you make will affect that number. If you're like me, you never want to see that number change unless it is to go up.

Just as you want to track your payment records, try to keep a good track of all your parts. Typically, you'll order a few of a part, then things will go well and you'll need to order a lot more. It's a total pain to go to order more of something and you forgot the part number.

The solution is to have some type of storage or bin system that will contain your parts. Get bins that can hold a couple hundred of the part type. There are various systems out there with different size bins in a single shelf unit. What I like to do is to tear off the part number label when I fill the bin and put it in with the parts or tape it to the front. Make sure you keep track of where you bought the parts.

A good source that I use for parts is Digi-Key. They have just about every part you'll ever need, except for Apple proprietary parts. Get familiar with the Digi-Key parts locator. Digi-Key even carries evaluation kits for various processors.

When you use Digi-Key or any other part supplier, be aware of what they have in stock. For example, when I went to order a bunch of PIC16F690 processors, Digi-Key only had about a hundred. I ordered them all, and a hundred would do me for a short while, but if I ever got even a moderate order, then I'd have to wait.

Two points to this story; if the supplier has a conspicuously low number, get them all then backorder some. Usually a supplier will order more than you have on back order so you're kind of forcing them to replenish their stock. Second, look for a second or even a third source for your parts.

Try to design using common parts. One of my credit card reader parts uses this funky connector that's only made and supplied by one Japanese manufacturer. Digi-Key carries it, but only a few at a time and it takes weeks to restock. I wound up changing the design to a more common connector type.

You may want to legitimatize your business by incorporating or getting a business license, if you don't already have one. For anything related to this area, seek legal advice specific to your region and circumstances. Why form a business? Ask yourself whether a company is likely to take you seriously if you go into them and say "My name is John and I want to sell you this." It may seem trivial, but I believe a business presence lends a little credibility to your project. If nothing else, it says that you had enough confidence in your project that you made it a "real" business. Hey, even Apple became a business at some point very early in its history.

Should you become a success, you'll want to have a record of all the things you did through the process in case you decide to file patents and/or trademarks. These are your discovery records and provide a paper trail so that you can prove your work was really your own. Filing a provisional patent on work can be a very good idea, not just to prove your work was your own in case it ever comes to that, but provisional patents are at least an order of magnitude lower than a formal patent. No one gets to see the papers; your patent attorney files them and they're never placed in public domain. Filing one gives you the right to put "patent pending" on your product. This is one of those little things that help to establish your legitimacy. Also, it provides your potential inventions with some level of comfort.

Same thing goes for trademarks. If you've got a catchy name or logo for something and want it to stay yours, consider filing trademark paperwork. Your App or product name could likely become your brand and you want to keep it safe, and your own.

Other than those very few tips, just take things seriously and not as a second hobby that you do in your spare time.

Summary

I've covered the basics of what an accessory is and the tools (EAAccessory Framework) that Apple provides to help you work with an accessory. I walked you step-by-step through an albeit simple application using an accessory. Hopefully, you realize that the software tools are there to make your life easier and, I believe, they do so admirably.

In the last part of the book, I opened my Kimono (I've always wanted to use that phrase somewhere) and revealed every secret that I had. Unfortunately, I couldn't go into as much detail as I would have liked because of the NDA I have with Apple. Hopefully, I've erred (erred, that's another one) on the side of conservatism and I won't be forever banned from the halls of Cupertino HQ.

I hate to say it, but it's time to part company and you can now go out and do it all yourself. I'll say it straightaway, I'm no expert in all (or much) of this, but I did go through it. I got beat up by the system, wanted to quit a hundred times, actually quit (or said so to my wife) five times, begged for money several times, and got money a very few times.

All in all though, I made it through the process and I believe that you can too.

Appendix

PongViewController.h interface listing

```
//
//   PongViewController.h
//
//


#import <UIKit/UIKit.h>
#include <AudioToolbox/AudioToolbox.h>


@interface pongViewController : UIViewController {
        //
        //          Define the outlets that will be updated
        //   as the game progresses
        //
        IBOutlet UIImageView *ball;
        IBOutlet UIImageView *playerPaddle;
        IBOutlet UIImageView *compPaddle;
        IBOutlet UILabel   *playerScoreView;
        IBOutlet UILabel   *compScoreView;
        IBOutlet UILabel   *winOrLoseView;

        //****************************************************
        //
        //   GENERAL NOTES ON THE PROPERTIES AND METHODS BELOW
        //
        //   Most, if not all, of the stuff below could be
        //   defined as simple instance variables within the
        //   the pongViewController and does not need to be
        //   defined here, in the interface section. While
        //   this would create slimmer (and probably better)
        //   code, I chose to put it here to force the condition
        //   that all properties be defined as accessible.
        //   Remember, this portion of the book describes a self-
        //   contained, touch-activated game, but we are planning
        //   to incorporate an additional controller to access
        //   the game controller accessory. So we want to make
        //   the pongViewController more open to expansion and
```

```
//    by putting things here, in the interface, we are
//    acting in a more forward-looking manner.
//****************************************************

//
//        ballSpeed - the X and Y velocity of the ball.
//        -- we use a CGPoint which is just a struct with two
//    floats (x and y) as its elements. We then just set
//    the x and y values to the speed.
//    Y is defined as movement along the vertical axis between
//    the player and the computer.
//    X is defined as the side-to-side movement
//
CGPoint ballSpeed;

//
// These are the images we're going to use for the player's paddle.
// In a very simple game, we would just use a rectangle, but here we
// do a couple of unique things. We flip the paddle (left-right) as
// it moves to either side of the centerline...to simulate forehand-
// backhand action (playerPaddleLeft and playerPaddleRight). Also,
// if we're at either edge of the table, in a real game we would angle
// the paddle more to bring it back into play. In this case, we "tilt"
// the image of the paddle a bit to simulate this (playerPaddleLeftUp and
// playerPaddleRightUp).
//
    UIImage         *playerPaddleLeft;
    UIImage         *playerPaddleLeftUp;
    UIImage         *playerPaddleRight;
    UIImage         *playerPaddleRightUp;

//
// These are some basic variables to keep track of things.
//
NSUInteger      playerScore;
NSUInteger      compScore;
NSUInteger      status;

//
//    We need these for handling the sound that the program generates
//
    CFURLRef                    paddleSoundFileURLRef;
SystemSoundID           paddleSoundObject;
}
@property (readwrite)     CFURLRef         paddleSoundFileURLRef;
@property (readonly)      SystemSoundID    paddleSoundObject;

@property (nonatomic,retain) IBOutlet UIImageView *ball;
@property (nonatomic,retain) IBOutlet UIImageView *playerPaddle;
@property (nonatomic,retain) IBOutlet UIImageView *compPaddle;
@property (nonatomic,retain) UILabel     *playerScoreView;
@property (nonatomic,retain) UILabel     *compScoreView;
@property (nonatomic,retain) UILabel     *winOrLoseView;


@property(nonatomic) CGPoint ballSpeed;
@property(nonatomic) NSUInteger      status;
```

```
@property     (nonatomic,retain) UIImage  *playerPaddleLeft;
@property     (nonatomic,retain) UIImage  *playerPaddleLeftUp;
@property     (nonatomic,retain) UIImage  *playerPaddleRight;
@property     (nonatomic,retain) UIImage  *playerPaddleRightUp;


@property NSUInteger    playerScore;
@property NSUInteger    compScore;

//
//  The object's method calls
//  serveAction is initiated by a user action (pressing the button)
//
-(IBAction) serveAction;

@end
```

PongViewController.m implementation listing

```
//
//  PongViewController.m
//
//

#import "pongViewController.h"

//
//      State Variables used by
//      compPlay method to determine
//  actions to take depending on
//  where we are in the game.
//
#define NOT_STARTED 0
#define IN_PLAY     1
#define POINT_OVER  2
#define GAME_OVER 3

//
// Points to win the game
//  I use 5 here to make the game
//  go by quickly
//
#define GAME_WON    5

//
//  Speed of the ball in both
//  the x and y directions.
//
#define BALL_DELTA_X  5
#define BALL_DELTA_Y  10

//
// Starting position of the ball.
//  Roughly the center of the table
```

```
//
#define BALL_STARTING_X    160.0
#define BALL_STARTING_Y    220.0


//
//  defines the performance
//  of the computer player.
//  higher number equals better
//  computer player
//
#define COMP_REACTION_TIME    15


//
//  COMP_SETUP_TIME is a variable
//  that also determines computer
//  performance. In general, it adjusts
//  how soon the computer reacts by
//  adding y-position info to the
//  check of where the ball is.
//
#define COMP_SETUP_TIME    40


//
//  WALL_MARGIN adds a delta distance
//  from the edges of the wall to check
//  when to "bounce" the ball. If it were
//  not added, then the ball might look like
//  it went "into" the wall before bouncing.
//
#define WALL_MARGIN    5

@implementation pongViewController

//
// Use @synthesis to create all the
// necessary getters and setters
//
@synthesize ball;
@synthesize playerPaddle;
@synthesize compPaddle;

@synthesize ballSpeed;
@synthesize        status;
@synthesize playerPaddleLeft;
@synthesize playerPaddleLeftUp;
@synthesize playerPaddleRight;
@synthesize playerPaddleRightUp;

@synthesize playerScore;
@synthesize playerScoreView;
@synthesize compScore;
@synthesize compScoreView;
@synthesize winOrLoseView;

@synthesize paddleSoundFileURLRef;
@synthesize paddleSoundObject;
```

```
//
//      setServePosition
// Place the ball at approximately the center of the table
// for the serve.
// -- the ball's center position and speed are both structs
//     containing an X and Y value. This way, what we call
//     speed is really just the delta position added to the
//     ball at each call of the timer expiration.
//
-(void) setServePosition {
        ball.center = CGPointMake(BALL_STARTING_X, BALL_STARTING_Y);
        ballSpeed = CGPointMake(BALL_DELTA_X, -BALL_DELTA_Y);
}


//
// compPlay - adjust the computer's paddle position to meet the ball
// This is basically the only AI in the program and it's just moving
// the comp's paddle towards the ball at a certain speed. Really,
// if the player is very, very lucky and has gotten a good angle on his
// return *and* the computer's paddle is at the extreme other side of the
// table, then it might just NOT make it to the ball in time and the
// player will score a point.
//
-(void) compPlay {

  if(ball.center.y <= self.view.center.y + COMP_SETUP_TIME)      { // is ball on computer's
side of court ?
     if(ball.center.x < compPaddle.center.x) {
     // does computer need to move racquet ?
        CGPoint compLocation = CGPointMake(compPaddle.center.x - COMP_REACTION_TIME,
compPaddle.center.y);
        compPaddle.center = compLocation;
    }
       if(ball.center.x > compPaddle.center.x) {
           CGPoint compLocation = CGPointMake(compPaddle.center.x + COMP_REACTION_TIME,
compPaddle.center.y);
           compPaddle.center = compLocation;
       }
     }
}

//
// gameLoop - the heart of the game
//
// This is called at every expiration of the NSTimer interval that we set at startup
time
// Typically, in this type of design, the first thing to do is check all the boundary
conditions:
//  has the ball hit an edge of something (the room), has a point been scored, is the
game over,
//  has the ball connected with the player's or computer's paddle.
//  Note that all the code in the entire function is contingent on the game status being
IN_PLAY. This
//  should be obvious that we only want the automatic part of the system to update if
we're in the
```

```
//   middle of play. In any other state (NOT STARTED, GAME WON, POINT OVER) the player
should determine
//   things (SERVE or not).
//
// Note also that this method also sets the game's status:
//   (1) If the ball is past the player's end, the computer has scored and we set
POINT_OVER
//   (2) Similarly, if the ball is past the computer's end, the player scored and
POINT_OVER as well.
//   (3) If the point total of a player is equal to the constant GAME_WON, we set status
= GAME_OVER
//   (4) NOT_STARTED is set at startup in the viewDidLoad method.
//
-(void)gameLoop {

    if(status == IN_PLAY) {
        ball.center = CGPointMake(ball.center.x + ballSpeed.x, ball.center.y +
ballSpeed.y); // move the ball

        // Has the ball hit the edge of the room ?
        if (ball.center.x > (self.view.bounds.size.width - WALL_MARGIN) || ball.center.x
< (0 + WALL_MARGIN)) {
            ballSpeed.x  = - ballSpeed.x;
        }

        if (ball.center.y > self.view.bounds.size.height || ball.center.y < 0) {
            ballSpeed.y = - ballSpeed.y;
        }

    // player scored against computer
    if (ball.center.y < 0) {
    // set status to hold
    status = POINT_OVER;
    playerScore++;
    playerScoreView.text = [NSString stringWithFormat:@"%d",playerScore];
    if (playerScore == GAME_WON)
     {
        winOrLoseView.text = @"YOU WIN";
        playerScore = 0;
        compScore   = 0;
        status     = GAME_OVER;
     }
      [self       setServePosition];

    } else
    // if player didn't score, did the computer score?

    if (ball.center.y > self.view.bounds.size.height) {
    // set status to hold
    status = POINT_OVER;
    compScore++;
    compScoreView.text = [NSString stringWithFormat:@"%d",compScore];
    if (compScore == GAME_WON)
    {
        winOrLoseView.text = @"YOU LOSE";
        playerScore = 0;
        compScore   = 0;
```

```
    status   = GAME_OVER;
    }
    [self     setServePosition];
}


// Did the player's paddle make contact with the ball
if(CGRectIntersectsRect(ball.frame, playerPaddle.frame)) {

    AudioServicesPlaySystemSound (self.paddleSoundObject);

    // Reverse front-to-back direction
    if(ball.center.y < playerPaddle.center.y) {
        ballSpeed.y = -ballSpeed.y;
    }

    // Reverse the X direction if we're off to one side of the table
    if ( (ball.center.x > (self.view.bounds.size.width /2)+100) ||
      (ball.center.x < (self.view.bounds.size.width /2)-100) )
    {
    // if we just reverse the delta-x, then we might get hung in a loop
    // so add a little offset from where the ball is to the center of the paddle

      ballSpeed.x = -ballSpeed.x + (ball.center.x - playerPaddle.center.x)/5;
    }
}


// Did the computer's paddle make contact withthe ball
if(CGRectIntersectsRect(ball.frame,     compPaddle.frame)) {

    AudioServicesPlaySystemSound (self.paddleSoundObject);

    // Reverse front-to-back direction
    if(ball.center.y > compPaddle.center.y) {
    ballSpeed.y = -ballSpeed.y;
    // each time the computer hits the ball, speed it up
    ballSpeed.y++;
    }

   // Let's change the X (side-to-side) direction if we're near the edge of the table
    if ( (ball.center.x > (self.view.bounds.size.width /2)+100) ||
    (ball.center.x < (self.view.bounds.size.width /2)-100) )
      ballSpeed.x = -ballSpeed.x;
    }
    //
    // Here is the only real action that this method does.
    // If none of the above conditions are met, then call
    //  the AI method that moves the computer's paddle towards
    //  the ball.
    //
    [self compPlay];
  } // end if
}

//
```

```
//     touchesBegan is the method that gets called when the player
//   interacts with the game (touches the screen to move his paddle).
//   this is just the method called by the system, and if the game
//   status is IN_PLAY, then our routine touchesMoved is called to
//   intercept and move the player's paddle.
//   REALLY, this is just a gateway that only allows the player
//   to move the paddle if the game is in play.
//
-(void)touchesBegan:(NSSet *)touches withEvent:(UIEvent *)event {
    if (status == IN_PLAY) {
      [self touchesMoved:touches withEvent:event];
      }
}


//
//   serveAction - Basically, this starts the game.
//   (1) Clear any startup text in the game window
//   (2) Initialize the scores
//   (3) change game status
//   (4) make a serve sound
//
// Note that this method really doesn't "serve" the ball. It
//   merely changes game status so that the next time the NSTimer
//   "fires", the gameLoop actually runs.
//
-(void)serveAction {
    winOrLoseView.text = @"";

    if (status == GAME_OVER) {
      compScoreView.text      = [NSString stringWithFormat:@"%d",0];
      playerScoreView.text  = [NSString stringWithFormat:@"%d",0];
      }
    status = IN_PLAY;

    AudioServicesPlaySystemSound (self.paddleSoundObject);


}

//
// touchesMoved:withEvent:
// This routine moves the player's paddle to the point on the
//   playing surface that he has placed his finger. NOTE that this
//   has the unnatural effect of instantly positioning his paddle
//   which is generally not how you want to play the game.
//   Also, depending on where the paddle is positioned (left or right)
//   or at the edges of the table, we change the image used by the player's
//   paddle to simulate forehand-backhand or to an angled shot back
//   into the game. We do not do this for the computer's paddle
//
-(void)touchesMoved:(NSSet *)touches withEvent:(UIEvent *)event {
    UITouch *touch = [[event allTouches] anyObject];     // returns one of the objects
in the set of all touches
    CGPoint location = [touch locationInView:touch.view];
    CGPoint xLocation = CGPointMake(location.x,playerPaddle.center.y);
    playerPaddle.center = xLocation;
    if (playerPaddle.center.x > (self.view.bounds.size.width /2))
```

```
        if (playerPaddle.center.x > (self.view.bounds.size.width /2)+101)
            playerPaddle.image = playerPaddleRightUp;
        else
            playerPaddle.image = playerPaddleRight;
        else
        if (playerPaddle.center.x < (self.view.bounds.size.width /2)-101)
            playerPaddle.image = playerPaddleLeftUp;
         else
                playerPaddle.image = playerPaddleLeft;
}


//
//   viewDidLoad - we use this to initialize our system.
// (1) Loads the images from the bundle to use for our variable player's paddle
//   (2) Displays the game name on the playing field
//   (3) Gets the sound file for the ball
//   (4) initializes the score to 0-0
//   (5) sets the game status to NOT_STARTED -- note that this is the only time
//       the game is in this condition
//   (6) set the serve position of the ball
//   (7) setup and start the timer
//
//   Note that for the game to actually start, the status must change to IN_PLAY
//   and that is only done by the serveAction method which fires when the player
//   taps the SERVE button --**** AND ***--- soon when the game controller's
//   serve button is pressed.
//
- (void)viewDidLoad {

    playerPaddleLeft    = [UIImage imageNamed:@"playerPaddleLeft.png"];
    playerPaddleLeftUp       = [UIImage imageNamed:@"playerPaddleLeftUp.png"];
    playerPaddleRight = [UIImage imageNamed:@"playerPaddleRight.png"];
    playerPaddleRightUp = [UIImage    imageNamed:@"playerPaddleRightUp.png"];

    winOrLoseView.text = @"PONG!";

  // SET UP SOUNDS
    CFBundleRef mainBundle;
    mainBundle = CFBundleGetMainBundle ();

    // Get the URL to the sound file to play
    paddleSoundFileURLRef =      CFBundleCopyResourceURL (
       mainBundle,    CFSTR ("paddleSound"),
       CFSTR ("aif"),
       NULL );
    AudioServicesCreateSystemSoundID (
       paddleSoundFileURLRef,
       &paddleSoundObject);

    playerScore   = 0;
    compScore = 0;

    status = NOT_STARTED;
    [self setServePosition];
    [NSTimer scheduledTimerWithTimeInterval:0.05 target:self
selector:@selector(gameLoop) userInfo:nil repeats: YES];
```

```objc
    [super viewDidLoad];
}



//
// The rest of the code is generated by Xcode and should
//  be setup in a "real" production level game.
//
- (void)didReceiveMemoryWarning {
    // Releases the view if it doesn't have a superview.
    [super didReceiveMemoryWarning];

    // Release any cached data, images, etc that aren't in use.
}

- (void)viewDidUnload {
    // Release any retained subviews of the main view.
    // e.g. self.myOutlet = nil;
}


- (void)dealloc {
    [super dealloc];

}

@end
```

GameController.h

```objc
/*

GameController.h

*/

#import <Foundation/Foundation.h>
#import "pongAppDelegate.h"
#import <ExternalAccessory/ExternalAccessory.h>

@interface GameController : NSObject <EAAccessoryDelegate> {
    EAAccessory *_accessory;
    EASession *_session;
    NSString *_protocolString;

    NSMutableData *_writeData;

        pongAppDelegate     *appDelegate;
}

+ (GameController *)sharedController;

- (void)setupControllerForAccessory:(EAAccessory *)accessory
withProtocolString:(NSString *)protocolString;
```

```
- (BOOL)openSession;
- (void)closeSession;

- (void)writeData:(NSData *)data;
- (void)_writeData;

// from EAAccessoryDelegate
- (void)accessoryDidDisconnect:(EAAccessory *)accessory;

@property (nonatomic, readonly) EAAccessory *accessory;
@property (nonatomic, readonly) NSString *protocolString;

@end
```

GameController.m

```
/*

GameController.m
*/

#import "GameController.h"

@implementation GameController

@synthesize accessory = _accessory, protocolString = _protocolString;


#pragma mark -
#pragma mark Externally Accessed writeData Method

- (void)writeData:(NSData *)data
{
    if (_writeData == nil) {
        _writeData = [[NSMutableData alloc] init];
    }

    [_writeData appendData:data];
    [self _writeData];
}

#pragma mark Instance Methods

- (void)_writeData {
    while ((([_session outputStream] hasSpaceAvailable]) && ([_writeData length] > 0))
    {
        NSInteger bytesWritten = [[_session outputStream] write:[_writeData bytes]
maxLength:[_writeData length]];
        if (bytesWritten == -1)
        {
            NSLog(@"write error");
            break;
        }
        else if (bytesWritten > 0)
        {
```

```
                    [_writeData replaceBytesInRange:NSMakeRange(0, bytesWritten) withBytes:NULL
    length:0];
            }
        }
}

#define EAD_INPUT_BUFFER_SIZE 128

- (void)_readData {

    //
    // get appDelegate (pongAppDelegate) so we can reference its properties
    //
    appDelegate = (pongAppDelegate *)[[UIApplication sharedApplication] delegate];

    uint8_t buf[EAD_INPUT_BUFFER_SIZE];

    while ([[_session inputStream] hasBytesAvailable])
    {
        NSInteger bytesRead = [[_session inputStream] read:buf
maxLength:EAD_INPUT_BUFFER_SIZE];
        NSLog(@"read %d bytes (%d) from input stream", bytesRead,buf[0]);

// for now, we only expect two different command bytes from the accessory
// 0x10 - means that the pushbutton was pressed and no additional data follows
// 0x20 - means that the knob (potentiometer) has changed position and an
//         additional  byte follows which represents the knob's position
        if (buf[0] == 0x10) {
        [[NSNotificationCenter   defaultCenter] postNotificationName:@"PBPRESSED"
object:self];   // no user data

        }
        if (buf[0] == 0x20) {
        //NSData *data = [[NSData alloc] initWithBytes:buf     length:bytesRead];

        //NSLog(@"Data = %@",data);
                unsigned char i = buf[1];
                NSNumber *posInt = [[NSNumber alloc] initWithUnsignedChar:i];
                NSLog(@"_readData position = %d",[posInt intValue]);
        // appDelegate.paddlePosition = i;

            NSMutableDictionary *dict = [[ NSMutableDictionary alloc]     // we use a
dictionary to send it via notification center
                init];
                [ dict     setObject:posInt forKey:@"parameter"];
                [[NSNotificationCenter     defaultCenter]
                postNotificationName:@"POTTURNED" object:self userInfo:dict];
                [dict release];
                [posInt   release];
        }
    }
}

#define EAD_INPUT_BUFFER_SIZE 128


+ (GameController *)sharedController
```

```
{
    static GameController *accessoryController = nil;
    if (accessoryController == nil) {
        accessoryController = [[GameController alloc] init];
    }

    return accessoryController;
}


#pragma mark -
#pragma mark Internal Methods

- (void)setupControllerForAccessory:(EAAccessory *)accessory
withProtocolString:(NSString *)protocolString
{
    [_accessory release];
    _accessory = [accessory retain];
    [_protocolString release];
    _protocolString = [protocolString copy];
}

- (BOOL)openSession
{
    [_accessory setDelegate:self];
    _session = [[EASession alloc] initWithAccessory:_accessory
forProtocol:_protocolString];
    //_session = [[EASession alloc] initWithAccessory:_accessory
forProtocol:@"COM.MACMEDX.P1"];

    if (_session)
    {
        [[_session inputStream] setDelegate:self];
        [[_session inputStream]
            scheduleInRunLoop:[NSRunLoop currentRunLoop]
                forMode:NSDefaultRunLoopMode];
        [[_session inputStream] open];

        [[_session outputStream] setDelegate:self];
        [[_session outputStream]
                scheduleInRunLoop:[NSRunLoop currentRunLoop]
                  forMode:NSDefaultRunLoopMode];
        [[_session outputStream] open];
    }
    else
    {
        NSLog(@"creating session failed");
    }

    return (_session != nil);
}

- (void)closeSession
{
    [[_session inputStream] close];
    [[_session inputStream] removeFromRunLoop:[NSRunLoop currentRunLoop]
            forMode:NSDefaultRunLoopMode];
```

```objectivec
    [[_session inputStream] setDelegate:nil];
    [[_session outputStream] close];
    [[_session outputStream] removeFromRunLoop:[NSRunLoop currentRunLoop]
            forMode:NSDefaultRunLoopMode];
    [[_session outputStream] setDelegate:nil];

      _session = nil;
    [_session release];


}



- (void)accessoryDidDisconnect:(EAAccessory *)accessory
{
    NSLog(@"Controller Removed");
}

#pragma mark NSStreamDelegateEventExtensions

- (void)stream:(NSStream *)aStream handleEvent:(NSStreamEvent)eventCode
{
    switch (eventCode) {
        case NSStreamEventNone:
            break;
        case NSStreamEventOpenCompleted:
            break;
        case NSStreamEventHasBytesAvailable:
            [self _readData];
            break;
        case NSStreamEventHasSpaceAvailable:
            [self _writeData];
            break;
        case NSStreamEventErrorOccurred:
            break;
        case NSStreamEventEndEncountered:
            break;
        default:
            break;
    }
}

#pragma mark -
#pragma mark Basic Object Methods

- (void)dealloc
{
    [self closeSession];
    [self setupControllerForAccessory:nil withProtocolString:nil];
    _writeData = nil;
    [_writeData release];


    [super dealloc];
}

@end
```

pongViewController.h

```
//
//  PongViewController.h
//
//


#import <UIKit/UIKit.h>
#include <AudioToolbox/AudioToolbox.h>
#import <ExternalAccessory/ExternalAccessory.h>
#import "GameController.h"
#import "pongAppDelegate.h"


@interface pongViewController : UIViewController {

    pongAppDelegate      *appDelegate;


    EAAccessory *_accessory;
    NSMutableArray *_accessoryList;

    EAAccessory *_selectedAccessory;
    GameController *_accessoryController;


    // Define the outlets that will be updated
    //  as the game progresses
    //
    IBOutlet UIImageView *ball;
    IBOutlet UIImageView *playerPaddle;
    IBOutlet UIImageView *compPaddle;
    IBOutlet UILabel  *playerScoreView;
    IBOutlet UILabel  *compScoreView;
    IBOutlet UILabel  *winOrLoseView;


//*****************************************************
//
//   GENERAL NOTES ON THE PROPERTIES AND METHODS BELOW
//
//   Most, if not all, of the stuff below could be
//   defined as simple instance variables within the
//   the pongViewController and does not need to be
//   defined here, in the interface section. While
//   this would create slimmer (and probably better)
//   code, I chose to put it here to force the condition
//   that all properties be defined as accessible.
//   Remember, this portion of the book describes a self-
//   contained, touch-activated game, but we are planning
//   to incorporate an additional controller to access
//   the game controller accessory. So we want to make
//   the pongViewController more open to expansion and
//   by putting things here, in the interface, we are
//   acting in a more forward-looking manner.
//*****************************************************
```

```
//
//      ballSpeed - the X and Y velocity of the ball.
//         -- we use a CGPoint which is just a struct with two
//      floats (x and y) as its elements. We then just set
//      the x and y values to the speed.
//      Y is defined as movement along the vertical axis between
//      the player and the computer.
//      X is defined as the side-to-side movement
//
CGPoint ballSpeed;



//
// These are the images we're going to use for the player's paddle.
// In a very simple game, we would just use a rectangle, but here we
// do a couple of unique things. We flip the paddle (left-right) as
// it moves to either side of the centerline...to simulate forehand-
// backhand action (playerPaddleLeft and playerPaddleRight). Also,
// if we're at either edge of the table, in a real game we would angle
// the paddle more to bring it back into play. In this case, we "tilt"
// the image of the paddle a bit to simulate this (playerPaddleLeftUp and
// playerPaddleRightUp).
//
    UIImage     *playerPaddleLeft;
    UIImage     *playerPaddleLeftUp;
    UIImage     *playerPaddleRight;
    UIImage     *playerPaddleRightUp;

//
// These are some basic variables to keep track of things.
//
    NSUInteger  playerScore;
    NSUInteger  compScore;
    NSUInteger  status;

//
// We need these for handling the sound that the program generates
//
CFURLRef        paddleSoundFileURLRef;
SystemSoundID   paddleSoundObject;
}
@property (readwrite)   CFURLRef        paddleSoundFileURLRef;
@property (readonly)    SystemSoundID   paddleSoundObject;

@property (nonatomic,retain) IBOutlet UIImageView *ball;
@property (nonatomic,retain) IBOutlet UIImageView *playerPaddle;
@property (nonatomic,retain) IBOutlet UIImageView *compPaddle;
@property (nonatomic,retain) UILabel    *playerScoreView;
@property (nonatomic,retain) UILabel    *compScoreView;
@property (nonatomic,retain) UILabel    *winOrLoseView;


@property(nonatomic) CGPoint ballSpeed;
@property(nonatomic) NSUInteger status;
```

```
@property (nonatomic,retain) UIImage *playerPaddleLeft;
@property (nonatomic,retain) UIImage *playerPaddleLeftUp;
@property (nonatomic,retain) UIImage *playerPaddleRight;
@property (nonatomic,retain) UIImage *playerPaddleRightUp;


@property NSUInteger    playerScore;
@property NSUInteger    compScore;

//
//  The object's method calls
//  serveAction is initiated by a user action (pressing the button)
//
-(IBAction) serveAction;

//
//   LED Control Routines
//
- (void)turnOnRedLED;
- (void)turnOffRedLED;
- (void)turnOnGreenLED;
- (void)turnOffGreenLED;
@end
```

pongViewController.m

```
//
//  PongViewController.m
//
//

#import "pongViewController.h"

//
//  State Variables used by
//  compPlay method to determine
//  actions to take depending on
//  where we are in the game.
//
#define NOT_STARTED     0
#define IN_PLAY         1
#define POINT_OVER      2
#define GAME_OVER       3

//
//   Points to win the game
//  I use 5 here to make the game
//  go by quickly
//
#define GAME_WON        5

//
//   Speed of the ball in both
//  the x and y directions.
//
```

```objc
#define BALL_DELTA_X        5
#define BALL_DELTA_Y        10


//
//    Starting position of the ball.
//    Roughly the center of the table
//
#define BALL_STARTING_X     160.0
#define BALL_STARTING_Y     220.0


//
//    defines the performance
//    of the computer player.
//    higher number equals better
//    computer player
//
#define COMP_REACTION_TIME      15


//
//    COMP_SETUP_TIME is a variable
//    that also determines computer
//    performance. In general, it adjusts
//    how soon the computer reacts by
//    adding y-position info to the
//    check of where the ball is.
//
#define COMP_SETUP_TIME        40


//
//    WALL_MARGIN adds a delta distance
//    from the edges of the wall to check
//    when to "bounce" the ball. If it were
//    not added, then the ball might look like
//    it went "into" the wall before bouncing.
//
#define WALL_MARGIN        5

@implementation pongViewController

//
// Use @synthesis to create all the
// necessary getters and setters
//
@synthesize ball;
@synthesize playerPaddle;
@synthesize compPaddle;

@synthesize ballSpeed;
@synthesize        status;
@synthesize playerPaddleLeft;
@synthesize playerPaddleLeftUp;
@synthesize playerPaddleRight;
@synthesize playerPaddleRightUp;

@synthesize playerScore;
@synthesize playerScoreView;
@synthesize compScore;
```

```
@synthesize compScoreView;
@synthesize winOrLoseView;

@synthesize paddleSoundFileURLRef;
@synthesize paddleSoundObject;


//
//    INSTANCE VARIABLES
//
BOOL    redLEDOn      = NO;
BOOL    greenLEDOn   = NO;

//
//    setServePosition
// Place the ball at approximately the center of the table
// for the serve.
//   -- the ball's center position and speed are both structs
//      containing an X and Y value. This way, what we call
//      speed is really just the delta position added to the
//      ball at each call of the timer expiration.
//
-(void) setServePosition {
     ball.center       = CGPointMake(BALL_STARTING_X, BALL_STARTING_Y);
     ballSpeed = CGPointMake(BALL_DELTA_X, -BALL_DELTA_Y);
}


//
//   compPlay - adjust the computer's paddle position to meet the ball
// This is basically the only AI in the program and it's just moving
// the comp's paddle towards the ball at a certain speed. Really,
// if the player is very, very lucky and has gotten a good angle on his
// return *and* the computer's paddle is at the extreme other side of the
// table, then it might just NOT make it to the ball in time and the
// player will score a point.
//
-(void) compPlay {

     if(ball.center.y <= self.view.center.y + COMP_SETUP_TIME)    {    // is ball on
computer's side of court ?
        if(ball.center.x < compPaddle.center.x) {    // does computer need to move racquet
?
         CGPoint compLocation = CGPointMake(compPaddle.center.x - COMP_REACTION_TIME,
compPaddle.center.y);
          compPaddle.center = compLocation;
       }
       if(ball.center.x > compPaddle.center.x) {
           CGPoint compLocation = CGPointMake(compPaddle.center.x + COMP_REACTION_TIME,
compPaddle.center.y);
            compPaddle.center = compLocation;
       }
      }
}

//
//   gameLoop - the heart of the game
//
```

```objc
// This is called at every expiration of the NSTimer interval that we set at
//    startup time
// Typically, in this type of design, the first thing to do is check all the
//    boundary conditions:
//    has the ball hit an edge of something (the room), has a point been scored,
//    is the game over,
//    has the ball connected with the player's or computer's paddle.
//    Note that all the code in the entire function is contingent on the game
//        status being IN_PLAY. This
//    should be obvious that we only want the automatic part of the system to
//        update if we're in the
// middle of play. In any other state (NOT STARTED, GAME WON, POINT OVER) the
//    player should determine
// things (SERVE or not).
//
//    Note also that this method also sets the game's status:
//    (1) If the ball is past the player's end, the computer has scored and we set
//        POINT_OVER
//    (2) Similarly, if the ball is past the computer's end, the player scored and
//        POINT_OVER as well.
//    (3) If the point total of a player is equal to the constant GAME_WON, we set
//        status = GAME_OVER
//    (4) NOT_STARTED is set at startup in the viewDidLoad method.
//
-(void)gameLoop {

    if(status == IN_PLAY) {
        ball.center = CGPointMake(ball.center.x + ballSpeed.x, ball.center.y +
ballSpeed.y); // move the ball

    //
    // If we turned on an LED in the last loop, then turn it off now
    //
        if (redLEDOn) {
          [self   turnOffRedLED];
          redLEDOn  = NO;
        }
        if (greenLEDOn) {
        [self    turnOffGreenLED];
        greenLEDOn  = NO;
        }

    // Has the ball hit the edge of the room ?
        if (ball.center.x > (self.view.bounds.size.width - WALL_MARGIN) || ball.center.x
< (0 + WALL_MARGIN)) {
            ballSpeed.x   = - ballSpeed.x;
        }

        if (ball.center.y > self.view.bounds.size.height || ball.center.y < 0) {
          ballSpeed.y = - ballSpeed.y;
        }

    // player scored against computer
        if (ball.center.y < 0) {
        // set status to hold
        status = POINT_OVER;
                playerScore++;
```

```
            playerScoreView.text = [NSString
                stringWithFormat:@"%d",playerScore];
          if (playerScore == GAME_WON)
          {

              winOrLoseView.text = @"YOU WIN";
              playerScore = 0;
              compScore   = 0;
              status    = GAME_OVER;

      }
      [self   setServePosition];


    } else
    // if player didn't score, did the computer score?

        if (ball.center.y > self.view.bounds.size.height) {
                // set status to hold
                status = POINT_OVER;
                compScore++;
                compScoreView.text = [NSString
                        stringWithFormat:@"%d",compScore];
                if (compScore == GAME_WON)
                 {

                     winOrLoseView.text = @"YOU LOSE";
                     playerScore = 0;
                     compScore   = 0;
                     status    = GAME_OVER;

                }
                [self        setServePosition];
            }


    // Did the player's paddle make contact with the ball
      if(CGRectIntersectsRect(ball.frame, playerPaddle.frame)) {


         AudioServicesPlaySystemSound (self.paddleSoundObject);
       // Reverse front-to-back direction
        if(ball.center.y < playerPaddle.center.y) {
           ballSpeed.y = -ballSpeed.y;
          }

      // Reverse the X direction if we're off to one side of the table
        if  ( (ball.center.x > (self.view.bounds.size.width /2)+100) ||
            (ball.center.x < (self.view.bounds.size.width /2)-100) )
        {
// if we just reverse the delta-x, then we might get hung in a loop
// so add a little offset from where the ball is to the center of the paddle

                ballSpeed.x = -ballSpeed.x +
                (ball.center.x - playerPaddle.center.x)/5;
        }
    //[self   turnOnRedLED];
    }


  // Did the computer's paddle make contact withthe ball
      if(CGRectIntersectsRect(ball.frame,        compPaddle.frame)) {
```

```
        AudioServicesPlaySystemSound (self.paddleSoundObject);

    // Reverse front-to-back direction
            if(ball.center.y > compPaddle.center.y) {
                ballSpeed.y = -ballSpeed.y;
    // each time the computer hits the ball, speed it up
                ballSpeed.y++;
            }

    // Let's change the X (side-to-side) direction if we're near
    // the /edge of the table
            if ( (ball.center.x > (self.view.bounds.size.width /2)+100) ||
                (ball.center.x < (self.view.bounds.size.width /2)-100) )
                    ballSpeed.x = -ballSpeed.x;
//[self    turnOnGreenLED];
    }
    //
    // Here is the only real action that this method does.
    // If none of the above conditions are met, then call
    //  the AI method that moves the computer's paddle towards
    //  the ball.
    //
    [self compPlay];
    } // end if
}


//
//   touchesBegan is the method that gets called when the player
//   interacts with the game (touches the screen to move his paddle).
//   this is just the method called by the system, and if the game
//   status is IN_PLAY, then our routine touchesMoved is called to
//   intercept and move the player's paddle.
//   REALLY, this is just a gateway that only allows the player
//   to move the paddle if the game is in play.
//
-(void)touchesBegan:(NSSet *)touches withEvent:(UIEvent *)event {
    if (status == IN_PLAY) {
      [self touchesMoved:touches withEvent:event];
      }
}


//
//   serveAction - Basically, this starts the game.
//   (1) Clear any startup text in the game window
//   (2) Initialize the scores
//   (3) change game status
//   (4) make a serve sound
//
//    Note that this method really doesn't "serve" the ball. It
//   merely changes game status so that the next time the NSTimer
//   "fires", the gameLoop actually runs.
//
-(void)serveAction {
      winOrLoseView.text = @"";
```

```
          if (status == GAME_OVER) {
            compScoreView.text    = [NSString stringWithFormat:@"%d",0];
            playerScoreView.text  = [NSString stringWithFormat:@"%d",0];
          }
          status = IN_PLAY;

      AudioServicesPlaySystemSound (self.paddleSoundObject);


}

//
//    touchesMoved:withEvent:
//    This routine moves the player's paddle to the point on the
//    playing surface that he has placed his finger. NOTE that this
//    has the unnatural effect of instantly positioning his paddle
//    which is generally not how you want to play the game.
//    Also, depending on where the paddle is positioned (left or right)
//    or at the edges of the table, we change the image used by the player's
//    paddle to simulate forehand-backhand or to an angled shot back
//    into the game. We do not do this for the computer's paddle
//
-(void)touchesMoved:(NSSet *)touches withEvent:(UIEvent *)event {
    UITouch *touch = [[event allTouches] anyObject];    // returns one of the objects in
the set of all touches
        CGPoint location = [touch locationInView:touch.view];
        CGPoint xLocation = CGPointMake(location.x,playerPaddle.center.y);
        playerPaddle.center = xLocation;
        if (playerPaddle.center.x > (self.view.bounds.size.width /2))
          if (playerPaddle.center.x > (self.view.bounds.size.width /2)+101)
            playerPaddle.image = playerPaddleRightUp;
          else
              playerPaddle.image = playerPaddleRight;
        else
          if (playerPaddle.center.x < (self.view.bounds.size.width /2)-101)
            playerPaddle.image = playerPaddleLeftUp;
          else
            playerPaddle.image = playerPaddleLeft;
}


//
// viewDidLoad - we use this to initialize our system.
//   (1) Loads the images from the bundle to use for our variable player's
          paddle
//   (2) Displays the game name on the playing field
//   (3) Gets the sound file for the ball
//   (4) initializes the score to 0-0
//   (5) sets the game status to NOT_STARTED -- note that this is the only time
//       the game is in this condition
//   (6) set the serve position of the ball
//   (7) setup and start the timer
//
//   Note that for the game to actually start, the status must change to IN_PLAY
//   and that is only done by the serveAction method which fires when the player
//   taps the SERVE button --****  AND ***--- soon when the game controller's
//   serve button is pressed.
```

```objc
//
- (void)viewDidLoad {

    [[UIApplication sharedApplication] setIdleTimerDisabled:YES];       // disable sleep
dimming
 //
 // get appDelegate (pongAppDelegate) so we can reference its properties
 //
    appDelegate = (pongAppDelegate *)[[UIApplication sharedApplication]
            delegate];


    [[NSNotificationCenter defaultCenter]
        addObserver:self
         selector:@selector(accessoryConnected:)
         name:EAAccessoryDidConnectNotification object:nil];
 [[NSNotificationCenter defaultCenter]
            addObserver:self
            selector:@selector(accessoryDisconnected:)
            name:EAAccessoryDidDisconnectNotification object:nil];
    [[NSNotificationCenter defaultCenter]
            addObserver:self
            selector:@selector(pbPressed:)
            name:@"PBPRESSED" object:nil];
    [[NSNotificationCenter defaultCenter]
            addObserver:self
            selector:@selector(potTurned:)
            name:@"POTTURNED" object:nil];
    [[EAAccessoryManager sharedAccessoryManager]
            registerForLocalNotifications];

    if ([[[EAAccessoryManager    sharedAccessoryManager]
        connectedAccessories] count] > 0) {
      NSLog(@"Connected accessories");
    } else {
      NSLog(@"NO Connected accessories");
    }


    _accessoryController = [GameController sharedController];
    _accessoryList    = [[NSMutableArray alloc]
        initWithArray:[[EAAccessoryManager sharedAccessoryManager]
        connectedAccessories]];




    playerPaddleLeft  = [UIImage imageNamed:@"playerPaddleLeft.png"];
    playerPaddleLeftUp  = [UIImage imageNamed:@"playerPaddleLeftUp.png"];
    playerPaddleRight   = [UIImage imageNamed:@"playerPaddleRight.png"];
    playerPaddleRightUp = [UIImage    imageNamed:@"playerPaddleRightUp.png"];

    winOrLoseView.text = @"PONG!";


// SET UP SOUNDS
    CFBundleRef mainBundle;
```

```
    mainBundle = CFBundleGetMainBundle ();

    // Get the URL to the sound file to play
    paddleSoundFileURLRef  =    CFBundleCopyResourceURL (mainBundle,
        CFSTR ("paddleSound"),CFSTR ("aif"), NULL );
    AudioServicesCreateSystemSoundID (
        paddleSoundFileURLRef  &paddleSoundObject  );

    playerScore        = 0;
    compScore = 0;

    status = NOT_STARTED;
    [self setServePosition];
    [NSTimer scheduledTimerWithTimeInterval:0.05
        target:self selector:@selector(gameLoop)
        userInfo:nil repeats: YES];
  [super viewDidLoad];
}



//
// The rest of the code is generated by Xcode and should
//  be setup in a "real" production level game.
//
- (void)didReceiveMemoryWarning {
 // Releases the view if it doesn't have a superview.
    [super didReceiveMemoryWarning];

 // Release any cached data, images, etc that aren't in use.
}

- (void)viewDidUnload {
    [[UIApplication sharedApplication] setIdleTimerDisabled:NO];    // enable sleep
dimming

    // Release any retained subviews of the main view.
    // e.g. self.myOutlet = nil;
}


- (void)dealloc {
    [super dealloc];

}

#pragma mark -
#pragma mark Accessory Methods

-(void) pbPressed:(NSNotification *)notification {
    NSLog(@"Pushbutton Pressed");
    [self   serveAction];
}

-(void) potTurned:(NSNotification *)notification {
    NSLog(@"Pot Turned");
    NSNumber   *position = [[notification userInfo] objectForKey:@"parameter"];
```

```objc
        int i = [position intValue];
        NSLog(@"Position Received = %d",i);
  //int i = appDelegate.paddlePosition;

    i = (-i + 256);

    float j = (float)i * (320.0/246.0);

    CGPoint xLocation = CGPointMake(j,playerPaddle.center.y);
       playerPaddle.center = xLocation;
    if (playerPaddle.center.x > (self.view.bounds.size.width /2))
    if (playerPaddle.center.x > (self.view.bounds.size.width /2)+101)
        playerPaddle.image = playerPaddleRightUp;
      else
        playerPaddle.image = playerPaddleRight;
      else
    if (playerPaddle.center.x < (self.view.bounds.size.width /2)-101)
        playerPaddle.image = playerPaddleLeftUp;
                    else
               playerPaddle.image = playerPaddleLeft;

}

#pragma mark -
#pragma mark LED Routines


- (void)turnOnRedLED
{
    const uint8_t buf[2] = {0x98, 0x01};
    [[GameController sharedController]
      writeData:[NSData dataWithBytes:buf length:2]];
      redLEDOn = YES;
}


- (void)turnOffRedLED
{
    const uint8_t buf[2] = {0x98, 0x02};
    [[GameController sharedController]
       writeData:[NSData dataWithBytes:buf length:2]];
}
- (void)turnOnGreenLED
{
    const uint8_t buf[2] = {0x98, 0x03};
    [[GameController sharedController]
       writeData:[NSData dataWithBytes:buf length:2]];
      greenLEDOn = YES;
}

- (void)turnOffGreenLED
{
    const uint8_t buf[2] = {0x98, 0x04};
    [[GameController sharedController]
       writeData:[NSData dataWithBytes:buf length:2]];
}
```

```
- (void)accessoryConnected:(NSNotification *)notification {

    NSLog(@"Game Controller Connected");

    EAAccessory *connectedAccessory = [[notification userInfo]
objectForKey:EAAccessoryKey];
    [_accessoryList addObject:connectedAccessory];
        _selectedAccessory = [[_accessoryList objectAtIndex:0] retain];   // select the
accessory from the "list" which is only one element

        [_accessoryController setupControllerForAccessory:_selectedAccessory
withProtocolString:[[_selectedAccessory protocolStrings] objectAtIndex:0]];
 [_accessoryController openSession];

}

- (void)accessoryDisconnected:(NSNotification *)notification {

    NSLog(@"Game Controller Disconnected");

    EAAccessory *disconnectedAccessory =
      [[notification userInfo] objectForKey:EAAccessoryKey];

    int disconnectedAccessoryIndex = 0;
    for(EAAccessory *accessory in _accessoryList) {
        if ([disconnectedAccessory connectionID] == [accessory connectionID]) {
            break;
        }
        disconnectedAccessoryIndex++;
    }

    if (disconnectedAccessoryIndex < [_accessoryList count]) {
        [_accessoryList removeObjectAtIndex:disconnectedAccessoryIndex];
    } else {
        NSLog(@"could not find disconnected accessory in accessory list");
    }
}

@end
```

pongAppDelegate.h

```
#import <UIKit/UIKit.h>

@class pongViewController;

@interface pongAppDelegate : NSObject <UIApplicationDelegate> {
    UIWindow *window;
    pongViewController *viewController;

    int paddlePosition;
}

@property (nonatomic, retain) IBOutlet UIWindow *window;
@property (nonatomic, retain) IBOutlet pongViewController *viewController;
```

```
@property int   paddlePosition;

@end
```

pongAppDelegate.m

```
#import "pongAppDelegate.h"
#import "pongViewController.h"

@implementation pongAppDelegate

@synthesize window;
@synthesize viewController;
@synthesize paddlePosition;


- (void)applicationDidFinishLaunching:(UIApplication *)application {

    // Override point for customization after app launch
    [window addSubview:viewController.view];
    [window makeKeyAndVisible];
}


- (void)dealloc {
    [viewController release];
    [window release];
    [super dealloc];
}


@end
```

GameController.h

```
#import <Foundation/Foundation.h>
#import "pongAppDelegate.h"
#import <ExternalAccessory/ExternalAccessory.h>

@interface GameController : NSObject <EAAccessoryDelegate> {
    EAAccessory *_accessory;
    EASession *_session;
    NSString *_protocolString;

    NSMutableData *_writeData;

     pongAppDelegate    *appDelegate;
}

+ (GameController *)sharedController;

- (void)setupControllerForAccessory:(EAAccessory *)accessory
      withProtocolString:(NSString *)protocolString;
```

```
- (BOOL)openSession;
- (void)closeSession;

- (void)writeData:(NSData *)data;
- (void)_writeData;

// from EAAccessoryDelegate
- (void)accessoryDidDisconnect:(EAAccessory *)accessory;

@property (nonatomic, readonly) EAAccessory *accessory;
@property (nonatomic, readonly) NSString *protocolString;

@end
```

GameController.m

```
#import "GameController.h"

@implementation GameController

@synthesize accessory = _accessory, protocolString = _protocolString;


#pragma mark -
#pragma mark Externally Accessed writeData Method

- (void)writeData:(NSData *)data
{
    if (_writeData == nil) {
        _writeData = [[NSMutableData alloc] init];
    }

    [_writeData appendData:data];
    [self _writeData];
}

#pragma mark Instance Methods

- (void)_writeData {
    while ((([_session outputStream] hasSpaceAvailable]) &&
        ([_writeData length] > 0))
    {
        NSInteger bytesWritten = [[_session outputStream]
            write:[_writeData bytes] maxLength:[_writeData length]];
        if (bytesWritten == -1)
        {
            NSLog(@"write error");
            break;
        }
        else if (bytesWritten > 0)
        {
            [_writeData replaceBytesInRange:NSMakeRange(0, bytesWritten)
                withBytes:NULL length:0];
        }
    }
```

```
    }

#define EAD_INPUT_BUFFER_SIZE 128

- (void)_readData {

    //
    // get appDelegate (pongAppDelegate) so we can reference its properties
    //
        appDelegate = (pongAppDelegate *)[[UIApplication sharedApplication]
            delegate];

    uint8_t buf[EAD_INPUT_BUFFER_SIZE];

    while ([[_session inputStream] hasBytesAvailable])
    {
        NSInteger bytesRead = [[_session inputStream]
            read:buf maxLength:EAD_INPUT_BUFFER_SIZE];
        NSLog(@"read %d bytes (%d) from input stream", bytesRead,buf[0]);

        if (buf[0] == 0x10) {
            [[NSNotificationCenter defaultCenter]
              postNotificationName:@"PBPRESSED" object:self];

        }
        if (buf[0] == 0x20) {
//NSData *data = [[NSData alloc]
//initWithBytes:buf length:bytesRead];

//NSLog(@"Data = %@",data);
        unsigned char i = buf[1];
// NSNumber *posInt = [[NSNumber alloc] initWithUnsignedChar:i];
// NSLog(@"_readData position = %d",[posInt intValue]);

            appDelegate.paddlePosition = i;

// NSMutableDictionary *dict = [[ NSMutableDictionary alloc]
// init];
// [ dict    setObject:posInt forKey:@"parameter"];
// [[NSNotificationCenter defaultCenter]
// postNotificationName:@"POTTURNED"
// object:self userInfo:dict];
        [[NSNotificationCenter    defaultCenter]
            postNotificationName:@"POTTURNED" object:self ];

// [dict release];
//[posInt release];
        }
    }
}

#define EAD_INPUT_BUFFER_SIZE 128

+ (GameController *)sharedController
{
    static GameController *accessoryController = nil;
```

```
        if (accessoryController == nil) {
            accessoryController = [[GameController alloc] init];
        }

        return accessoryController;
}


#pragma mark -
#pragma mark Internal Methods

- (void)setupControllerForAccessory:(EAAccessory *)accessory
        withProtocolString:(NSString *)protocolString
{
        [_accessory release];
        _accessory = [accessory retain];
        [_protocolString release];
        _protocolString = [protocolString copy];
}

- (BOOL)openSession
{
        [_accessory setDelegate:self];
        _session = [[EASession alloc]
          initWithAccessory:_accessory forProtocol:_protocolString];
        //_session = [[EASession alloc]
          initWithAccessory:_accessory forProtocol:@"COM.MACMEDX.P1"];

        if (_session)
        {
            [[_session inputStream] setDelegate:self];
            [[_session inputStream] scheduleInRunLoop:[NSRunLoop currentRunLoop]
                forMode:NSDefaultRunLoopMode];
            [[_session inputStream] open];

            [[_session outputStream] setDelegate:self];
            [[_session outputStream] scheduleInRunLoop:[NSRunLoop currentRunLoop]
                forMode:NSDefaultRunLoopMode];
            [[_session outputStream] open];
        }
        else
        {
            NSLog(@"creating session failed");
        }

        return (_session != nil);
}

- (void)closeSession
{
        [[_session inputStream] close];
        [[_session inputStream] removeFromRunLoop:[NSRunLoop currentRunLoop]
                forMode:NSDefaultRunLoopMode];
        [[_session inputStream] setDelegate:nil];
        [[_session outputStream] close];
        [[_session outputStream] removeFromRunLoop:[NSRunLoop currentRunLoop]
                forMode:NSDefaultRunLoopMode];
```

```objc
        [[_session outputStream] setDelegate:nil];

        _session = nil;
        [_session release];


    }



    - (void)accessoryDidDisconnect:(EAAccessory *)accessory
    {
        NSLog(@"Controller Removed");
    }

#pragma mark NSStreamDelegateEventExtensions

    - (void)stream:(NSStream *)aStream handleEvent:(NSStreamEvent)eventCode
    {
        switch (eventCode) {
            case NSStreamEventNone:
                NSLog(@"stream %@ event none", aStream);
                break;
            case NSStreamEventOpenCompleted:
                NSLog(@"stream %@ event open completed", aStream);
                break;
            case NSStreamEventHasBytesAvailable:
                NSLog(@"stream %@ event bytes available", aStream);
                [self _readData];
                break;
            case NSStreamEventHasSpaceAvailable:
                NSLog(@"stream %@ event space available", aStream);
                [self _writeData];
                break;
            case NSStreamEventErrorOccurred:
                NSLog(@"stream %@ event error", aStream);
                break;
            case NSStreamEventEndEncountered:
                NSLog(@"stream %@ event end encountered", aStream);
                break;
            default:
                break;
        }
    }

#pragma mark -
#pragma mark Basic Object Methods

    - (void)dealloc
    {
        [self closeSession];
        [self setupControllerForAccessory:nil withProtocolString:nil];
        _writeData = nil;
        [_writeData release];


        [super dealloc];
    }

@end
```

pongViewController.h

```objc
#import <UIKit/UIKit.h>
#include <AudioToolbox/AudioToolbox.h>
#import <ExternalAccessory/ExternalAccessory.h>
#import "GameController.h"
#import "pongAppDelegate.h"


@interface pongViewController : UIViewController {

    pongAppDelegate    *appDelegate;


    EAAccessory *_accessory;
    NSMutableArray *_accessoryList;

    EAAccessory *_selectedAccessory;
    GameController *_accessoryController;


//
//      Define the outlets that will be updated
// as the game progresses
//
IBOutlet UIImageView *ball;
IBOutlet UIImageView *playerPaddle;
IBOutlet UIImageView *compPaddle;
IBOutlet UILabel     *playerScoreView;
IBOutlet UILabel     *compScoreView;
IBOutlet UILabel     *winOrLoseView;


//****************************************************
//
//   GENERAL NOTES ON THE PROPERTIES AND METHODS BELOW
//
//   Most, if not all, of the stuff below could be
//   defined as simple instance variables within the
//   the pongViewController and does not need to be
//   defined here, in the interface section. While
//   this would create slimmer (and probably better)
//   code, I chose to put it here to force the condition
//   that all properties be defined as accessible.
//   Remember, this portion of the book describes a self-
//   contained, touch-activated game, but we are planning
//   to incorporate an additional controller to access
//   the game controller accessory. So we want to make
//   the pongViewController more open to expansion and
//   by putting things here, in the interface, we are
//   acting in a more forward-looking manner.
//****************************************************


//
// ballSpeed - the X and Y velocity of the ball.
// -- we use a CGPoint which is just a struct with two
//      floats (x and y) as its elements. We then just set
```

```
//     the x and y values to the speed.
//     Y is defined as movement along the vertical axis between
//     the player and the computer.
//     X is defined as the side-to-side movement
//
   CGPoint ballSpeed;




//
//   These are the images we're going to use for the player's paddle.
//   In a very simple game, we would just use a rectangle, but here we
//   do a couple of unique things. We flip the paddle (left-right) as
//   it moves to either side of the centerline...to simulate forehand-
//   backhand action (playerPaddleLeft and playerPaddleRight). Also.
//   if we're at either edge of the table, in a real game we would angle
//   the paddle more to bring it back into play. In this case, we "tilt"
//   the image of the paddle a bit to simulate this (playerPaddleLeftUp and
//   playerPaddleRightUp).
//
UIImage      *playerPaddleLeft;
UIImage      *playerPaddleLeftUp;
UIImage      *playerPaddleRight;
UIImage      *playerPaddleRightUp;


//
// These are some basic variables to keep track of things.
//
   NSUInteger    playerScore;
   NSUInteger    compScore;
   NSUInteger    status;


//
// We need these for handling the sound that the program generates
//
CFURLRef         paddleSoundFileURLRef;
SystemSoundID    paddleSoundObject;
}
@property (readwrite)    CFURLRef         paddleSoundFileURLRef;
@property (readonly)     SystemSoundID    paddleSoundObject;

@property (nonatomic,retain) IBOutlet UIImageView *ball;
@property (nonatomic,retain) IBOutlet UIImageView *playerPaddle;
@property (nonatomic,retain) IBOutlet UIImageView *compPaddle;
@property (nonatomic,retain) UILabel      *playerScoreView;
@property (nonatomic,retain) UILabel      *compScoreView;
@property (nonatomic,retain) UILabel      *winOrLoseView;


@property(nonatomic) CGPoint ballSpeed;
@property(nonatomic) NSUInteger    status;

@property    (nonatomic,retain) UIImage    *playerPaddleLeft;
@property    (nonatomic,retain) UIImage    *playerPaddleLeftUp;
@property    (nonatomic,retain) UIImage    *playerPaddleRight;
@property    (nonatomic,retain) UIImage    *playerPaddleRightUp;
```

```
@property NSUInteger    playerScore;
@property NSUInteger    compScore;

//
//  The object's method calls
//  serveAction is initiated by a user action (pressing the button)
//
-(IBAction) serveAction;

//
//  LED Control Routines
//
- (void)turnOnRedLED;
- (void)turnOffRedLED;
- (void)turnOnGreenLED;
- (void)turnOffGreenLED;
@end
```

pongViewController.m

```
#import "pongViewController.h"

//
//  State Variables used by
//  compPlay method to determine
//  actions to take depending on
//  where we are in the game.
//
#define NOT_STARTED     0
#define IN_PLAY         1
#define POINT_OVER      2
#define GAME_OVER       3


//
//   Points to win the game
//  I use 5 here to make the game
//  go by quickly
//
#define GAME_WON    5


//
//   Speed of the ball in both
//  the x and y directions.
//
#define BALL_DELTA_X    5
#define BALL_DELTA_Y    10


//
//   Starting position of the ball.
//  Roughly the center of the table
//
#define BALL_STARTING_X     160.0
#define BALL_STARTING_Y     220.0
```

```
//
//   defines the performance
//   of the computer player.
//   higher number equals better
//   computer player
//
#define COMP_REACTION_TIME   15


//
//   COMP_SETUP_TIME is a variable
//   that also determines computer
//   performance. In general, it adjusts
//   how soon the computer reacts by
//   adding y-position info to the
//   check of where the ball is.
//
#define COMP_SETUP_TIME      40


//
//   WALL_MARGIN adds a delta distance
//   from the edges of the wall to check
//   when to "bounce" the ball. If it were
//   not added, then the ball might look like
//   it went "into" the wall before bouncing.
//
#define WALL_MARGIN      5

@implementation pongViewController

//
// Use @synthesis to create all the
// necessary getters and setters
//
@synthesize ball;
@synthesize playerPaddle;
@synthesize compPaddle;

@synthesize ballSpeed;
@synthesize      status;
@synthesize playerPaddleLeft;
@synthesize playerPaddleLeftUp;
@synthesize playerPaddleRight;
@synthesize playerPaddleRightUp;

@synthesize playerScore;
@synthesize playerScoreView;
@synthesize compScore;
@synthesize compScoreView;
@synthesize winOrLoseView;

@synthesize paddleSoundFileURLRef;
@synthesize paddleSoundObject;


//
//   INSTANCE VARIABLES
//
```

```objc
BOOL   redLEDOn     = NO;
BOOL   greenLEDOn   = NO;

//
//      setServePosition
// Place the ball at approximately the center of the table
// for the serve.
//   -- the ball's center position and speed are both structs
//      containing an X and Y value. This way, what we call
//      speed is really just the delta position added to the
//      ball at each call of the timer expiration.
//
-(void) setServePosition {
    ball.center = CGPointMake(BALL_STARTING_X, BALL_STARTING_Y);
    ballSpeed = CGPointMake(BALL_DELTA_X, -BALL_DELTA_Y);
}


//
//   compPlay - adjust the computer's paddle position to meet the ball
// This is basically the only AI in the program and it's just moving
// the comp's paddle towards the ball at a certain speed. Really,
// if the player is very, very lucky and has gotten a good angle on his
// return *and* the computer's paddle is at the extreme other side of the
// table, then it might just NOT make it to the ball in time and the
// player will score a point.
//
-(void) compPlay {

    if(ball.center.y <= self.view.center.y + COMP_SETUP_TIME)     { // is ball on
computer's side of court ?
        if(ball.center.x < compPaddle.center.x) { // does computer need to move racquet ?
            CGPoint compLocation = CGPointMake(compPaddle.center.x - COMP_REACTION_TIME,
compPaddle.center.y);
            compPaddle.center = compLocation;
        }
        if(ball.center.x > compPaddle.center.x) {
            CGPoint compLocation = CGPointMake(compPaddle.center.x + COMP_REACTION_TIME,
compPaddle.center.y);
            compPaddle.center = compLocation;
        }
    }
}


//
//   gameLoop - the heart of the game
//
// This is called at every expiration of the NSTimer interval that we set at startup
time
// Typically, in this type of design, the first thing to do is check all the boundary
conditions:
//   has the ball hit an edge of something (the room), has a point been scored, is the
game over,
//   has the ball connected with the player's or computer's paddle.
//   Note that all the code in the entire function is contingent on the game status being
IN_PLAY. This
//   should be obvious that we only want the automatic part of the system to update if
we're in the
```

```
//  middle of play. In any other state (NOT STARTED, GAME WON, POINT OVER) the player
should determine
//  things (SERVE or not).
//
//       Note also that this method also sets the game's status:
//  (1) If the ball is past the player's end, the computer has scored and we set
POINT_OVER
//  (2) Similarly, if the ball is past the computer's end, the player scored and
POINT_OVER as well.
//  (3) If the point total of a player is equal to the constant GAME_WON, we set status
= GAME_OVER
//  (4) NOT_STARTED is set at startup in the viewDidLoad method.
//
-(void)gameLoop {

    if(status == IN_PLAY) {
      ball.center = CGPointMake(ball.center.x + ballSpeed.x, ball.center.y +
        ballSpeed.y); // move the ball

  //
  // If we turned on an LED in the last loop, then turn it off now
  //
      if (redLEDOn) {
        [self   turnOffRedLED];
        redLEDOn = NO;
      }
  if (greenLEDOn) {
            [self   turnOffGreenLED];
            greenLEDOn  = NO;
      }

// Has the ball hit the edge of the room ?
      if (ball.center.x > (self.view.bounds.size.width - WALL_MARGIN) ||
          ball.center.x < (0 + WALL_MARGIN)) {
          ballSpeed.x  = - ballSpeed.x;
      }

      if (ball.center.y > self.view.bounds.size.height || ball.center.y < 0) {
        ballSpeed.y = - ballSpeed.y;
        }

// player scored against computer
      if (ball.center.y < 0) {
// set status to hold
        status = POINT_OVER;
        playerScore++;
        playerScoreView.text = [NSString
            stringWithFormat:@"%d",playerScore];
        if (playerScore == GAME_WON)
        {
                winOrLoseView.text = @"YOU WIN";
                playerScore = 0;
                compScore  = 0;
                status  = GAME_OVER;
          }
            [self   setServePosition];
```

```
        } else
// if player didn't score, did the computer score?
        if (ball.center.y > self.view.bounds.size.height) {
// set status to hold
        status = POINT_OVER;
        compScore++;
        compScoreView.text = [NSString
        stringWithFormat:@"%d",compScore];
        if (compScore == GAME_WON)
        {
            winOrLoseView.text = @"YOU LOSE";
            playerScore = 0;
            compScore   = 0;
        }
          [self   setServePosition];
        }


// Did the player's paddle make contact with the ball
        if(CGRectIntersectsRect(ball.frame, playerPaddle.frame)) {

                AudioServicesPlaySystemSound (self.paddleSoundObject);

// Reverse front-to-back direction
                if(ball.center.y < playerPaddle.center.y) {
                    ballSpeed.y = -ballSpeed.y;
                }

// Reverse the X direction if we're off to one side of the table
                if ( (ball.center.x > (self.view.bounds.size.width /2)+100) ||
                    (ball.center.x < (self.view.bounds.size.width /2)-100) )
                        {
// if we just reverse the delta-x, then we might get hung in a loop
// so add a little offset from where the ball is to the center of the paddle

                    ballSpeed.x = -ballSpeed.x +
                    (ball.center.x - playerPaddle.center.x)/5;
                }
//[self   turnOnRedLED];
}


// Did the computer's paddle make contact withthe ball
        if(CGRectIntersectsRect(ball.frame,    compPaddle.frame)) {
            AudioServicesPlaySystemSound (self.paddleSoundObject);

// Reverse front-to-back direction
        if(ball.center.y > compPaddle.center.y) {
            ballSpeed.y = -ballSpeed.y;
// each time the computer hits the ball, speed it up
            ballSpeed.y++;
        }


// Let's change the X (side-to-side) direction if we're near the edge of the table
        if ( (ball.center.x > (self.view.bounds.size.width /2)+100) ||
            (ball.center.x < (self.view.bounds.size.width /2)-100) )
```

```
                        ballSpeed.x = -ballSpeed.x;
    //[self        turnOnGreenLED];
        }
    //
    //    Here is the only real action that this method does.
    //    If none of the above conditions are met, then call
    //  the AI method that moves the computer's paddle towards
    //  the ball.
    //
        [self compPlay];
    } // end if
}


//
//    touchesBegan is the method that gets called when the player
//  interacts with the game (touches the screen to move his paddle).
//  this is just the method called by the system, and if the game
//  status is IN_PLAY, then our routine touchesMoved is called to
//  intercept and move the player's paddle.
//  REALLY, this is just a gateway that only allows the player
//  to move the paddle if the game is in play.
//
-(void)touchesBegan:(NSSet *)touches withEvent:(UIEvent *)event {
    if (status == IN_PLAY) {
        [self touchesMoved:touches withEvent:event];
    }
}


//
//      serveAction - Basically, this starts the game.
//  (1) Clear any startup text in the game window
//  (2) Initialize the scores
//  (3) change game status
//  (4) make a serve sound
//
//      Note that this method really doesn't "serve" the ball. It
//  merely changes game status so that the next time the NSTimer
//  "fires", the gameLoop actually runs.
//
-(void)serveAction {
    winOrLoseView.text = @"";

    if (status == GAME_OVER) {
      compScoreView.text     = [NSString stringWithFormat:@"%d",0];
      playerScoreView.text   = [NSString stringWithFormat:@"%d",0];
    }
    status = IN_PLAY;

    AudioServicesPlaySystemSound (self.paddleSoundObject);


}


//
// touchesMoved:withEvent:
// This routine moves the player's paddle to the point on the
// playing surface that he has placed his finger. NOTE that this
```

```
//  has the unnatural effect of instantly positioning his paddle
//  which is generally not how you want to play the game.
//  Also, depending on where the paddle is positioned (left or right)
//  or at the edges of the table, we change the image used by the player's
//  paddle to simulate forehand-backhand or to an angled shot back
//  into the game. We do not do this for the computer's paddle
//
-(void)touchesMoved:(NSSet *)touches withEvent:(UIEvent *)event {
        UITouch *touch = [[event allTouches] anyObject];   // returns one of the objects
in the set of all touches
        CGPoint location = [touch locationInView:touch.view];
        CGPoint xLocation = CGPointMake(location.x,playerPaddle.center.y);
        playerPaddle.center = xLocation;
        if (playerPaddle.center.x > (self.view.bounds.size.width /2))
         if (playerPaddle.center.x > (self.view.bounds.size.width /2)+101)
            playerPaddle.image = playerPaddleRightUp;
         else
            playerPaddle.image = playerPaddleRight;
         else
          if (playerPaddle.center.x < (self.view.bounds.size.width /2)-101)
             playerPaddle.image = playerPaddleLeftUp;
          else
             playerPaddle.image = playerPaddleLeft;
}


//
//  viewDidLoad - we use this to initialize our system.
//  (1) Loads the images from the bundle to use for our variable player's paddle
//  (2) Displays the game name on the playing field
//  (3) Gets the sound file for the ball
//  (4) initializes the score to 0-0
//  (5) sets the game status to NOT_STARTED -- note that this is the only time
//      the game is in this condition
//  (6) set the serve position of the ball
//  (7) setup and start the timer
//
//  Note that for the game to actually start, the status must change to IN_PLAY
//  and that is only done by the serveAction method which fires when the player
//  taps the SERVE button --**** AND ***--- soon when the game controller's
//  serve button is pressed.
//
- (void)viewDidLoad {

    [[UIApplication sharedApplication] setIdleTimerDisabled:YES];  // disable sleep
dimming
 //
 // get appDelegate (pongAppDelegate) so we can reference its properties
 //
        appDelegate = (pongAppDelegate *)[[UIApplication sharedApplication]
                delegate];


        [[NSNotificationCenter defaultCenter]
            addObserver:self selector:@selector(accessoryConnected:)
            name:EAAccessoryDidConnectNotification object:nil];
        [[NSNotificationCenter defaultCenter]
```

```
                addObserver:self selector:@selector(accessoryDisconnected:)
                    name:EAAccessoryDidDisconnectNotification object:nil];
        [[NSNotificationCenter defaultCenter]
                addObserver:self selector:@selector(pbPressed:)
                name:@"PBPRESSED" object:nil];
        [[NSNotificationCenter defaultCenter]
                addObserver:self selector:@selector(potTurned:)
                name:@"POTTURNED" object:nil];
        [[EAAccessoryManager sharedAccessoryManager]
                registerForLocalNotifications];

        if ([[[EAAccessoryManager sharedAccessoryManager]          connectedAccessories]
count] > 0) {
            NSLog(@"Connected accessories");
        } else {
            NSLog(@"NO Connected accessories");
        }


        _accessoryController = [GameController sharedController];
        _accessoryList   = [[NSMutableArray alloc]
        initWithArray:[[EAAccessoryManager sharedAccessoryManager]
            connectedAccessories]];




        playerPaddleLeft    = [UIImage imageNamed:@"playerPaddleLeft.png"];
        playerPaddleLeftUp  = [UIImage imageNamed:@"playerPaddleLeftUp.png"];
        playerPaddleRight   = [UIImage imageNamed:@"playerPaddleRight.png"];
        playerPaddleRightUp = [UIImage    imageNamed:@"playerPaddleRightUp.png"];

        winOrLoseView.text = @"PONG!";


// SET UP SOUNDS
    CFBundleRef mainBundle;
    mainBundle = CFBundleGetMainBundle ();

    // Get the URL to the sound file to play
    paddleSoundFileURLRef =    CFBundleCopyResourceURL (mainBundle,
        CFSTR ("paddleSound"), CFSTR ("aif"), NULL);
    AudioServicesCreateSystemSoundID (paddleSoundFileURLRef,
            &paddleSoundObject);

    playerScore  = 0;
    compScore    = 0;

        status = NOT_STARTED;
        [self setServePosition];
        [NSTimer scheduledTimerWithTimeInterval:0.05
            target:self selector:@selector(gameLoop) userInfo:nil repeats: YES];
        [super viewDidLoad];
}
```

```
//
//   The rest of the code is generated by Xcode and should
//   be setup in a "real" production level game.
//
- (void)didReceiveMemoryWarning {
 // Releases the view if it doesn't have a superview.
    [super didReceiveMemoryWarning];

 // Release any cached data, images, etc that aren't in use.
}

- (void)viewDidUnload {
    [[UIApplication sharedApplication] setIdleTimerDisabled:NO];       //
enable sleep dimming

 // Release any retained subviews of the main view.
 // e.g. self.myOutlet = nil;
}


- (void)dealloc {
    [super dealloc];

}

#pragma mark -
#pragma mark Accessory Methods

-(void) pbPressed:(NSNotification *)notification {
    NSLog(@"Pushbutton Pressed");
    [self        serveAction];
}

-(void) potTurned:(NSNotification *)notification {
    NSLog(@"Pot Turned");
 //NSNumber      *position = [[notification userInfo]
//objectForKey:@"parameter"];

 //int i = [position intValue];
    int i = appDelegate.paddlePosition;
    NSLog(@"Position Received = %d",i);

    i = (-i + 256);

    float j = (float)i * (320.0/246.0);

    CGPoint xLocation = CGPointMake(j,playerPaddle.center.y);
    playerPaddle.center = xLocation;
  if (playerPaddle.center.x > (self.view.bounds.size.width /2))
    if (playerPaddle.center.x > (self.view.bounds.size.width /2)+101)
       playerPaddle.image = playerPaddleRightUp;
    else
       playerPaddle.image = playerPaddleRight;
  else
    if (playerPaddle.center.x < (self.view.bounds.size.width /2)-101)
        playerPaddle.image = playerPaddleLeftUp;
        else
```

```
              playerPaddle.image = playerPaddleLeft;

}

#pragma mark -
#pragma mark LED Routines


- (void)turnOnRedLED
{
    const uint8_t buf[2] = {0x98, 0x01};
    [[GameController sharedController]
        writeData:[NSData dataWithBytes:buf length:2]];
        redLEDOn = YES;
}

- (void)turnOffRedLED
{
    const uint8_t buf[2] = {0x98, 0x02};
    [[GameController sharedController]
        writeData:[NSData dataWithBytes:buf length:2]];
}
- (void)turnOnGreenLED
{
    const uint8_t buf[2] = {0x98, 0x03};
    [[GameController sharedController]
      writeData:[NSData dataWithBytes:buf length:2]];
        greenLEDOn = YES;
}

- (void)turnOffGreenLED
{
    const uint8_t buf[2] = {0x98, 0x04};
    [[GameController sharedController]
        writeData:[NSData dataWithBytes:buf length:2]];
}

- (void)accessoryConnected:(NSNotification *)notification {

    NSLog(@"Game Controller Connected");

    EAAccessory *connectedAccessory = [[notification userInfo]
        objectForKey:EAAccessoryKey];
    [_accessoryList addObject:connectedAccessory];
    _selectedAccessory = [[_accessoryList objectAtIndex:0] retain];     // select the
accessory from the "list" which is only one element

    [_accessoryController setupControllerForAccessory:_selectedAccessory
        withProtocolString:[[_selectedAccessory protocolStrings]
      objectAtIndex:0]];
 [_accessoryController openSession];

}

- (void)accessoryDisconnected:(NSNotification *)notification {

    NSLog(@"Game Controller Disconnected");
```

```objc
    EAAccessory *disconnectedAccessory = [[notification userInfo]
        objectForKey:EAAccessoryKey];

    int disconnectedAccessoryIndex = 0;
    for(EAAccessory *accessory in _accessoryList) {
        if ([disconnectedAccessory connectionID] == [accessory connectionID]) {
            break;
        }
        disconnectedAccessoryIndex++;
    }

    if (disconnectedAccessoryIndex < [_accessoryList count]) {
        [_accessoryList removeObjectAtIndex:disconnectedAccessoryIndex];
    } else {
        NSLog(@"could not find disconnected accessory in accessory list");
    }
}


@end
```

Index